CROOKED RIVER CITY

American Made Music Series

ADVISORY BOARD

David Evans, General Editor
Barry Jean Ancelet
Edward A. Berlin
Joyce J. Bolden
Rob Bowman
Susan C. Cook
Curtis Ellison
William Ferris
John Edward Hasse
Kip Lornell
Bill Malone
Eddie S. Meadows
Manuel H. Peña
Wayne D. Shirley
Robert Walser

CROOKED RIVER CITY

The Musical Life of Nashville's
WILLIAM PURSELL

TERRY WAIT KLEFSTAD

University Press of Mississippi / Jackson

www.upress.state.ms.us

Designed by Peter D. Halverson

The University Press of Mississippi is a member of the
Association of University Presses.

Copyright © 2018 by University Press of Mississippi
All rights reserved

All photographs are courtesy of the William Pursell Archive,
Lila D. Bunch Library, Belmont University unless otherwise noted.

First printing 2018

∞

Library of Congress Cataloging-in-Publication Data

Names: Klefstad, Terry Wait, 1971– author.
Title: Crooked River City : the musical life of Nashville's William Pursell / Terry Wait Klefstad.
Description: Jackson : University Press of Mississippi, [2018] | Series: American made music series | Includes bibliographical references and index. |
Identifiers: LCCN 2018012514 (print) | LCCN 2018017768 (ebook) | ISBN 9781496818652 (epub single) | ISBN 9781496818669 (epub instititional) | ISBN 9781496818676 (pdf single) | ISBN 9781496818683 (pdf institutional) | ISBN 9781496818638 (cloth : alk. paper) | ISBN 9781496818645 (pbk. : alk. paper)
Subjects: LCSH: Pursell, Bill. | Composers—United States—Biography. | Musicians—United States—Biography.
Classification: LCC ML410.P966 (ebook) | LCC ML410.P966 K54 2018 (print) | DDC 781.64092 [B]—dc23
LC record available at https://lccn.loc.gov/2018012514

British Library Cataloging-in-Publication Data available

CONTENTS

A Note on the William Pursell Archive VII

Introduction: Bill Pursell and the Nashville Sound IX

Prelude: Crooked River Town XVII

1: A California Childhood. 3

2: Two Fathers 24

3: High Flight 39

4: A Student Again, and Then, Not 58

5: Nashville Sessions 76

6: Our Winter Love 93

7: Nashville and Beyond 113

8: Heritage 140

9: Dr. Pursell 163

Postlude: Crooked River Town 183

List of Compositions 189

Discography 195

Notes 205

Bibliography 217

Index 221

A NOTE ON THE WILLIAM PURSELL ARCHIVE

When I began this project, I thought that my chief source would be my recorded interviews with Bill. We met almost weekly for a period of about three years, and in subsequent years had countless conversations, emails, and phone calls to clear up questions that I had. However, my timing was incredibly fortunate. In the summer of 2014, Bill sold his house, the sprawling limestone mansion on Curtiswood Lane in Nashville that he had purchased in 1971. By this time, we had gotten to know each other fairly well, and he accepted with alacrity my offer to help him clear out his basement and various areas of his house, with the idea that many of the documents and recordings we hauled away would form the heart of a new archive, to be housed in the special collections of the Lila D. Bunch Library at Belmont University.

Thus, I had unlimited access to a lifetime of letters, photographs, business correspondence, union time sheets, etc. Then, in May 2017, Bill retired from thirty-seven years of service to Belmont University, and I helped him clear out his office, also an enormous and overwhelming task. My reward was more letters and more original manuscripts of his compositions.

Most scholars approach archivists hat in hand, humbly begging permission to access the sacred materials, housed in antiseptic quarters, many to be examined only with gloved hands. I was incredibly lucky. Not only did Bill decide to move and retire before my book was finished, but these major life events came after our time of regular interviews, and we had built up a great degree of trust with each other. Thus, my sources for this biography became not just the over fifty interviews I had recorded and transcribed, but also countless documents from a lifetime. Bill never threw anything away, as far as I could tell, and although that made moving a chore for him, it was a treasure trove for a musicologist like me.

I had been able to corroborate many of Bill's statements through research in outside sources, such as the Nashville Symphony Archives, the California State Library in Sacramento, and of course many secondary sources like newspapers and books. But the hundreds of documents that were made unconditionally available to me further corroborated everything Bill had told me, down to dates and places and names. For a nonagenarian, his mind is incredibly sharp, and it seems that he has forgotten almost nothing from his long life lived in the musical world. And I was able to affirm that by reading long-hoarded letters, newspaper clippings, and music manuscripts.

Those documents have found a new home in the Lila D. Bunch Library special collections. They will be (further) organized and stored in archival boxes, in the event that another scholar might want to expand on the work presented herein.

INTRODUCTION: BILL PURSELL AND THE NASHVILLE SOUND

Accounts of the transformation in country music in the late 1950s and 1960s known as the Nashville Sound usually begin with Chet Atkins and Owen Bradley, and mention Eddy Arnold in the mix. Then come the Jordanaires and the Anita Kerr Singers, Nashville session vocal groups that were key to the new style of country music. Pianist Floyd Cramer is often mentioned as Chet Atkins's favorite sideman and another force in the rise of the Nashville Sound. Almost never does one read of the pianist Bill Pursell, who came to Nashville in 1960 at the invitation of Eddy Arnold, and who was an active session keyboardist through the crucial years of the rise of the Nashville Sound. Many of the major figures mentioned in the rise of the Nashville Sound, including Bob Moore, Grady Martin, Marty Robbins, Jean Shepard, Harold Bradley, Patsy Cline, Johnny Cash, and Chet Atkins, worked with Pursell at one time or another, and most of the minor figures too. Why then is Pursell absent from these accounts of Nashville in the 1960s? In the 2010s, he has watched many of his friends become inductees of the Country Music Hall of Fame, and when Belmont University held a Columbia Studio B reunion (a studio where he did most of his session work), somehow they forgot to invite Pursell. This rankles.

The most obvious reason for his absence from the story of the Nashville Sound is that he was always considered to be an outsider among the Nashville musicians. Pursell is from California, not the South, and he is a highly trained classical musician, keyboardist, composer, and arranger who can read music like a native language. He moonlighted as a concert pianist with the Nashville Symphony. And he was not savvy enough, at least at first, to conceal his abilities.[1] Unlike many classically trained musicians, Pursell can improvise in just about any style, so he could have blended in. But he was eager to demonstrate his skill during his first sessions in Nashville, and this did not endear him to the other session musicians. He was an outsider from the beginning, though he learned quickly to play simply, "like Floyd Cramer." To Nashville musicians, his ability to read music and play Rachmaninoff was just one more sign that the traditional Nashville country sound was fading.

Another possible reason Pursell was never considered a key figure in the rise of the Nashville Sound is that as a pianist and keyboard player, he was part of the rhythm section. Travis Stimeling's work with Nashville string players shows that their moonlighting with the Nashville Symphony was not much of an issue—they were called in to sessions but were not considered solo artist material, for the most part. Pianists were in a slightly different category, but not on the same level as singers or guitarists. However, Floyd Cramer was a pianist who is widely recognized as part of the Nashville Sound. So Pursell's status as pianist cannot be a major reason for the lack of attention to his work.

One further reason may be Pursell's relationship with his producer Don Law and Columbia Records, a situation that is described in chapter 6. Pursell never made money off his 1963 hit, "Our Winter Love," as an angry 1966 letter to Columbia attests, and he did not have a good relationship with Law, nor did he receive artist promotion from Columbia on his second and third solo albums. Thus, record label politics played some role in the silencing of his work.

His neglect in studies of the Nashville Sound is likely a combination of all of the above reasons: his status as a country music outsider (not even really a country musician), his role as keyboardist, and his relationship with his record label. Perhaps his fellow session musicians forgot to mention him when scholars came for interviews, or perhaps they just didn't consider him part of the club. For whatever reason, Pursell's story has been neglected, and this book is an attempt to remedy that loss.

Pursell is barely aware of his role as one of the architects of this profound change in the style of country music. To Bill, it was work, and he was a working musician. He had to earn a living, and that meant playing jazz in downtown Nashville, playing country riffs in the recording studios, and performing Gershwin and Grieg with the Nashville Symphony. Later, he arranged and produced countless recordings in the Nashville studios. His skills at arranging for strings were especially welcome, as strings were part of the essence of the Nashville Sound. His story, then, is intertwined with the story of 1960s Nashville. The difference is that Nashville country music was only one part of his career, however important a part. Music in Nashville is about much more than country, but a brief examination of the Nashville Sound in relation to Pursell's musical life is in order, to provide some valuable context for the broad sweep of his career.

From the founding of the radio station WSM and Grand Ole Opry's barn dance broadcasts in the 1920s to the famous Quonset Hut that Owen and Harold Bradley added to their recording studio on Music Row in 1955, Nashville has been a center of musical entrepreneurship. Many scholars have told in many ways how Nashville became Music City U.S.A., from the collection of quotes and anecdotes gathered by Michael Kosser (*How Nashville Became Music City, U.S.A.*) to the fascinating history of WSM told by Craig Havighurst (*Air Castle of the South: WSM and the Making of Music City*), to the history of the Grand Ole Opry told by Paul Kingsbury. These accounts and more are listed in the bibliography if you want to know more about country music and Nashville.

The roots of country music in Nashville lay in the Grand Ole Opry performers, with their fiddles, rural accents, and upright bass. Ernest Tubb was the iconic figure of the original Grand Ole Opry, along with the Carter family and Roy Acuff (Hemphill 2015, 38–39). The Opry's audience was widespread, rural, and middle-aged. Joli Jensen (1998) asserts that the front-porch sets and folksy costumes used at the live Opry shows established the authenticity of the Opry as "down-home," traditional, and rural (14–15). Pursell's uncles and aunts in the foothills of the California Sierra Nevada Mountains religiously listened to the Grand Ole Opry on Saturday nights; the radio station WSM reached across the continent to them (and is still broadcasting today, with a heavy emphasis on traditional country music).

By the 1950s, however, American culture had changed significantly, and music in Nashville changed too. As recording studios began to spring up on Music Row, one after the other, the twangy, folksy sound of the Opry gave way to a more polished, commercialized sound, "countrypolitan," as Jensen calls it. Upright bass gave way to electric bass, vocal timbres were smoothed, and full string sections began to replace the fiddle solos. The banjo was replaced by the piano, and the electric guitar and drum set were added. Background vocals with "oohs" and "aahs" (the kind of thing that we now call "Disney voices") also intruded. Eventually, critics found a name for this new kind of country music: the Nashville Sound. The term was coined in 1958 in *Music Reporter* magazine and now is used to denote the shift in the style of country music as it was recorded and performed in Nashville from the late 1950s through the 1960s.

In the late 1950s, Bill Pursell was performing gigs in Florida, first with a pop music band called the Interludes and then as a solo act when the Interludes disbanded. It was in Florida that he met Eddy Arnold, who is now recognized as one of the pioneers of the Nashville Sound (Streissguth 2009). Eddy Arnold liked what he heard in Pursell's playing and assured him that if he moved to Nashville, he would get plenty of work. In 1960 Pursell moved to Nashville, and his musical career took another bend down the path of that crooked river when he became a Nashville session musician.

Most accounts of the Nashville Sound credit Chet Atkins, Owen Bradley, and Don Law with its development. Chet Atkins, a guitarist from Luttrell, Tennessee, was hired by RCA Victor as their head of A&R (artists and repertoire) after being a session musician. Owen Bradley, a pianist, worked closely with Decca's A&R man, Paul Cohen, and became Decca's main A&R rep for Nashville in 1958. Owen and his brother Harold Bradley are famous for founding the first music recording studio on Music Row in a renovated house, and adding a real Quonset hut to its back to serve as a recording area in 1955. Today the Quonset Hut, Columbia's famed Studio B, is owned by Belmont University (Pursell's employer 1980–2017) and is used by its students to learn the recording industry. Don Law was a producer for Columbia and thus essentially Pursell's boss during the years of his Columbia contract, 1962–67. Pursell worked with Harold Bradley on many sessions for Columbia and Decca, and when he first came to Nashville he played jazz with Chet Atkins at the Carousel in Printer's Alley. He knew all of these men well.

One distinctive facet of the Nashville Sound was its use of background vocalists. Two groups, the Anita Kerr Singers (female) and the Jordanaires (male), became regulars in Nashville sessions, and Pursell worked frequently with both groups. The "Anita Kerrs," as he calls them, sang wordless syllables on his 1963 hit song "A Winter Love." Another distinctive part of the Nashville Sound was its use of strings. Pursell's extensive experience as a young arranger for the Air Force Orchestra in the 1940s paid great dividends from the 1960s and beyond in Nashville. His skills at string arranging were just what Chet Atkins and Eddy Arnold were looking for when he began to arrange for Nashville sessions.

Floyd Cramer, another key figure in the Nashville Sound, was a pianist who worked closely with Chet Atkins. As you will read in chapter 5, Pursell was advised from the beginning of his time in Nashville to "play like Floyd," and eventually he did. Cramer developed a signature lick, a slip-note gesture. Jensen (1998) notes that Cramer's special piano style "offered a way for a softened steel guitar-like sound to fit in 'uptown'" (79). Pursell doesn't have much good to say about Cramer, a self-taught musician from Louisiana. See chapter 5 for a good story about Atkins, Cramer, and Pursell. Another pianist who appears on many Nashville recordings of this time is Hargus "Pig" Robbins. Some of the arrangements Pursell made in the late 1960s use Pig Robbins as session pianist.

Guitarists were central to the creation of the Nashville Sound. Chet Atkins's role was mainly as A&R man and producer, but Hank Garland, Grady Martin, and Harold Bradley were regulars in the 1960s Nashville sessions. Rich Kienzle calls them the triumvirate of guitar players (Kienzle 1983, cited in Jensen). Pursell worked with all of them, especially the latter two.

Country music fans have bemoaned the loss of the traditional, rural country style that had been celebrated in the early decades of WSM and the Grand Ole Opry. The relative merits and demerits of the new style is not a matter for this study. However, it is worth noting that the reason most offer for the shift in country music in the late 1950s is the rising popularity of rock 'n' roll music. The change in country music coincided with the advent of Elvis Presley and other rock musicians, and with this rise, a significant drop in sales of country albums, and thus a loss of radio airplay.

The rise of rock 'n' roll certainly created financial difficulties for country musicians in Nashville during the late 1950s, and Kosser points out that it happened almost overnight (37). The burgeoning Nashville recording industry had to find some way to compete with rock and revitalize sales and airplay of country music, and a shift in style was the solution they found. Much later (in 1999), bluegrass musicians Larry Cordle and Larry Shell even wrote a song about it: "Murder on Music Row" (Schaefer 2012). Their lyrics blame "drums and rock 'n' roll guitars" but also "the almighty dollar and the lust for worldwide fame" for the "death" of country music. Ironically, a popular cover of this tune features Alan Jackson and George Strait, both in the requisite cowboy hats and carrying acoustic guitars but backed up with electric bass and a drum set.[2] At least they used two fiddles.

Some would argue that the Nashville Sound saved country music rather than murdered it. Jensen's book-length analysis of the phenomenon points out that the myth of rock 'n' roll music's death blow served the country music world well; it gave them a justification for the shift in musical style toward a more commercialized sound. As the music industry in Nashville grew and more recording studios were founded, it is no surprise that the style of country music would evolve with growing technologies. Jensen (1998) also notes that new relationships between radio stations and record companies necessitated a change (121). Bill Ivey (1994) points to shifting business practices as another reason for the change in musical style. With growth comes change.

I would add that the obsession with creating hits must have contributed to these changes. Pursell talks about the atmosphere in a studio when a hit has been cut. He says that there is a special feeling among musicians at the end of a session if the recording is going to be a hit. He remembers talking with Chet Atkins the day that he and Floyd Cramer cut "Last Date" and how he knew it would be a hit (see ch. 5). Getting a hit meant attention from the record label, more opportunities to make music, and of course, hopefully, money. The *Billboard* charts became something to watch and something to aspire to by the 1960s, and this surely made artistic decisions seem more like business decisions than ever before. In 1963 Pursell paid close attention to the rise of "Our Winter Love" on the charts.

One of the results of the perceived threat to the survival of country music was the founding of the Country Music Association, an organization with which Pursell is only peripherally involved, but which has an unexpected connection to the story of Pursell's musical life. In 1958 the Country Music Disc Jockey Association met in Florida to form the Country Music Association, with the purpose of promoting country music within the music industry. In 1958 Bill Pursell was also in Florida, performing with the Interludes, and it was there that he met Eddy Arnold. Thus, his move to Nashville in 1960 coincides with the rise of the CMA, a startling coincidence that perhaps has a deeper meaning, for it is alongside the founding of the CMA that the style of country music began to change, and Pursell was invited to Nashville to be a key player in that change.

Pursell's hit solo recording "Our Winter Love" (released in 1962; achieved hit status in early 1963) shows many characteristics of the Nashville Sound, even though it is not a country song. The simple piano slap-back motive and melody are in the foreground, of course, because Pursell is a pianist, and the album was to feature his playing. But right behind him are massed strings, with sustained chords and soaring melodies, and then the Anita Kerr Singers with their wordless ooos and aaahs. Then in the second chorus, Harold Bradley enters with his electric bass and the "fuzz box" sound that was made so famous by Grady Martin. Pursell was working Martin's session when the sound was first discovered, as you will read in chapter 6. "Our Winter Love" hit #4 in "Middle Road Singles" in March 1963 and was listed as a Hot R&B single in April. It was not on the "Country" lists. But right on the recording were the stalwarts of the Nashville Sound: Harold Bradley on bass, the Anita Kerr Singers, and a group of session string players.

Pursell is not a country musician, and the listing on the *Billboard* R&B and "Middle Road" charts in the early 1960s affirms that. There are country tunes on his solo albums, but even these seem either smoothed into a gentle easy-listening style, or transformed into a jazz tune, like Johnny Cash's "I Walk the Line," which appears on the *Our Winter Love* album, or "Crying" on *Chasing a Dream*. The most "country"-sounding tune on *Our Winter Love* is "I Can't Help It If I'm Still in Love with You," a tune he later arranged for the Nashville Symphony. On the album the strings and Anita Kerrs are still present, but even on "I Can't Help It," his piano solos have a tinge of jazz with their blue notes and bebop-styled riffs. He may have used a bit of Floyd Cramer's slip-note style in the verses, but the chorus is all Pursell. He may have been able to adjust his style as a session player, but his solo albums reveal his deep lack of country credentials.

What follows is an account of Pursell's life, and because he is not a country musician, this is not a country music book. It is also not a book about a classical musician, because although Pursell has composed symphonies, a concerto, and sonatas, he worked with all styles of music and played many different musical roles during his lifetime. Instead, the story of Pursell's life is the story of a musical life lived in America during the rise of popular music in both radio and recordings. It is the story of many choices made, and the crooked, winding path that a musical life can take, given the skills and musicianship that Pursell had worked so hard to develop.

PRELUDE

CROOKED RIVER TOWN

THE
GENERAL JACKSON BLUEGRASS
AMERICANUS ! ! !
CUCKOLD & POLTROON
& MISSIES PRISSY & HANNAH
& HANNAH WITH THE RED BANDANNA
& SWEET RACHEL
SHOW

Scene: The town square in Nashville, Tennessee, in front of the Red Heifer Tavern. It is 1815. Everyone in town has turned out to await the arrival of the hero of the Battle of New Orleans, General Andrew Jackson. The orchestra plays a fanfare, but we hear the band leader call out in disappointment that the man walking down the road is not the eagerly awaited General Jackson. The chorus of townspeople sings: "Here comes the Cuckold comin' down 'at road. Here comes the Cuckold, the worst we ever knowed."

William Pursell paused in his description of his new opera, and played some broken octaves on the piano.

"Isn't that interesting? That's Borodin, that's exactly what he did in the Polovtsian Dances. He did the same modulation. That leaked through! That thing goes back to my childhood." Pursell played some more octaves, and then moved into the riff that underlies the chorus, singing about Robards, the man whose wife, Rachel, would eventually marry Andrew Jackson. "Here comes the Cuckold."

And then he played a phrase on the piano that could be right out of a Mozart sonata, designated for the strings in the opera. "Then he [the Cuckold] says, 'See, am I well fit, with gold buttons and a hat?'"

I asked him, "Would you say this musical style is more like a Broadway kind of opening?"

Pursell replied, "It's a combination of Broadway and classical and light opera, almost Gilbert and Sullivan. It's a comedy in a way, but there are some parts of this thing that are quite soul-searching, especially with Rachel and her heart problem."

The opera *Crooked River Town* is based on the true story of Andrew Jackson and his romance with Rachel Donelson Robards, a doomed romance because of her first marriage, heart problems, and early death before Jackson entered the White House as president of the United States. Pursell's friend Fred Burch, a prominent songwriter, wrote the libretto, and Pursell provided music that is every bit as eclectic and interesting as Pursell himself. Parts of it would be comfortable on a Broadway stage, parts at the Station Inn (a famous bluegrass venue in Nashville), and other parts on the stage of the Metropolitan Opera. There is comedy, drama and pathos, a ball, a duel, and a death scene—classic elements of any opera or Broadway show.

If this were Pursell's last large-scale masterwork, none other could be better fitting for a man who lived his life in a variety of musical worlds. *Crooked River Town*, scored for a string octet and bluegrass band, is a masterful blend of musical styles, classical and popular, every bit of it a postmodern American opera. It tells the story of Pursell's life in music, from Borodin to Boots Randolph, and by the end leaves one longing for more.

William Pursell, known as Bill to just about everyone, loves to tell stories. At the age of ninety, his memory is as sharp and vivid as it was when he first came to Nashville in 1960. Bill has been my colleague for the more than ten years that I have been a music history professor at Belmont, and I have grown to value his insight, his teaching skills, and his musical skills. No one else I know has the keyboard skills, the orchestration skills, and the ear that Bill has. He can spontaneously break out into Rachmaninoff's Piano Concerto No. 3 on the piano, improvise it into a boogie woogie tune, then shift to Gershwin's *Rhapsody in Blue*. He can orchestrate any kind of music and can hold forth on music history from the medieval era to the present day. He is a musician of the sort they don't make anymore, not just a performer, not just a composer or an arranger, but all and everything in between.

This book has grown out of the stories he loves to tell, his memories of an active life in a very lively period of American music history, and countless letters and documents that verify and expand upon his stories. I have spent the past several years interviewing Bill, scouring symphony archives and libraries for corroborating documents, and organizing and digesting the vast personal archive that Bill has accumulated from his seventy or so years in the music business. As far as I can tell, he never threw anything away. From business letters to family letters to union time sheets to news clippings and concert programs and original manuscripts, these archives hold a wealth of information, not just on Bill's life, but on what it meant to be a working musician in mid-twentieth-century America.

Bill has experienced a life that coincided with the rise of popular music in the United States. He had a hand in writing and arranging music for 1940s radio shows, toured with bands in the 1950s, recorded in and out of Nashville with some of the most famous American popular musicians in the 1960s and 1970s, and produced and arranged albums for a variety of clients. He had a *Billboard* Top 10 hit record in 1963, "Our Winter Love," and went on to record two more solo albums for Columbia. He played no small role in the rise of the Nashville Sound that arose during the peak of his career as a session musician. From the 1980s, he served as a music professor at the Belmont University School of Music, sharing his vast knowledge and experience with several generations of college music majors.

Pursell, like many American composers, has regularly crossed the quixotic line between classical and popular music, but he is unique in the ease with which he moved between the worlds, and the consistency, quality, and simultaneity of his efforts. Born in 1926, he was raised in the aftermath of what Lawrence Levine (1988) calls the sacralization of American culture, when the performance of what we now call classical music was given its rituals and social prestige, and when popular music began to be derided as lower class and not appropriate for polite society. Pursell's father, Arthur Pursell, only listened to classical music and carefully nurtured the young Bill's talents as a classical pianist, yet Bill himself did not harbor these same anti-popular prejudices. Like the famed American poet Walt Whitman, or the American composers Charles Ives and George Gershwin, Pursell was not afraid to embrace all aspects of American musical culture, and at times to even combine the "high" and "low" in his compositions. He did all of this while maintaining a lively career as a performer, arranger, producer, and composer. He participated on every level of musical life in mid-twentieth-century America, and did so successfully and with an ease that belied his natural gifts for music, his unfailing optimism, and a capacity for hard work.

Pursell's early training as a classical pianist and his years of study at prominent American music schools gave him a solid keyboard technique and impressive orchestration skills. Unlike many classically trained pianists, he finds improvisation easy, and music a native tongue. While Pursell was playing by day with Johnny Cash and Patsy Cline and other stalwart figures of the Nashville Sound in the recording studios of Nashville, he was concertizing by night with Nashville Symphony conductors Willis Page, Thor Johnson, and Kenneth Schermerhorn. He is not just a classical composer who dabbles in contemporary styles, nor is he a country keyboardist who can also play Gershwin. Pursell is able to do it all, and do it well.

He easily could have become a concert pianist, or lived his life fully as a touring rhythm and blues musician, or a studio pianist and arranger. But Pursell made key decisions along the way that took him from a seemingly straight path around an unexpected bend, just as the Cumberland River, also known to locals as the Crooked River, winds through Middle Tennessee. Pursell's life as an American musician did not flow along the currents his parents or teachers laid out for him, or even the currents he chose for himself. Rather, he was swept along, around various bends and curves, and managed to make a successful and satisfying musical life in spite of it all. This book, then, is the story of Pursell's life in music: the story of a California childhood, elite American music schools, music in the United States military, bands on the road, the Nashville recording industry, the rise of the Nashville Sound, and higher education in music in the United States. William Pursell is not a household name, but many have heard his music without knowing it, whether on hit albums from the 1960s or on television, films, and commercials, or in the music of his students. Here, then, is his story.

CROOKED RIVER CITY

I. A CALIFORNIA CHILDHOOD

In 1968 Arthur Pursell sent his son some home movies. After watching them with his family, Bill Pursell reflected on the experience in a letter to his father (January 7, 1968):

> In the first part of the film, which starts at the Pursell house on H Street, there is an almost dream-like feeling in watching these very dear people pass in front of the camera. . . . Eldon, Aunt Pearl, Grandma and Grandpa, made me think of the poem you wrote, Dad, called Reverie. The thought of people from the past coming out on a stage in your mind's eye, smiling at you and then leaving.
>
> And then, there was me. A rather self-conscious child, with large protruding boyish ears, and baggy pants, especially down by the shoes. Not too serious, still somewhat of an enigma, even to himself. A kind of crackley, big toothed grin, that said: "I'm awfully glad to be here, but where am I?" I can see parts of my present self there in this boy on the film. There is a difference, naturally, in the physique, and even in features and shape of the head, but it's me alright.

William Whitney Pursell was born on June 9, 1926, in an Oakland hospital. He was adopted as an infant by Arthur and Delia Pursell and was raised in the small California town of Tulare as an adored only son. Many of his obsessions later in life—trains, Russian orchestral music, and rural mountain culture—can be traced back to his rich and varied California childhood. A brief tour of Pursell's early years gives us a picture, not only of how he grew up and the reasons for his likes and dislikes, but also of small-town California in the 1930s and 1940s, and a way of life in America that has long been romanticized (or the opposite) in films and novels.

Tulare in the 1930s was the California depicted in John Steinbeck's epic American novel *The Grapes of Wrath* (1939).[1] Pursell's Tulare childhood is colored by memories of sitting behind his mother at the Red Cross depot, watching her hand out food and clothing to migrant workers who had come to California seeking work picking crops. He also remembers

Young William Pursell

them coming to his back door to ask for food: "I imagine the word got out around the Brotherhood that there was this nice lady on King Street, at the house with the front porch covered with vines with the rocking chair, that you could depend on for a hand-out."²

Pursell also remembers the steam train coming through town, summers at the local public pool, nights sleeping on the floor at his father's hand-built observatory, and weeks spent hiking and camping in the Sierra Nevada Mountains. This is not a childhood that one would suspect would lead to a successful career as a professional musician. Pursell's father did not force him to spend hours practicing the piano (though the boy and his mother did have some conversations about his reluctance to practice), nor did he grow up in a major city, surrounded by a lively cultural scene. But in addition to a fairly normal, easygoing childhood spent mostly outdoors and with friends, Pursell benefited from his father's love of music and parents who sought out the best teachers for him that they could find. When little Billy began playing tunes by ear on the piano at age three, his parents knew they had something special, and encouraged their son throughout the years to take his music more seriously, without ever forcing it on him or trying to make him into a concertizing prodigy.

Classical music did shape his early years, however. One of Pursell's earliest memories is the pattern on the living room carpet, where he crawled around as a toddler while listening to his father's records of the Russian orchestral greats. He especially remembers Tchaikovsky's

Eleven-year-old Bill Pursell and his mother Delia

Nutcracker Suite and Borodin's Polovtsian Dances, which have, thanks to their distinctive rhythms, forever become joined to memories of his cat and the neighborhood fire siren.

Pursell's adoptive parents were exceptional in their own ways. His father, Arthur Pursell, was a grammar school principal (seventh and eighth grade), and his mother was a nurse for the Red Cross. Delia Peterson Pursell, Bill's mother, had moved to San Francisco from Minnesota with her Swedish-Norwegian family, after a prairie fire destroyed their farm. She was a resilient woman who knew how to persevere through hardship. Her father committed suicide when she was a young teenager, and she had to go to work to help support her family. Later, one of her brothers would commit suicide, and two of her other brothers would eventually spend the last years of their lives in a mental institution.[3]

Delia earned a nursing certificate from the Merritt Hospital School of Nursing in Oakland, and when the United States entered World War I in 1917 she volunteered as an army nurse and served at an army hospital in

Fort Logan, Colorado. She would later work at the hospital in Berkeley, California, where Arthur Pursell, having returned from military duty in France, arrived with a case of the measles. Delia's fair hair, laugh, and sunny disposition captured Arthur's attention.[4] They were married on June 8, 1921, and soon moved to Arthur's hometown of Tulare. On May 18, 1922, Delia gave birth to Robert Lewis Pursell, but Arthur wrote: "To our dismay he did not survive the period of delivery." Four years later, Arthur and Delia adopted Bill from the Native Sons and Daughters orphanage in San Francisco and brought him home to be raised in Tulare, a small town of about fifteen thousand in the San Joaquin Valley.

The peaceful idyll of small-town California was disturbed by the extreme poverty brought on by the Depression and the migration of farm workers from Arkansas and Oklahoma to California. Pursell's encounters with poverty during his childhood were not limited to sitting behind his mother at the Red Cross depot; he also learned about what it means to be poor in the schoolyard. Pursell's family never had much money, but they did have plenty to eat. Pursell remembers one particular family at his school:

> The Pyrtle kids went to school with us, and at lunchtime, when Mrs. Schafer used to blow the whistle, they would go out and stand underneath the trees until she blew the whistle to come back in for class. We finally figured out they didn't have any lunch. So what we did was that we would bring extra food in our lunchbox. We were just kids, second grade, and we would do that to make sure they got fed. Kids will do that.

Pursell lived and saw these things through the eyes of a young child, and his family played a role different from what is usually depicted in the classic stories of American literature, which are most often told from the point of view of the poor. His father and mother were both employed, and he was secure at home, even if money was tight at times. Hobos were knocking at his back door while he was composing little marches on the piano or listening to the Polovtsian Dances on his father's record player.

One of the advantages of being raised in a small town was the freedom Pursell enjoyed as a child and later as a teenager. Pursell says that he did not get serious about the piano until he was about twelve years old. He had two uncles who were coaches, track and football, and he received balls and bats and other sports equipment from them for Christmas and birthday gifts. Pursell also liked trains as a boy, and just running around the neighborhood with his friends. In his own words, "I goofed away my life." Pursell says that his love for sports and play did keep him away from the piano at times.

Pursell's fondest childhood memories are from summer. He remembers summers spent at the Blue Moon pool: "Mom used to give me a buck in dimes for Tootsie Rolls, and she had to do her work as a Red Cross nurse. So she would leave me alone down there all summer. And I would do nothing but swim. Forget practicing, I was out there swimming. I used to have a way of treading water with my feet, so it would look like I was standing up in the pool. I'd say, 'Come on in, it's shallow!' and I'd be there, and they'd sink down. I was a good swimmer."

Pursell also spent a great deal of his summers in the nearby Sierra Nevada Mountains. His father's family was scattered throughout the San Francisco and Los Angeles areas, but they had deep roots in the mountains that Arthur Pursell so loved. Some of Pursell's aunts and uncles who lived up there were quite eccentric. This large and unique family deserves some description, as they played an important part in helping raise Bill. His childhood adventures in the Sierra Nevada gave him a strong sense of place and of family roots. He describes their home as "high in the foothills, almost to the mountains, and the brush up there grows very close to the earth. It's a very interesting place."

One of his cousins, Lizzie McGee, lived in Orosi. Pursell remembers:

> It was wild country; when you'd go up there at night, you'd hear the pumas, the wildcats. On Easter, they would have an Easter sunrise service up there, and all these people from around Dunlap would come, and they'd all go up on this hill, about five o'clock, six o'clock in the morning, Cousin Lizzie would say, and the "imported musicians" would come. Actually, they were just three trumpet players from the Valley. They'd go up and start playing these hymns at the top of the mountain, and all of these people would go up, and they'd have their sermon. Then they'd break open their picnic baskets and have their picnic up there, on Easter sunrise. And that was a real sunrise service.

Arthur's cousin Lizzie lived near a close family friend, Sally Evans. Pursell remembers visiting Sally regularly as a child, probably so that his father could check on her well-being. Again, as with the hobos and migrant workers in Tulare, there is no prejudice or judgment in Pursell's memories of Sally, merely a twinkle in his eye, and a sense of amazement at this unique individual. Her story is best read in his own voice.

> In my memory, I think from the time I was old enough, two or three, I remember Dad and Mom and I would drive up in that area, and we'd always stop at a certain spot along the mountain road. There would be a picket fence. And we'd go up there, but we wouldn't go beyond that fence, and Dad would call, "Sally." And at the very end, in this little lean-to hut would emerge this little old woman, with a pioneer bonnet on and long dresses, and her legs wrapped with gunny sacks to keep her from the cold. As she walked towards us, you noticed that she had this sort of leathery skin, like she'd been out a lot. But she had the clearest blue eyes, and she'd say, "Hello, Art," to my Dad, and "Sally, how you doin'?" "I'm fine, Art, except that the beast has been bothering me." Later on I found out that the beast was what she called the "catamount," which lived in the trees, and at night she'd bang pots and pans to get rid of it.

Sally Evans had been a close friend of the Pursell family since the turn of the century and had even rocked Arthur as a baby. She was a schoolteacher who had a bad love affair and was so bitter about her rejection that she suddenly decided to move to the mountains and become a hermitess.

> She built her own little shack, on the other side of the mountain, and that's where she lived during the First World War. Now, she said, and she claimed that the Indians told her, that the Kaiser Wilhelm had buried gold at the bottom of the creek, at the bottom of this mountain. And she went down and dug a big hole and tried to find it.

She had run a lunch stand for the wagon-drivers but then became afraid that they too were after the Kaiser's gold or her property, and she removed herself deeper into the mountains. Cousin Sally came to a mysterious end. Pursell's cousin Lizzie and her husband looked up one day and saw smoke, and when they arrived at Sally's cabin, it was burned to the ground. They never did find her body. And one year later, their own house burned. Only the chimney was left standing, and Pursell remembers camping out under it as a child.

The young William Pursell likely did not notice the contrast between his country cousins and his educated, more cosmopolitan parents.

Children accept life as it comes, and these jaunts into the hills to see his aunts and uncles were a regular event for him. But I wonder how his father saw it, and how his country relatives saw it: Arthur, a World War I veteran and grammar school principal, and Delia, a trained nurse, bringing their boy up to the hills for a visit. Were there late-night talks about the boy's education, his obvious intelligence and musical abilities? Did the country cousins understand how different Bill's life would be? Although Arthur and Delia did not cultivate Bill for a high-powered life like some parents might have (imagine a Leopold Mozart or a Frederick Wieck for a father), they clearly valued education and would later ensure that Bill's potential would be developed. They had left the mountains, and even small-town Tulare seemed like an opportunity. This is not to say that the country Pursells were ignorant or unintelligent. They were curious people, artistic and creative, but they had chosen to remain in the mountains. Arthur had moved on.

A mutual love of the stars brought the two worlds together on at least one occasion. Bill recalls:

> Lizzie wanted to learn something about astronomy. So Dad made her a six-inch Newtonian reflector telescope. He ground the mirror himself, and then he put the prism at the top. Lizzie would sit there with her green eyeshade on when she was quite old, and she would look out the window at the constellations. She'd say, "Art, I saw all of these wonderful stars last night." When she died, they published a poem she wrote, "God's Garden of Stars." She was really something.

Later in life, when Pursell was living in Nashville, Tennessee, and played on the stage of the Grand Ole Opry for the first time, his California family finally believed that he had arrived. Scholarships to the most prestigious music school in the country, the Peabody Conservatory and the Eastman School of Music, did not impress them, nor did his numerous classical compositions. It was when he got up on that famous stage with country music star Eddy Arnold that his family sat up and took note. After all, they had listened for years to the Saturday night broadcasts of the Grand Old Opry from their homes in the foothills of the Sierra Nevada Mountains, and for them, the Opry was more real than any orchestra performance or classical piano recital.

One of his closest childhood friends was Daniel DaFoe, and they had in common a great love for music. Pursell remembers that they would test each other for pitch names, one playing a note on the piano and the other guessing the note, then switching. Daniel played the clarinet and would later become the principal clarinet in the San Joaquin Symphony. Pursell remembers playing harmonicas with Daniel when they were children, and spending time camping together in the Sierra Nevada Mountains.

Another important part of his childhood summers, besides visiting his aunts and uncles in the foothills of the Sierra Nevada, was Camp Tulequoia, a YMCA summer camp. These adventurous summers formed a crucial part of his sense of identity and helped foster strong bonds between father and son. From the age of five Bill would spend a large part of his summers at the camp. His father was in charge of a cabin, and his mother was the camp nurse. When Bill got older, he had his own cabin under his charge. These summers fed what would become for Pursell a lifelong sense of adventure.

Pursell spent a great deal of his childhood hiking the Sierra Nevada Mountains with his father. These hiking and camping trips developed in Pursell a strong sense of discipline and self-reliance, and an almost fearless love of adventure, all of which would later serve him well as a working musician.

> I had this wonderful outlet of going to the mountains all the time with Dad. I was getting asthma attacks when I was about twelve or thirteen. I'd go near a cotton dummy, or my Uncle Carl's cotton farm, and I would literally tie up. And Mom, who was a nurse, had these ephedrine capsules, so that if I got tied up, I would take an ephedrine capsule; it would open my lungs up. Dad got the idea, he never discussed it with Mom, but I started hiking through the mountains with him. I was a skinny little kid, and I had to carry my own pots and pans, but he hiked it out of me. We would hike steadily for eight hours at a time, going up. I ended up with tremendous vital capacity, no asthma, he just drummed it out of me.

Sometimes his father and his uncle Frank Pursell would take Bill and a friend (usually Daniel DaFoe or Henry Bramer) camping, and they would leave the boys at a tent and disappear into the mountains for a few days. Bill and his friends would have to fend for themselves. He remembers that they used to go down to the Giant Forest supply store to purchase bacon and other food, and they would hoist it high up into a tree to protect it from animals at night. But on one trip there was a bear that figured out how to get the food, and several mornings in a row, the boys would wake to find the basket on the ground and the bacon gone. Pursell remembers that this was getting quite expensive, purchasing all of this bacon, and not being able to eat it. So he told Henry to wake him if he heard the bear in the night. That night, Henry shook him, and sure enough, the bear was going after the basket, just outside their tent. Bill was so mad that he took his ax, left the tent, and threw it into the darkness as hard as he could, straight toward the noise. He heard a cry of pain, and then the bear ran away. The boys were told the next day that in the morning, a park ranger had been attacked by a wounded bear and had shot it dead. "I was so stupid," Pursell recalls. "That bear could have gone after me."

The second great love of Pursell's life, aside from music, is flying, which became another outlet for his sense of adventure. As an adult, he earned a pilot's license and spent his free time in between studio sessions flying various small planes. He often has said that if he were not a pianist, he would be a pilot. Pursell learned to fly at a young age, illegally, flying without a license with other underage pilots. Tulare was close to an aviation school, the Rankin Aeronautical Academy. A stunt pilot, J. G. "Tex" Rankin, received a contract from the United States Army to establish a training school for their pilots in World War II. The Rankin Academy was open from 1941 to 1944, and trained thousands of cadets.[5] Pursell remembers watching the pilots train and even spending time at the field. His friends Conrad and Mervyn Fulton had a Bellanca plane and he would go up with them. They would find a dust devil, fly right into it, and watch the altimeter go up and up. It wasn't until 1962 that Pursell took official pilot lessons, and his instructor noticed that he already knew the basics of being a pilot.

All of these experiences—camping, swimming, flying—were interwoven with a love of music, nurtured by his father Arthur, who himself was an amateur musician and played recordings of classical music constantly at home. Pursell writes about the time that his parents first realized he was musically gifted, when he was three years old:

> There was a particular instance, one evening at supper, which I can still see in my mind; the shape of the dining room, how the chairs were around the table, my mother and father sitting at each end, Mother near the kitchen, myself in the middle near Dad's desk, and the little upright piano across from me on the other side of the wall. My mother and I had come back from the circus that afternoon

which was held at the county fairgrounds. There had been a band playing for the different circus acts, and that evening during dinner I got down from my chair at the table, went over to the piano and started playing "Yankee Doodle" with both hands. I remember hearing my mother drop some kind of utensil, a spoon perhaps, on to a plate at her end of the table, which startled me. I looked back at my dad, who (I can still see) continuing to chew his food, calmly, making no comment, and simply looking down at me.

Somewhere later in time, possibly a week or more, he asked me to play a little piece of music I had made up, and he slowly started to write it out in manuscript. Seeing him do this was the beginning of my learning how note symbols were put down on paper. He named it "Billy's Orchestra."

By the age of five, Bill was studying piano with a local Tulare teacher, Lucy Lee, and would remain her student through his sophomore year in high school.[6] Ms. Lee played the organ for a show on weekends, and Bill decided he wanted to learn the organ. It is a credit to his parents that they did not discourage his natural musical curiosity. The only place that he could find to practice was the Hamilton Peers funeral parlor, which had a Hammond organ. Pursell tells the story that one day, he was experimenting on the organ, making sounds like he would hear on radio serials, tremolos, diminished chords, anything that sounded ominous. Mr. Peers came into the room where he was playing and told him that he had to stop, because he was frightening the people who were coming to the office to make arrangements for their dearly departed.

By the time he was a teenager, his musical world began to expand. One summer, Pursell was up in the Sierra Nevada Mountains with his family. There was a talent show in the park, and Pursell played the *Rondo alla turca* by Mozart. The audience's response helped Pursell begin to understand what it meant to be a performer: "I got an ovation from these people, and I remember it hooked me. I remember thinking, my God, this is something else. And I remember the ranger standing there saying, 'He's only fourteen,' and everybody was cheering and whistling, and I thought, wow, there's something in this. And then I started playing a lot."

Around the same time, Pursell attended a concert by Alexander Brailowsky at a concert series in the neighboring town of Visalia and heard him perform Domenico Scarlatti and Carl Tausig's *Pastorale Cappriccio* and Manuel De Falla's *Ritual Fire Dance*. Pursell was inspired to go out and find the music and try to learn it himself. He says that his teacher was unhappy with him because these pieces had not been assigned, and that was the beginning of the end of his studies with Ms. Lee. She said to him, "Why don't you play the pieces I assign you?" and Pursell replied, "Why don't you assign me pieces I can play?" After they cooled down, though, Ms. Lee realized that perhaps it was time for another teacher, and so she suggested that Pursell go up to San Francisco and play for Elizabeth Simpson, a well-known concert coach.

The decision by his parents to live in Berkeley for a summer and allow the young Bill to study with Mrs. Simpson was a turning point in his life, away from the carefree Tulare small-town childhood and toward a more serious, focused study of music. That summer, his father took summer courses in Berkeley and Pursell studied piano with Mrs. Simpson. By the end of the summer, Mrs. Simpson told Pursell's parents that she wanted to continue to teach him, and so they made arrangements for him to move to Berkeley, board with a family, and continue his lessons. Pursell was sixteen in the fall of 1942 when he left his home in Tulare, and he spent his last two high school years at Berkeley High. This was the first major bend in the crooked river of Pursell's career, a shift toward high-level classical training.

When he first arrived in Berkeley, Mrs. Simpson told his parents that he was about three years behind in terms of repertoire, and he reports that he worked very hard to catch up. Pursell remembers his lessons with Mrs. Simpson fondly.

> Every week I would get on the College Avenue streetcar, and go up to Webster Street and get off and walk up to Mrs. Simpson's house, very ornate. She would come to the door, and she looked like Queen Mary, "Come in William." So I would go into this inner sanctum, this place where this famous woman taught all these remarkable pianists. She had a Mason and Hamlin, and a Steinway, sitting next to each other, shiny black, seven feet long, which in those days, considering that I grew up in Tulare, laboring over a little Byron Mausey upright, I thought, this was just royalty personified. I was in her good graces and so she would have me in there, and we would work, and she had repertoire classes on Saturday.

Pursell's new teacher insisted that he learn the orchestra part of a piano concerto before he learned the solo piano part. (A piano reduction of the orchestral part rather than a full orchestra is often used to accompany young pianists in concert.) Pursell says that Mrs. Simpson insisted on this method so that the pianist would know the whole of the concerto well, instead of just his own part. A concert program of three recitals from Mrs. Simpson's studio at this time shows Pursell accompanying Tchaikovsky's Concerto in B flat Minor, with Floyd Sharp as the soloist. On another recital, Pursell performed Mendelssohn's *Capriccio Brillante* as soloist. The year is not listed on the program, but it must have been 1943 or 1944, the years of Pursell's study with her. A note at the bottom says: "Realizing the present need for music as a builder of morale, this series of recitals is given by these pianists as a wartime service. To enable those desiring to cooperate in this service to do so, a silver offering for the benefit of the American Red Cross will be accepted at the door after the program."[7] In the next two years, the war would become terribly real to him, as he would turn eighteen and be eligible for the draft. His time in Berkeley was invaluable to his growth as a musician, and if he had been two years older, he likely would not have experienced it. The draft was looming.

Pursell did not limit his musical study to piano performance while living in Berkeley. He was able to study composition and harmony at the high school, and enjoyed further studies with a private tutor. His composition/counterpoint tutor was Herman Trutner, and his harmony teacher at the high school was Dorah O'Neil.[8] Pursell traveled to Oakland once a week to study with Mr. Trutner, the first horn player of the San Francisco Symphony at the time. They worked their way through the classic counterpoint text by Johann Joseph Fux, *The Steps to Parnassus*. This is the kind of musical study that most students only encounter when they enter college, and indeed, Pursell would later study the same concepts as a music major at the Peabody Conservatory. These studies, along with music theory classes at Berkeley High School with Mrs. O'Neil and his piano studies with Mrs. Simpson, gave Bill a strong foundation as a young musician. Pursell's later skills as a composer, arranger, and organizer are doubtlessly indebted to these early studies in harmony.

Most of Pursell's compositions from this time were for solo piano. A recital program for Dorah Dooley O'Neil's harmony class shows that Pursell played a suite of piano pieces, "The Dream," "Day in the City," and "Lullaby," in June 1943. One piece that Pursell composed during this time, *Waltz Conflict*, was a portrayal of a waltz in conflict with itself, and another, *Mad Player Piano*, imagined a player piano out of control. *Mad Player Piano* has a steady stride pattern in the left hand, interspersed with

Manuscript of "Mad Player Piano"

Manuscript of "Waltz Conflict"

broken chords in the right hand on the off beats. There is a lot of wrong-note harmony, sharps and flats intermingled, and half step conflicts between the right hand and the left hand. The ragtime broken chords in the right hand gradually dissolve into scale-like runs and tremolos, as the music gets faster and faster. At the end there is a Lisztian descending run, alternating hands, to a final return of the ragtime patterns in both hands. Pursell's hands are very large, and the intervals in the left hand span a tenth.

Mad Player Piano is an early harbinger of the wonderful intersection between popular and classical musical styles that makes Pursell's music appealing and unique. The ragtime and jazzy rhythms marry with Romantic gestures influenced by Rachmaninoff and Liszt, whose music Pursell was learning in his piano lessons. *Waltz Conflict*, for both piano and orchestra, survives only as a sketch, with chord symbols for the orchestra and instructions for the piano like "French waltz" and "piano plays busy background."

In 1943 Pursell's composition teacher at Berkeley, Mrs. O'Neil, submitted two of his songs to a composition contest that was sponsored by *Scholastic Magazine*, the RCA Victor recording company, and the Music Educators' National Conference. "The Dead" and "The Wanderers' Night Song" were songs he had composed before he came to Berkeley, and they won both first prize and honorable mention. The songs were first performed at Berkeley High School's annual composers' recital. Seventeen-year-old Bill won thirty-five dollars for first prize and the *Victor Book of Opera* as honorable mention.[9] One of the judges was the composer William Schumann.

"The Dead," set to a poem by Ernest Stockman, uses a rising two-note motive, introduced by the piano and then incorporated into the voice, to unify the piece. This song is in E minor, with a brief excursion into E flat major near the end. Pursell uses a three-note descending gesture in the bass to cycle through harmonies that are at once sophisticated and simple. Pursell explores secondary dominants in this piece, for example, using the tonic E minor as an E major seventh chord to tonicize IV. He moves outside and around the key in ways that do not sound unconventional, but are sophisticated. For example, the first verse is sung over this progression in the piano: i-i7-IV-VII7-III-I7-iv-V7-i. He uses the two-note motive to create passing tones between these chords. The voice is given longer notes on words like "rest," "near," "weep," "still," "soul," and "graves," to heighten the meaning of the key words.

"Wanderer's Night Song" is written to a well-known poem by the German romantic poet Johann Wolfgang Goethe. The poem was most famously set by the prolific nineteenth-century composer of songs, Franz Schubert. Pursell's setting begins with a rocking pattern in the left hand and chords in the right hand. The piece is set in B flat minor, and on beat three of the opening measures an A natural in the left hand evokes a harmonic poignancy.[10] Pursell's harmonies are rich, lush, and sometimes even a little bluesy. But this is thoroughly a classical art song in the Schubertian tradition, with its use of repeated patterns in the left hand to accompany the voice and its attention to text. In the second verse ("O'er all the hill tops is quiet / In all the tree tops hearest thou hardly a breath / The birds are asleep in the trees / Wait! Soon like these thou too shalt rest"), the birds are depicted by triplets in the right hand set against duplets in the left hand. At "rest" (symbolizing the ultimate rest, death), there is an upwards leap and a reassuring major chord. The compositional language is well-formed and sophisticated, not what one would expect of an American teenager in the 1940s.

Pursell describes his time at Berkeley High School as one of incredible artistic and intellectual stimulation. One of his friends there, James Cahill, would go on to become a world-renowned authority on Chinese painting. Another friend, Hans Baerwald, would become a historian of Japan. Being a student at Berkeley High, Pursell says, was to be one of many gifted teenagers.

Almost all of Elizabeth Simpson's piano students were exceptional talents. One of her students, whom she taught before Pursell came to Berkeley to study with her, was Ruth Slenczenska. Her childhood was very different from the one Pursell had enjoyed. Ruth's father had groomed her for a career as a concert artist, and he would make her practice nine hours a day or more. Pursell says that his mother often would point Ruth out to him as fellow gifted young pianist. Ruth, however, would have trouble with the incredible amount of pressure her father exerted on her, and would later elope, much as Clara Schumann had, a century before, and become estranged from her father. Ruth later wrote about her troubles in a book, *Forbidden Childhood* (1957). In the 1930s, she was studying with Mrs. Simpson in Berkeley, and she was still living there (though no longer Mrs. Simpson's student) when Pursell moved to town. Pursell remembers seeing her getting off the College Avenue streetcar to visit her friend's house to put some makeup on before a date, because her father would not allow her to wear makeup. He also remembers seeing her backstage after a concert one day. She was signing autographs, but there was a moment when her father held up her cloak, and without another word, she stopped signing, her father put the cloak over her shoulders, and they left. It was, Pursell says, like they were communicating without words. Mrs. Simpson told Pursell that she had had to release Ruth as a student, because her father interfered too much with her artistic development and with Mrs. Simpson's authority as a teacher.

The very different lives of the two young pianists are a case study for stage parents everywhere. Slenczenska endured a childhood of work and little play (her father would not even allow her to have dolls, according to Pursell), and Pursell spent his summers hiking in the mountains and swimming at the local pool. Slenczenska had a career as a concert artist but ended up estranged from her father. Pursell would go on to have a life as a professional musician, not exclusively as a concert artist, but as a versatile and happy virtuoso. Pursell could have pursued the concert artist path, if he had made different choices (to be addressed in later chapters). But perhaps because he had been given a large measure of freedom in his youngest years, he did not see his life as a narrow, proscribed path, but one with many different possibilities, twists and turns, musical and otherwise.

Pursell returned home to Tulare in January 1944 to perform a concert with the Gavlan Symphony Orchestra in the Tulare High School auditorium. A news clipping, likely from the Tulare *Advance Register*, states that the orchestra brought "the finest piano available in the San Joaquin Valley," a Steinway piano from Fresno, so that Pursell could "give the best rendition of" Beethoven's "Moonlight" Sonata.[11] On the concert, Pursell played the "Moonlight" and Chopin's "Black Key" Etude in G Flat Major.[12] The Steinway on which he performed became a cause of some consternation—Steinway mistakenly billed the Gavlan Symphony for the entire cost of the piano, six thousand dollars, rather than just a rental fee.[13]

Living in Berkeley allowed Pursell more than one encounter with greatness. One day, Pursell had gotten off the bus to go home, and a little car came up the street, with a man who "filled up the whole front seat." The man leaned out, said "Bonjour," and asked directions to a different house on Spruce Street. Pursell, who could understand the broken English and French, gave him the directions, the man said, "Merci," and went his way. It was Darius Milhaud, who was teaching at Mills College at the time. Pursell would later see him at concerts going backstage to meet the famous conductor Pierre Monteux.

Berkeley High School had an exchange program with the University of California, and Bill and his fellow students would often go to the campus to hear lectures. They offered the opportunity to personally encounter major composers and other important musical figures. He remembers attending a workshop by composer Ernest Bloch, who was discussing his seminal work, *Schelomo*. He sat close to the composer and had a strong reaction to the piece. "The piece of music itself is just astonishing. It is like a proclamation and a picture of Jewish suffering." Pursell was only sixteen years old, and the founding of Israel was only a few years in the future. But he remembers responding more to the music of the work than its deeper meaning.

The Berkeley lecture exchange was not Pursell's only opportunity to learn from major musical figures. Bill and his friends would often volunteer to usher at concerts of the San Francisco Symphony, where they would hear Pierre Monteux conduct.

> We would go in and we would usher, and then afterwards we would march down Market Street in San Francisco on the way to the train with hot dogs in our hands. I would say, now you be the brass, and you be the woodwinds of the Brahms First (Symphony), and you be this, and we would sing all of these parts while we were marching down Market Street. We were kids, you know? It was just great stuff. We were all sixteen and took ourselves incredibly seriously. We were all into the arts.

Pursell began to experience some ambition as a young musician. One of the many concerts that Pursell attended in San Francisco was given by the famous pianist Rudolph Serkin, and after the concert, he went backstage with Mrs. Simpson to meet the artist. He recalls standing backstage with several people, and Mrs. Simpson asked Pursell if he wanted to play for him. Pursell was intimidated by the great artist and said no, and went home. He regretted his shyness and knew he had passed up an opportunity to play for one of the great pianists of his time.

This incident is what prompted him, sometime later, to travel via train to Philadelphia to play for Serkin. Mrs. Simpson, when she discovered his plan, told Pursell that he was not ready for such an audition, and told his parents not to let him go, but Pursell was adamant, and with his typical stubbornness and surety of purpose, he went. He took a 3,000-mile train ride, accompanied by his Aunt Naomi, across the country. Pursell

Elizabeth Simpson

Presents

William Pursell, Pianist

Assisted by

Arabelle Hong, Soprano

Floyd Everett Sharp, Accompanist

BERKELEY WOMEN'S CITY CLUB
2315 Durant Avenue

SUNDAY, MAY TWENTY-EIGHTH
Three O'clock

■

PROGRAM

I

Prelude and Fugue, C minor .... *Bach*
Pastorale .... *Scarlatti*
Capriccio .... *Scarlatti*

II

Sonata, C sharp minor .... *Beethoven*
Adagio sostenuto — Allegretto — Presto agitato

III

Nocturne, Op. 9, No. 2 .... *Chopin*
Nocturne, Op. 55, No. 1 .... *Chopin*
Etude, Op. 10, No. 5 .... *Chopin*

IV

*The Dead .... *William Pursell*
Wanderer's Night Song .... *William Pursell*

ARABELLE HONG

V

A Dream .... *William Pursell*
Danse de Puck .... *Debussy*
The White Peacock .... *Griffes*
Ritual Fire Dance .... *De Falla*

VI

Concerto, A minor .... *Grieg*
Allegro molto moderato

■

This recital illustrates a part of the work in piano and composition accomplished by William Pursell during his high school period. His compositions were completed under the supervision of Dorah Dooley O'Neill.

* These songs have just won first prize in a nationwide competition sponsored by the Educator's National Conference, Scholastic Magazine, and R. C. A. Victor, and open to high school composers only.

This is the first of a series of three recitals by members of Elizabeth Simpson's piano class. The second will be given by Violet Caldwell, assisted by Harriett Westling, 'cellist, at the Berkeley Piano Club on June eleventh at three o'clock. You and your friends are invited to attend.

Concert program, May 28, 1944

```
CLASS OF SERVICE                WESTERN         1201   SYMBOLS
This is a full-rate                                    DL = Day Letter
Telegram or Cable-                                     NL = Night Letter
gram unless its de-              UNION                 LC = Deferred Cable
ferred character is in-                                NLT = Cable Night Letter
dicated by a suitable        A. N. WILLIAMS            Ship Radiogram
symbol above or pre-           PRESIDENT
ceding the address.
The filing time shown in the date line on telegrams and day letters is STANDARD TIME at point of origin. Time of receipt is STANDARD TIME at point of destination.

    FC98 NL PD=B BALTIMORE MD 26
    MR AND MRS A L PURSELL=
    738 EAST KING ST TULARE CALIF=

    HAVE JUST WON THE THREE YEAR BOISE COMPOSITION SCHOLARSHIP
    AM TAKING PIANO FROM ALEXANDER SKLAREVSKI CONCERT ARTIST
    WHOOPEE=
        WILL.
```

Telegram from Baltimore

says that he worked himself into a "nervous wreck" during the long train ride, with no piano to practice on, and when he went to play for Serkin, he was so nervous that he played badly. While there, he also played for Isabella Vengerova and Mstislav Hvorostovsky. He played one of his own compositions for them, among other repertoire.

After his return to Berkeley, his parents received a letter stating that although the great pianists were impressed with his tremendous musicality, the other students had played better, with better technique. Pursell sees this event as one of the biggest mistakes of his life, and one of the most important and costly lessons learned: "I made up my mind that I would never again ever be as nervous as that when I played. And I never was. But that was a lesson, and it cost me. But I'm sorry, because it cost a lot of money to do it. It took 6,000 miles for me to learn that lesson, to never be intimidated again by anyone. Because I almost made it." Pursell's unique character shines through in this reflection—someone else might have regretted not listening to Mrs. Simpson, but Pursell's only regret was getting nervous. He did not admit that he was not ready to play for these great pianists, but instead felt that they intimidated him and that he did not do his best. This episode in Pursell's early musical life shows the grit, determination, and confidence that would later serve him well as a working musician.

After he returned to California, Pursell performed his first recital under Mrs. Simpson. His teacher had a special way of preparing him to enter the stage: "I remember Mrs. Simpson came backstage and she said, 'William, I want you to do something for me,' and I said, 'What's that?' She said, 'I want you to sit here and say to yourself, I am Arthur Rubinstein, over and over again.' And I did, and if you had asked me who I was when I went on the stage, I'd say Arthur Rubinstein. But the concert went off fantastically."

The program took place on May 28, 1944. The music Pursell played represented various time periods of classical piano music, from Bach to De Falla. It also included Pursell's prize-winning songs, sung by Arabelle Hong. Pursell's mother Delia wrote, "He met with instant approval, holding his audience with his excellent interpretations and responding to numerous calls for encores." Pursell remembers that at his next piano lesson after the concert, Mrs. Simpson sat down with him and said, "I think you can do it."

He was ready. He had not been ready when he took the train to see Rudolph Serkin, but with this concert behind him, he was prepared to continue his work toward a career as a concert pianist. Pursell graduated from Berkeley High School in 1944, and that fall he entered the Peabody Conservatory of Music in Baltimore, Maryland, as a composition student. On September 25, 1944, Arthur and Delia Pursell received a Western Union telegram: "Have just won the three year Boise composition scholarship am taking piano from Alexander Sklarevski concert artist whoopee = Will."

2. TWO FATHERS

When he was very young, about four years old in his estimation, Bill Pursell heard a conversation between his parents that made him wonder whether they really were his parents. He asked his mother, who told him that he had been "chosen." William Pursell had been adopted as an infant.

A few years later, the precocious seven-year-old was rummaging through a trunk in his mother's room when he found his certificate of adoption. He read it quickly without telling his mother, and put it back. Now he knew that not only was he adopted, but that his origins were dark and mysterious, and had something to do with something called "rape" and his real father being in jail. That was all he knew for a long time, except for the occasional comment from his mother that his natural father was in prison. When he was in his fifties, still curious about his origins, he would seek out and find his birth father, Raymond Clawson.

This early knowledge of his status as "chosen" shaped the young Pursell's psyche. He knew his adoptive parents loved him and would do anything for him, but he also knew that he was different, not a blood relation. One day when he was about thirteen years old, his father called him into his office. The clerk at the local hardware store, Lender's, had called him and told him that Bill had bought a great deal of candy on the family's credit account. Arthur Pursell asked Bill to explain himself. Bill denied any knowledge of this; growing up with such a strict father ensured that he would never dare do something so obviously dishonest. But Arthur and Delia marched Bill right down to Lender's, and asked the clerk if it was true. Fortunately, Bill's neighbor and friend, another boy about his age, was just going out the door, and the clerk said, "No, it was *that* boy," and pointed to the other boy.[1] It was only then that Bill's parents believed him. Decades later, looking back, Pursell remembered wondering as a child if his parents doubted him because his birth father was a criminal. "I remember thinking, 'Was it because of my background that you didn't believe me?' because Mom had said several times, 'Your father was in jail.' I remember thinking, 'Why didn't you take my word for it?' I was thirteen. Was it because of that? I remember that very clearly. I thought,

Arthur Pursell

'You had to take me all the way down there before you believed me?"' Any parent would understand why the Pursells handled the situation as they did, but for thirteen-year-old Bill, that moment awoke in him a spark of self-doubt, defensiveness, and a bit of anger. How could they suspect him of buying candy without permission? Wasn't he their son? But he wasn't, technically. This sense of not-quite-belonging, of being tainted, remained with Pursell for most of his life, in spite of a happy childhood in a loving home. There was always that small, quiet voice inside, saying, "Your father was in jail."

Bill's adoptive father, Arthur Pursell, was a widely respected man of profound character and fortitude, who raised Pursell with a firm ethical and moral spirit and gave him a strong foundation for a successful life. Arthur was a school principal, an amateur astronomer, and an avid hiker. He was notorious in small-town Tulare for agitating against the dangers of alcohol and tobacco. Pursell's birth father, Raymond Clawson, on the other hand, was jailed at the age of nineteen as a rapist, was later released, and tore through his family's fortune while conducting various unscrupulous business dealings. He later would be jailed for income tax evasion.[2] Clawson had no direct influence on Pursell's upbringing, but perhaps a genetic predisposition to intelligence and adventure was passed on to his son. It was surprising to Arthur and Delia Pursell that Bill would embark on such an unconventional career as a touring musician, and then continue a life in the commercial music industry, in spite of his extensive training as a classical concert pianist. Maybe there was after all a little of Raymond Clawson in Pursell's personality in his willingness to leap out into the world and try something new and uncertain.

Pursell did not follow the straight and narrow path that his parents had so carefully built for him, from piano lessons with a famous coach during high school, to college at the Peabody Conservatory, one of America's top music schools. The next step would have been to perform in competitions, find an agent, and build a concert career. But Pursell's college years were interrupted by military service at the end of World War II, and although he did return to school (albeit a different one, the Eastman School of Music) to finish his education, he again turned from that path to tour with a rhythm and blues band. The crooked river of his career continued throughout his professional life.

I would not go so far as to attribute Pursell's occasional turn toward the unconventional to the legacy of Raymond Clawson, but maybe Pursell inherited something from his birth father after all, at the very least a very high level of intelligence and a love of adventure. There is a twinkle that appears in Pursell's eye sometimes when he tells a story of a mishap on the road, or the eccentricities of Johnny Cash in the studio, and one can tell that he has lived a full and satisfying life. That mischievous smile, the zest for life, the charm and vivacious wit, must have come from somewhere. They enabled Pursell to set forth on the crooked and winding path of his musical life and ensured his success in an industry that favors a quick wit and good people skills. And although it certainly cannot be proven that any of these are the legacy of Pursell's birth father, one has to wonder, because these are not qualities evident in Arthur Pursell, regardless of how wonderful a father he was to Bill. It is worth taking a few moments, then, to explore the lives of both of Pursell's fathers, and speculate on how their influence (or genes) may have shaped the young Pursell and made such a diverse and rich career possible.

RAYMOND CLAWSON

The document that seven-year-old Bill had found in his mother's cedar chest came from the Native Sons and Native Daughters Central Committee on Homeless Children. It described a child named Donald Humphrey (né Robert Humphrey), his mother, Eleanor Humphrey, age twenty-three, and his father, Raymond Clawson, age twenty-two (this was a lie; Eleanor was twenty-six and Clawson nineteen at the time of Bill's birth). A section titled "Additional History" described an unwed mother and a father in jail. The young William knew somehow that this child was him. Years later, in 1973, after his mother died, the adult Bill Pursell was going through his mother's cedar chest and found the same document, only the "Additional History" section had been carefully cut off. Pursell writes "It was obvious she had intended on my never seeing it, and that I was right in assuming when I was seven that it would be better to keep it quiet."[3]

Pursell's first attempt to find his birth father came in 1969, when his parents sent to him a copy of his birth certificate in order to apply for a passport. This birth certificate, amended to reflect his adoption, listed Delia and Arthur Pursell as his parents. They also sent him the Certificate of Relinquishment, which listed his mother as Eleanor Humphrey, and his birthday as June 9, 1926. Pursell, curious about his history, wrote a letter to the Native Sons and Native Daughters asking for information. He posited several details that were on target, even though he didn't know it, and one can't help but imagine what an adoption clerk must have thought upon opening this request for sealed adoption records.[4] Pursell gave two compelling reasons, beyond simple curiosity, for his desire to know about his real birth father and birth mother: medical history and religious history.

He did not receive a response until April 9, 1970, and it was unsatisfactory. Peter Conmy, the director of historical research, had lost track of his letter, after doing some work on it, and asked for a fresh copy of Pursell's materials and information. In February 1971, Pursell received a letter from attorney Bernard G. Hiss, informing him that the Native Sons and Native Daughters was terminated and their files were sent to the Department of Social Welfare in Sacramento. This letter included a carbon copy of a letter from Conmy to Hiss, with the information that there was a sealed birth certificate on file for Pursell under the name of Donald Humphrey. After this, Pursell became busy with work and family, and let the matter rest for some time.

Ten years later, Pursell sent another letter (dated January 4, 1981) to the Department of Social Services in Sacramento asking for information on his birth parents, listing all the information he had to date—his mother's name, his birth name (Donald or Robert Humphrey), and copies of the documents he had already received. He received a phone call at his home from a clerk named Chuck, who told him to expect a package in the mail. On January 16, Pursell received the package via certified mail with this handwritten note:

Mr. Pursell:
   God bless you. I pray that I have done you no harm. I wish I could be more open with you but I fear for my job.
   Again, God bless you and your family.
   Chuck

   p.s. The first time in 12 yrs I've broken the principles of social work.[5]

Enclosed were Pursell's complete adoption records and several newspaper clippings on his birth father, Raymond Clawson, who was convicted of the rape of Eleanor O'Connell and sent to prison at San Quentin. Bill Pursell today marks the receipt of this handwritten note as one of the major turning points of his life. Chuck's brave, kind, and illegal act allowed Pursell to answer questions he had been asking for most of his life.

The official State Board of Health birth certificate listed the names of both child and father as Robert Humphrey, but the adoption and relinquishment certificates show Raymond Clawson to be the father. Also included was a copy of the document that young William had found in his mother's cedar chest so many years before. Under Additional History, the section that his mother had removed, it stated:

This is a very confidential case. The mother of this baby had met the father on several occasions. She went riding with him in the Berkeley Hills where she was accousted [sic] by him. After this affair she was in a very serious physical condition for some time. The doctors and her mother kept her true condition from her in fact told her that she was not pregnant and that possibly due to the shock that she would never menstrate [sic] again. However after she did learn that she was pregnant her mother wanted her to sue the man for damages but the girl refused to sue for money and only wanted the man punished and her name cleared. At this her mother turned against her.

This little mother married her present husband about 4 months ago. They told his family that they had been married for some time and allowed them to believe the baby was theirs. However, she could not live under this falsehood so told his mother. Her husband is of a very nice family and is protecting her in every way.

The case against the father comes up in a week or so.

The father of the baby is from a supposedly good family. As near as the little mother knows he is well educated and he apparently had money. This father has been in jail but they do not know his present whereabouts.

Thus, at the age of fifty-four, William Pursell received positive confirmation that he was the child of rape. However, later research of court documents revealed many affidavits that put the mother's character in question, and it became clear to him over time that the act in question was possibly consensual and not a rape. Several of Eleanor's friends and acquaintances said in court affidavits that she often went out at night, and stayed out, with various men.

Raymond Clawson was from a wealthy family, and it is possible that Eleanor's family wanted to gain financially from the situation, as the document cited above attests, and Pursell suspects. The nineteen-year-old Clawson was married at the time, and his wife was three months pregnant.[6] Eleanor had been engaged at the time of Pursell's conception to Charles Gilkyson. This was an enormously complicated situation, and the year was 1926, a time when unwed pregnancy was treated very differently than it would be today. Pursell says that such a trial (and conviction) would never take place today. Thus, although this discovery was a profound one, Pursell himself has not expressed any guilt or bad feelings toward his birth father. But surely this awareness of his biological father's time in jail, his association with rape charges, and his sexual promiscuity must have affected Pursell's sense of self-identity. Having grown up with the idea that he was loved by his adoptive family but never a true blood relative, and discovering the unstable and possibly criminal nature of his natural family, may have confirmed his instinctive sense of being an outsider.

Also included in the documents sent by Chuck was a record of a court visit with the young Bill, named "Donald Humphries" in the report, and his adoptive parents, Arthur and Delia Pursell. It paints a portrait of a happy baby and very happy parents.

Chuck was careful to cover his tracks; Pursell also received an official letter from him dated January 19, 1981, informing Pursell that he would have to petition the Superior Court of his county in order to obtain sealed adoption records. Enclosed with the letter was a brief document listing ethnicity and health of parents, but no names. In November 1982, Chuck informed Pursell that he could find no vital statistics records on Eleanor Gilkyson O'Connell. Later, Pursell's daughter Laura would locate a death certificate for Eleanor listing her death in March 1977. This document also lists her birth in the year 1900, which means Eleanor would have been twenty-six, not twenty-three, at the time of Pursell's birth.

Pursell eventually found a research consultant, Nancy O'Neill, who agreed to find Raymond Clawson for him. She asked for pictures of Pursell and his family to assure Clawson that Bill was indeed a real person who had some physical resemblance to him. O'Neill speculated that Clawson might be at the age where he desired to resolve issues from his past, especially if Pursell appeared nonthreatening.[7] She found Clawson and sent a letter to Pursell dated August 30, 1982, with an address.

Pursell wrote a letter to Raymond Clawson, his birth father, on September 16, 1982. He kept several drafts of this letter in his personal archive—clearly this was a difficult letter to write. Early drafts mention a brochure listing his professional accomplishments, but this was cut in the final letter, which is cautious, extremely polite, and carefully nonthreatening. Pursell cites his reasons for searching out Mr. Clawson as a desire to know more about his nationalistic (changed from "racial" in earlier drafts) and religious background. Some of the phrases in the letter are taken directly from communications from Nancy O'Neill, such as the desire to "tie up loose ends," and the enclosed photos.

Raymond Clawson responded with a letter dated October 5, 1982. He wrote that he was typing a response within four hours of receipt of Pursell's letter, which he described as "a very touching experience." There was, as in Pursell's first letter, no mention of the rape trial or the jail sentence, but merely this: "At the time of your birth I was in a very desperate situation. All I knew was that your mother had had a child. While the dates indicated that there was good reason to believe I was the father, we could not be sure because of your mother's life style." He wrote that from the pictures, he was convinced that no blood test was necessary to prove that he is indeed Pursell's father.

During one of their first conversations, Clawson made a comment to Pursell that revealed he had known a little more than the mere fact of Pursell's birth. He said that he had heard there was a talented kid out there. He did not reveal anything more of this to Pursell, but Pursell does remember being taken by his mother as a very young child to Berkeley for regular visits with a Mrs. Carlson. This was the name used by Clawson's mother, he would learn much later. The record of Clawson's trial reveals that Clawson often went under the name of "Raymond Carlson." He thinks he was around the age of three or four at the time of these visits. This is also the time that Pursell began to play the piano by ear, so news of his musical talent must have reached Clawson. These events, though, were not discussed by Pursell and Clawson in the 1980s.

One thing they did discuss, however, was the trains that went through Tulare. On the phone, Pursell related to Clawson his memories of the trains going through town at night, and the distinctive sound of the steam whistle that would keep him awake as a child. Clawson said to him, "Bill, I was on that train many times, going through Tulare on the way up to San Francisco on business." During Pursell's childhood, his birth father was closer than he thought.

Pursell and Clawson would exchange several letters and pictures over the following weeks, and Pursell would eventually find his half brothers and sister, the children of Raymond Clawson. Pursell would also, with the help of his daughter Laura, research Clawson's history, and learn more about the story of his origins, and of his father's shrewd intelligence.

Clawson had been sentenced in 1926 to San Quentin for one to fifty years for rape, a vague and confusing sentence. It was the practice in California at the time for the prisoner to receive sentence after the prisoner had already served some time; Clawson's sentence was, after having served two years, determined to be twenty years.[8] Clawson, however, studied law, and filed a brief as an application for a writ of habeas corpus, claiming that his sentencing was illegal because it was performed by a non-judicial body, in this case the State Board of Prison Directors.[9] He also protested the way that parole hearings were conducted, and that is what got him out of prison on parole.

When Clawson penned his brief he was only twenty-four years old. The vocabulary of the document is complex and technical, and it is clear from his lengthy discussion of numerous court cases that he studied law extensively while in prison at San Quentin. The brief is evidence of a tenacious and brilliant mind, one that seeks out details and is able to construct

William Pursell, Russ Clawson, and Ron Clawson

a lengthy and multifaceted argument. Pursell certainly inherited many of these qualities—he is highly intelligent, able to work small musical details into a cohesive whole, and has a marvelous memory.

The *Oakland Tribune* reported on February 1, 1930, that Clawson won a mandamus order (which was appealed by the parole board) to a hearing for parole. A mandamus order is a command to action from a superior body, in this case, from a judge to a parole board, commanding them to meet. The judge who issued the mandamus order, Superior Judge Edward A. Butler, ruled that the board must hear pleas for all prisoners after their first year in prison (this was not the usual practice; they often waited as long as half the maximum sentence before allowing a parole hearing). The *Tribune* reported that prison officials said this ruling would affect three thousand prisoners in San Quentin.[10] Thus, Clawson not only won his own parole, but a fair hearing for many of his fellow prisoners, and a significant change in how convicts were sentenced.

Clawson would go on to become an oil developer, stockbroker, and geophysics consultant. Pursell suspects that he was not always the most honest and forthright businessman (his words are "a confidence man"). When Clawson came to visit Pursell in Nashville in the 1980s, Pursell had suspicions that he would try to swindle him out of money. They did not develop a close relationship, but Pursell was able to learn something of his genetic and cultural heritage, and he also learned that he had brothers and sisters.

Clawson would father five other children by three of his five wives (these are the siblings that Pursell has discovered; there may be more), and Pursell today remains in touch with his half siblings Raymond Walden Clawson, Ron Clawson, Bud Clawson, and Janet Clawson. Pursell was raised as an only child, with several aunts and uncles, and the news that he had half siblings was welcome. His half-brother Russell Clawson is three months older than Pursell, an unusual situation made possible only by the events that landed their father in jail.

Raymond Clawson died in April 1995. Pursell only knew his birth father for twelve and a half years. He says that in the later years, he did not see Clawson very much, that his curiosity had been satisfied. He did, however, gain siblings, with whom he meets on a regular basis.

ARTHUR PURSELL

Pursell's adoptive parents, Arthur and Delia Pursell, lived in Tulare, California, a small town of about fifteen thousand in the San Joaquin Valley. Arthur Pursell could not have been more different from Raymond Clawson. Arthur was the local grammar school (seventh and eighth grade) principal, a widely admired and respected man in his community. Pursell describes him as a very strict father, who did not tolerate alcohol, tobacco, or dancing.[11] Arthur's letters to Bill during Bill's early adult years often included spelling corrections from Bill's previous letters, and references to be wary of the "pagans" who were plentiful in the Washington, D.C., area, where Pursell was stationed during World War II. However, Arthur was also a loving and encouraging father, who frequently expressed his pride for his only son, both in his letters to Bill and in conversation to his friends in Tulare.

Arthur and Delia had one other child, Robert Lewis, who had died as an infant before Bill was adopted. Pursell was raised as an only child and received all of their best parental energies and attention. After he left home, it is clear from their letters how sorely they missed him, in their frequent requests for him to write them letters, for news of what he was doing out East.

Tom Hennion, the editor of the local newspaper in Tulare, the *Advance Register*, told this story about Arthur Pursell as part of his eulogy in 1986:

> I had been on the job only a few days (as editor) when the mail brought an envelope bearing Arthur's return address. Inside was a clipping from my favorite newspaper of two days earlier, bearing a sticker with a concise but unmistakably clear message printed on its face. The sticker read: "I do not like to see this kind of advertising in my newspaper." The ad that had drawn Arthur Pursell's wrath was for a Tulare liquor store.
>
> I wondered what kind of person would go to so much trouble to protest such a perfectly legal, perfectly normal run-of-the-mill ad in a community newspaper, so I called Arthur. I found out in a hurry.
>
> After he had lectured me at length on the evils of drink, and the kind of newspapers that permit themselves to be used to promote its consumption, he permitted me to have my inning.
>
> I explained that a newspaper had no right whatever to sit in moral judgment on such matters, so long as the product advertised was not in violation of the law. Besides, I asked him, would he want me to censor out of the newspaper something else in which he might believe just because another reader might get upset over its publication?
>
> He chuckled at that, in the manner that only Arthur Pursell could chuckle, and said "Of course not." He never returned another liquor ad—and a warm and lasting understanding was born. The fairness he demonstrated then, I think, said a great deal about the fine man to whom we are paying our last respects today.[12]

Hennion described Arthur's teaching career and strict policies as a school principal, and went on to say: "The influence of Arthur Pursell's teaching, counseling, and friendship of countless young Tulare people, and particularly those with special gifts, was enormous." One of these students was Charles Campbell, who would become part of the Manhattan Project, in Oak Ridge, Tennessee, to help build the first atomic bomb. Campbell spent a summer with Arthur building a telescope, and called Arthur his "scientific father." Campbell was a little older than Pursell, but they became close friends, and the two would stay in touch throughout the years.

Arthur Pursell had a keen interest in astronomy, and in 1935 was one of the founders of the Tulare Astronomical Society. With friends, he

The observatory in Tulare

pooled money to purchase a three-inch refractor telescope, which he kept in his backyard. Arthur, who wanted a larger telescope but could not afford to purchase one, would later build his own ten-inch telescope and install it into a home-made observatory on his brother-in-law's land. Arthur ground the lens for the telescope himself and had it silvered by a company (Glick) who said it was a near-perfect mirror. Pursell remembers sleeping in the observatory many nights when he was a boy. Arthur notes in his autobiography that over a thirty-year period, around five thousand people signed the registry at his observatory. Arthur was featured in several local newspaper articles, and served as an astronomical consultant on various issues. In his later years, he gave regular lectures to student and community groups on astronomy. In 1980 the Tulare Observatory, which he had helped design and build, was named the Arthur L. Pursell Observatory.[13] In 1982, Hennion notes, the California Legislature passed a resolution calling Arthur a "musician, astronomer, natural scientist, teacher and Renaissance Man who passed his knowledge and enthusiasm in many areas to thousands of young people (and old) fortunate to have come in contact with him."

Arthur Pursell in France and Belgium (image taken from Arthur's scrapbook)

Bill did not acquire Arthur's enthusiasm for the stars, but his love for music was fostered from a very young age thanks to his father's equal enthusiasm for music. Arthur played the clarinet for most of his life. As a soldier in World War I, he marched around the trenches of France, carrying his clarinet and playing as part of the Army Band.[14] Later, he was a member of the Tulare County Symphony and helped organize the Tulare Civic Music Association in 1949, remaining its president until 1955.[15] Hennion wrote that Arthur learned to play the cello in only one month and performed on it frequently in his church. Arthur's letters to Bill often describe musical evenings at his house, where friends and family would gather to listen to phonograph recordings of classical music. His letters also mention how he would adjust his equipment to get the best sound, the optimum balance of bass and treble. He tinkered with his musical devices as an engineer would, evidence of his scientific mind at work. Thus, although Arthur was not a professional musician, Bill remembers growing up in a house full of music.

When drafted into World War I, Arthur served as a clarinetist in the Army band. He compiled a detailed record of his Army experiences into an unpublished volume that he entitled "I'm in the Army Now." Musicians conducted first aid on the battlefront, carrying stretchers and providing help to wounded soldiers. Arthur saw action in the Meuse-Argonne

Arthur Pursell near the summit of Mt. Whitney (image taken from Arthur's scrapbook)

offensive and the Ypres-Lys offensive. The letters he wrote during this time document some of these days. Arthur was a meticulous man, concerned with detail, and his writings describe such things as dates and times of events, numbers of troops, training encampments, and more. In these surviving written records the mind of the scientist is clearly evident.

Arthur loved the mountains and would visit them regularly, from his boyhood well into his adult years. In his autobiography, Arthur describes in detail a trip up Mt. Whitney with his father, just before 1917. They had mules to carry food and equipment, and upon reaching the summit, he writes, "It was a supreme moment when we looked out over Owen's Valley but soon a let-down feeling came to us as we realized there was no place left to go but down!"[16]

It is clear from their correspondence and my conversations with Pursell that Arthur and Delia Pursell provided a stable and stimulating home environment for him. The regular presence of music in the household surely influenced his later choice to become a full-time professional musician. And Arthur's moral certainty gave Bill a firm grounding from which to enter the world outside Tulare with confidence.

It would be difficult to imagine two fathers more different from each other: Raymond Clawson, the wealthy confidence man who was convicted of rape at the age of nineteen, who wrote a lengthy brief that changed California sentencing policy; and Arthur Pursell, community leader, who built his own telescopes and gramophone players, who loved to hike in the mountains and play the clarinet, who became a mentor to many of the young people in his home town. Pursell may have inherited parts of his personality from both of his fathers—from Clawson, the risk-taking, the shrewd intelligence, the zest for an unusual life; from Arthur, a depth of character and honesty and a strong sense of responsibility to those around him. If he had been raised by his birth father or birth mother, it is likely that he would have gained none of these things, and Pursell himself admits that he was very lucky that the Pursell family found him as an infant. He says, "I think out of that whole thing, I hit the jackpot. I mean, when they found me in San Francisco, someone was looking after me, because I could have gone anywhere. It was really the good luck of the draw that I got into that family."

As a working musician, Pursell relied heavily on a strong work ethic and sense of decency and respect for those around him. But he also was able to tolerate and even embrace the uncertainties of such a life, always looking for the next gig, never sure what was around the corner. He moved with ease between the classical and commercial music worlds, not even imagining that perhaps a classically trained pianist did not belong in the country music studios of Nashville. Bill Pursell claimed for himself a unique place in American music as a virtuoso jazz pianist, classical concert pianist, session musician, composer of both popular and classical music, and orchestral arranger. Everywhere he went, he both belonged and didn't belong, and was always aware that he had been relinquished at birth, but embraced wholeheartedly by a family who loved and wanted him.

3. HIGH FLIGHT

William Pursell arrived in Baltimore in the fall of 1944, one week late for the start of the semester at the Peabody Conservatory. At the age of eighteen, Pursell was eligible to be drafted into the military to serve in World War II, but the draft had not yet caught up with him. The move across the country would delay his draft when it came, as he had registered when living in Tulare, and his family would have to forward all correspondence to Baltimore.

Pursell had been accepted to Peabody as a composition major and piano minor, but all of the piano scholarships had already been given out, and with limited funds, he was faced with the unhappy prospect of returning to Tulare. However, the director of the Conservatory suggested to Pursell that he apply for the composition scholarship, which was still available. Pursell remembers returning to his rented room and spending an entire night copying out his compositions. "I went in the next morning, in front of the entire composition faculty and Reginald Stewart (who was director of the Conservatory and conductor of the Baltimore Symphony at that time). I was interviewed; they tried me out for perfect pitch, knowledge in theory, and that kind of thing, and then I left. And they sent me to sit out in the hall. He (Stewart) came out and said, we've decided to give the composition scholarship to you. The Boise Composition Scholarship, a three-year scholarship, and that was it."

The Peabody Conservatory was founded in the mid-nineteenth century and has long been one of the most prestigious music conservatories in the United States. To be accepted to attend Peabody was a mark of Pursell's potential as a musician; to be given the composition scholarship was a vote of confidence by the conservatory's faculty that Pursell would fulfill his potential. Although (thanks to the draft) he was only able to attend Peabody for a year and a half, Pursell's experience at the conservatory was life-changing. His piano teacher was the Russian émigré concert pianist Alexander Sklarevski and his composition teachers were Nicolas Nabokov, the famed Russian émigré composer, and Franz Bornschein, composer and music critic. He would later remember his piano studies

Alexander Sklarevski

with Sklarevski as the most formative of his musical life; his composition studies with Nabokov, however, were not as successful.

Nicolas Nabokov's aristocratic family had fled Russia during the Bolshevik Revolution, and after some time in Berlin and Paris, Nabokov came to the United States to seek his fortune as a musician, writer, and teacher. He became an American citizen in 1939, and taught composition at various schools in the Eastern United States, including the Peabody Conservatory. His most famous compositions are those for the ballet, and he worked with both Sergei Diaghilev and George Balanchine, important figures in modern ballet.[1]

Pursell did not get along with Professor Nabokov, perhaps due to his teaching style: "Our lessons together were just a travesty: 'This is stupid, stupid, how can you bring something like that to me?' Mainly about harmony, but different things of that sort. Finally I went down to Dean Carty and I said, 'Look, I can't do it, can you switch me?' So she gave me Franz Bornschein. He was a wonderful teacher, and I studied with him until I finally got the greetings from the army to go in." Professor Bornschein also later wrote a letter of support for Pursell when he entered the military, in the hopes that Pursell might be placed in a position where he could continue to use and develop his musical skills.[2]

On the other hand, Pursell greatly valued his time at the Peabody Conservatory with his piano teacher Sklarevski: "Sklarevski did so much for me when I was studying with him. He was a Busoni pupil; he also went to the Petrograd Conservatory. He taught me this Russian flat-fingered way of playing; he gave me the technique. He gave me the approach where you could make it up; if something went wrong, you could do it."

Pursell remembers a concert he performed at Peabody that was a major success for him as a young pianist. Inexperienced musicians will often try to play difficult pieces as fast as they can to show off their technical skill. Professor Sklarevski had finally convinced Pursell that faster was not necessarily better. Pursell remembers that he decided to take a different approach on this concert, and that it worked.

> At the middle of the (Liszt Hungarian) Rhapsody, there was this arpeggio. Instead of going into it at a certain speed, I went slowly, started off so that when I finally got up to the point of tempo, I was playing very easily, but in contrast to the way I started that section. It sounded like I was very fast. I got through and sped up at the very end with the final section arpeggios and everything else, and they started thumping their feet on the floor. Somebody told me Sklarevski was running around backstage saying, "I finally slowed him down!" The next morning, Madame Longy said, "Willie, don't let that go to your head."[3]

Eighteen-year-old Pursell finally knew he was in the right place and had the right teachers and was finding success, not only as a composer, but as a pianist. He insists that Renée Longy, who had taught theory at the Juilliard School of Music and the Curtis Institute before she had come to Peabody, was the best teacher he ever had.[4]

Reginald Stewart, who was the director of the Peabody Conservatory at the time, and also the conductor of the Baltimore Symphony, heard Pursell perform, was impressed with his playing, and began to invite him to attend concerts as his guest. Pursell would sit in Maestro Stewart's private box with his wife and daughter for concerts on a regular basis, and would attend rehearsals when famous soloists came to play with the symphony. Pursell was able to hear (and meet) artists like pianist Vladimir Horowitz and cellist Gregor Piatigorsky. These rehearsals and concerts were, for Pursell, a door opening into the world of the concert artist. He suspects that Stewart was grooming him as a piano soloist with the orchestra.

There is little written record of Pursell's two years at Peabody that survives. In his personal papers exists one curiosity, a bill from the Peabody Conservatory to his parents for piano practice time, at 25 cents an hour. (Today music schools do not bill for hours of practice time, though they might charge a fee for private lessons.) The total cost of Pursell's practicing, forty-one hours, in April 1945 was $10.25. This means that his scheduled practice time (students reserve practice rooms) was about ten hours a week, but Pursell remembers that he practiced a great deal more than that. A budding concert artist would have to practice several hours every day.

Also surviving in Pursell's papers are several letters from his father, beginning in 1945, his second year at Peabody, when Europe was embroiled in war. These letters express his parents' worries that Bill would be drafted into the military. Conscription in the United States had been introduced in 1941. Pursell was eighteen, the minimum eligible age for the draft, when he began his studies at Peabody in 1944. If he had been two or three years older, it is possible that he would not have ever made it to Peabody. The greatest need for troops from the United States was during the years preceding Pursell's eighteenth birthday, 1941–44. His father's letters from 1945 show an increasing concern that the government would call Pursell to service.

By 1945, the tides had turned in Europe, the Allies were clearly at an advantage, and the major troop offensives were mostly over. In August 1945, as Pursell was preparing to begin his second year at Peabody, the United States dropped two atomic bombs in Japan, which signified to most that the war would soon end. Japan formally surrendered on September 2. Therefore, Pursell was facing conscription at the end of World War II, rather than at its beginning or middle, and so his prospects were better than they might have been a year or two earlier. The war was officially over by the time Pursell entered service; the obligation to report for service remained, however.

When Pursell moved to Baltimore in 1944, he had to write to the draft board to transfer his records, which may have caused a delay in his being called to service. According to a letter from his father, the Berkeley draft board tried to contact Pursell in California at the end of the summer 1945, but he was in Baltimore. Arthur Pursell wrote to Bill on September 29, 1945:

> We keep wondering what the service is going to ask you to do. You have, of course, received Mother's letter explaining that we received notice from the Berkeley board. Before you receive this letter we shall

have heard from you and you may have additional information for us. Of course, you know that we hope they will not take you now. There seems so much that you might lose.

Arthur Pursell, who had served in France during World War I, knew all too well what his son had to lose. By his second year at Peabody and at age nineteen, young Pursell was aware that he would likely be drafted. But apparently the wheels of bureaucracy were turning slowly, and Pursell was able to devote himself fully to his studies at Peabody during the fall of 1945. A letter from his father in December 1945 mentioned hopefully, "(I) hope that draft board forgets about you for a few months anyway."[5] Delia Pursell later wrote (in a handwritten biography of her son) that they knew the draft board would "send him greetings" in February 1946.

Pursell had learned that if he enlisted voluntarily, he would only have to serve an eighteen-month term of service, and he would be able to return to Peabody to finish his education. Sometime near the end of 1945, then, Pursell decided to enlist.[6] In November, Pursell wrote to his parents with the news that his physical exam for the military was successful, and he was awaiting orders. Arthur Pursell advised him to stay put in Baltimore until after his induction, after which he would be allowed to have a visit home in California. This meant not coming home for Christmas, which Pursell could not afford anyway. Arthur wrote some words of encouragement and advice:

> Surely they will place you where you can do the most good. I have heard so often that people with special talents are given special service that there must be something to it. Of course, there will be some advantages to military routine. As you say, there will be fewer worries. The ease with which one's life flows on in the army during peace has made a bum out of many a fellow and unfitted him for the struggle of life as a free man. I know that you will be plenty glad to get out after serving a time, even though you have to worry about board and bed. Regimentation is an irksome thing.
>
> Mother thinks we should suggest that you sign up for the minimum time. I do not know whether you have any choice or not.[7]

It is fairly clear from these letters that Pursell's parents were unaware that he had decided to enlist, and that they thought he was still facing the draft. A letter from Arthur in January commiserates with Bill that there is "still no word about your induction." Arthur encourages Bill to try to put thoughts of the draft aside as much as possible, while he is waiting, and to enjoy his time remaining.[8]

Pursell must have told his parents of his decision to enlist in January 1946. On February 3, Arthur wrote to Bill: "Whoa! Hold everything a minute! So you want to enlist?" His father was full of questions whether Peabody would hold his scholarship for him, how long he would serve, and the like. He also expressed a concern that perhaps Bill should think very carefully before making such a decision, but overall his letter was supportive and expresses confidence in Pursell's ability to make the right choice. Pursell says today that he decided to enlist voluntarily because he knew he could be out of the military in eighteen months, whereas with the draft, he was not sure how long he would be required to serve.

Pursell enlisted in the military in January 1946.[9] By late February 1946, Pursell was attending basic training at Keesler Field in Mississippi. Aptitude tests were pointing him in the direction of cryptography, but his destiny was the Air Force Orchestra. How he got there is a study in military politics.

Pursell made a fast friend in basic training, Bernard Lipshitz, who was from the Bronx, and who initially was assigned to the Air Force Orchestra in Washington, D.C. He met "Bernie" on the train that was taking them to Biloxi for basic training, and as they were both musicians, they quickly discovered that they were kindred spirits, and became at times, partners in crime. Bernie and Bill both suffered from good-natured ribbing in basic training, and perhaps that's what drew them together. Pursell remembers: "We would get out there in the morning for roll call, and he would say, 'Pursell,' 'here,' 'Smith,' 'here,' 'Jones,' 'here,' 'Lipshitz,' 'ha-ha.' Everybody would laugh their heads off, and Bernie would say, 'That's me, goddammit!' And Bernie went around with a pipe in his mouth." Bill, on the other hand, gained the nickname "'Fesser,'" because of his education. He says:

> There was this guy who had these milky white glasses. Obviously these were store-bought glasses, as we used to say. He looked like he was right from the hills, and he would say, "Well, you use them long words, you know, I'm gonna call you 'Fesser!'" And I think I used a word like *analyze*. But I can tell you that going through basic training with this character, he'd say "I can't stand that long-haired music," and I used to think he was an absolute walking idiot, you know. He

just doesn't have any brains. It turns out that he had an AGCT (Army General Classification Test) rating about as high as mine. His specialty was math! So you can't judge a book by its cover.

This incident might illuminate Pursell's difficulties in the 1960s when he moved to Nashville. Working as a musician among people who were probably not all that different from the man with the milky white glasses, he could not conceal his training. And this made him an outsider.

Bernie and Bill stuck together during basic training, through thick and thin. One afternoon they were out on the shooting range together, and they were wearing their helmets.

> They started throwing stones around on our helmets, because it was just fun, but when it hits, doink, like that, it creates tinnitus because it's so loud inside. So finally, Bernie turns around and says, with this Bronx accent, "Once is funny, but twice is too much!" And this guy says "Ah, you're nothing but a Goddamn Jew." And I saw my fist go out, and his went out, we caught the guy on both sides of his head. This lieutenant came along, as we were all getting into it. He yelled, "Stop, halt!" And so that was it. We almost caused a riot out there.

Lipshitz would eventually change his last name to Linden, much to the chagrin of his father, and his brother became Hal Linden, the famous actor.

In 1946, after basic training, Lipshitz was stationed in Washington, D.C., and he made repeated attempts to get Pursell transferred up there. He became aware that the arranger for the Air Force Orchestra, Fred Kepner, was approaching the end of his service, and wrote a letter to Major George S. Howard about Pursell, who was serving in Mississippi at the time.

Major Howard sent a script of an episode (the orchestra played for the weekly *Radio Hour*) as a trial arrangement for Pursell. This was a little intimidating for the twenty-year-old young musician. He had no experience writing for a large ensemble like an orchestra, having only written chamber music in school. But he wrote the arrangement and sent it to Washington, D.C., and they liked it. Pursell decided that he would call Warrant Officer Wolfe at his own base and ask for the loan of an orchestration book, to signal that he was writing something for Washington. This worked, because Wolfe decided to transfer Pursell to the band at

Keesler Field, which gave him credentials as a military musician. He was hoping that this would be an intermediary position on the way to an appointment to Washington, D.C. However, Pursell was soon shipped down to Boca Raton, Florida, where Warrant Officer Azulina had heard of Pursell's talents and was trying to build a band himself.[10]

There was no military title for "composer," so at Keesler Field and then in Boca Raton, Pursell was designated a bass drum specialist. He had to carry a glockenspiel in parade drill, and rigged the straps around his neck so that he could march and play with two mallets. Pursell remembers that he bumped into a tuba in front of him at one point, marching in parade dress.

Pursell was afraid he would never get to Washington, D.C. After a long delay, he wrote his friend Bernie Lipschitz, only to discover that the now-Colonel Howard had been sending orders to get Pursell transferred up to Washington. They found out from a friend in the mail room that Warrant Officer Azulina's son, who was a captain at Scott Field, had been throwing the orders away. In the end, Colonel Howard sent some orders with an adjutant general's signature on them, as a show of power, and that finally succeeded in putting the transfer through. Lipshitz's letter had been sent in May, so it was sometime after that that Pursell was transferred to Bolling Field.[11]

Having finally arrived in Washington, D.C., twenty-year-old Pursell's job was to write arrangements for the Air Force Orchestra's *Radio Hour* broadcasts and for a series of documentaries. This job provided Pursell invaluable on-the-job training as a working composer, something very different from what he had experienced at Peabody, where the focus had been on his skills as a piano performer. At Bolling Field he was able to make the best use of his classical musical training, and combine it with new skills along more popular lines. It was a major turning point in his life as a musician, another significant bend in the crooked river of his musical life, though he did not know it at the time.

Pursell began his service with the Air Force Orchestra as an assistant to the chief arranger Fred Kepner, who was preparing to leave the service. Pursell did his composing and arranging in the orchestral library, where he discovered Glenn Miller's arrangements for the Air Force Band. He spent time studying Miller's arrangements and learning everything he could. Eventually he received commutational pay and was allowed to live off-base, so he found an apartment, secured a piano, and only wore his uniform during rehearsals and special events.[12]

Pursell remembers his years with the Air Force Orchestra as incredibly busy and fulfilling. "Finally getting into the Air Force Orchestra, with that big orchestra there, to write, was really an opportunity to learn it from the ground up, and that's what I did. And of course it was do it right or get shipped out. I was doing a pretty big load of music every week, documentary music as well as arrangements and things like that. I learned to write fast. By the time I got out, when I was twenty-three, I had a lot of writing under my belt."

The radio broadcasts encompassed a variety of subjects and took advantage of Pursell's musical versatility. They performed many shows about World War II, of course, and the pilot Jimmy Doolittle. They even did an Air Force version of *A Christmas Carol*, where the three ghosts of Christmas Past, Present, and Future visited an American Air Force pilot. The ghost of Christmas Future took the pilot for a visit to an America that had been hit by a nuclear bomb. Pursell remembers it being a lot of hard work.

Pursell's new job was certainly sink or swim. He had never written for a full orchestra before, and after his arrival at Bolling Field, he had an entire sixty-five-piece orchestra to perform his works on a regular basis. He acknowledges that as a composer, one just has to jump in and compose from the beginning. Some experiments were more successful than others.

> I had never heard anything of mine played by an orchestra before I got into the Air Force band. So gradually, doing all of these documentaries gave me a chance to experiment with the orchestra and try out different things. But I really got over my head one time; I remember that I was under the gun, and I just threw caution to the winds and I put down every atonal sounding thing you could ever imagine. We got into rehearsal, and Colonel Howard brought the baton down, and of course this explosion went off, and he turned to me and said, "Pursell, what have you done?" And I tried to explain to him what it was, then he tried it again, and I heard this "flick" and I saw my score going through the air towards the back of the studio, so I went back to retrieve it, and at the next cue, I saw the next score coming back at me. He threw them all at me, pages of scores. He didn't like anything, he didn't understand, it was all quite atonal.

Hazing is not limited to football teams or fraternities; the young Pursell experienced some uniquely musical hazing during his first weeks as arranger for the Air Force Band. It is common for an orchestra to challenge a new arranger; stories are numerous about trumpet players asking the conductor about a wrong pitch, or others challenging the arranger's authority. Pursell's trouble was with the French horns, and he called them out on it. With every new arrangement, a French horn player would ask the conductor (Colonel Howard) what this or that note was, as though Pursell had made a mistake in the score. Finally, Pursell decided to check the parts before rehearsal, and they were all correct. When the horns again began to question his part, he walked back through the stands, looked directly at their scores, and then said to them, quietly: "Don't ever do that again." This took care of that problem.

Pursell also was allowed to conduct his music from time to time, and another issue that he had, albeit a small one, was that the orchestra played a little behind his beat. Pursell says that this is fairly typical. The famed conductor Arturo Toscanini was the exception: when his baton went down, the sound began at the bottom of the sweep. But for most conductors, the baton goes down, and then the sound begins as it is coming up. This confused the young Bill, who was having his initial experience as an orchestral conductor: "When I conducted the Air Force Orchestra for the first time, I didn't know that. And I got up there, and everything was behind my beat, and finally I just slowed down to meet their beat, and they just kept getting slower. So I turned to Colonel Howard, and I said, 'What in the world is going on?' He said, 'Watch me,' and he got up there and was always in front of the beat." A similar effect occurs playing an organ in a large church. There is a significant delay between the time one presses the key down and the sound returns to the player, so the player must play just ahead of what he or she is hearing. It takes a conscious effort at first to accommodate for the delay in sound.

Pursell was cutting his musical teeth not just on arranging, but on conducting and managing an orchestra on a regular basis, in every style from light classical to jazz and various other popular styles. Pursell's writing even got the attention of Stan Kenton, a pianist and famous jazz band leader, who asked him to be his band arranger after hearing his arrangement for "Jingle Bells." But Pursell liked to work with strings, and the Kenton job would have been for big band, so he turned down the offer. He still has a signed picture from Kenton in his office that reads "You and your music will be famous someday, I believe in you, Stan Kenton."

Pursell's position with the Air Force orchestra offered him more musical variety than a position with a jazz band, or even another type of

Archival album of the United States Air Force Band, "High Flight"

touring band, could offer. He was composing and arranging volumes of music for a full string orchestra, every week, and hearing the results instantly. The work was challenging and fulfilling, and came at a crucial time in his life—in his early twenties—when his creativity and energies were at their best. Although he had entered the military under the threat of conscription, he couldn't have asked for a better training ground as a young musician. This job set the tone for the remainder of his life, where his skills at orchestration would be cause for great praise, whether he was arranging hymns for an orchestra or composing his own classical pieces. For a time, his endeavors as a classical pianist had to be laid aside as he focused on his new challenges.

One of Pursell's fondest memories of his years at Bolling Field is a radio broadcast of the poem "High Flight," for which he composed the music. This is a famous poem by John Gillespie Magee Jr., an Englishman who flew for the Canadian Royal Air Force. Magee wrote this poem in

September 1941 when he was nineteen years old, and he died in December in a mid-air collision over England. The most famous lines are "Oh I have slipped the surly bonds of Earth / and danced the skies on laughter-silvered wings." The producer of the *Air Force Radio Hour*, Captain Robert Keim, brought the poem to Pursell and asked him what he thought. They ended up compiling a show about Magee, his childhood in England, and his love of flying. This poem (with different music) was used for years as a television station nighttime sign-off, and was quoted by President Ronald Reagan in 1986 when the space shuttle *Challenger* exploded in air. But Pursell claims to have been the first to compose music to it in 1948.

Pursell describes his music for "High Flight" as Debussy-like, similar to *La Mer*. Unlike Debussy, it is fully tonal, but Pursell's use of woodwind (mostly clarinet and flute) solos and a free-flowing rhythm are indeed Debussy-like. The background music is unified by a leaping dotted-note motto, introduced by the solo clarinet and then repeatedly played by the strings under soaring woodwind melodies. The music drops out, most effectively, when the narrator relates how Magee died in a mid-air crash.[13] Pursell's love of flying dates back to his Tulare childhood, so "High Flight" surely had special meaning to Pursell personally. Its topic also made it a natural fit for the *Air Force Radio Hour*.

Pursell made many friends while working for the Air Force Orchestra, thanks to the hours spent in rehearsal. One of his closest lifelong friends, clarinetist Bob Marcellus, comes from this time. Marcellus had already had experience as a professional musician, playing in the National Symphony Orchestra under Hans Kindler. Pursell wrote many clarinet solos for Marcellus during their time together in the Air Force Orchestra, and they became lifelong friends. Marcellus would later become first clarinet for the Cleveland Orchestra under George Szell. One of Pursell's regrets is that he never wrote a Rhapsody for Clarinet and Orchestra for his friend, something Marcellus repeatedly requested of him.

Pursell remembers his time in the Air Force Orchestra as a time of almost overwhelming hard work. "I was working all night sometimes. I'd get up, get in the car at 4:00 in the morning, drive across D.C. to Al Perata's house, slide my score under his door, get in my car, drive back to where I was living, and go to bed. Stayed up all night. Used to take a brick of cheese, slice it while I was writing, and I was smoking at that time, piles of ashes." When Pursell began, he was under the supervision of chief arranger Fred Kepner, but by the time he was finished, he was writing the shows entirely on his own: "At one point when Fred Kepner got out, I was handling the whole thing. So I came out of the Service weighing about 145 pounds, from overwork and coffee. I remember Dean Burton at Eastman [School of Music] asking me, 'Why are you so thin?' and I said, 'I'm tired.'"

While Pursell was in Washington developing his skills as a composer and orchestrator, back home in Tulare his father and mother were dealing with health and financial problems. Arthur continued to faithfully write letters to Bill, almost weekly, describing Bill's mother's increasing weakness and happenings in Tulare. Delia Pursell had fallen ill during Bill's first years at Peabody, and she was diagnosed with tuberculosis of the spine. She had surgery in late September 1945, but by the time Bill was in the military, her illness had grown worse, and Arthur informed Bill in May 1946 that she was likely to be an invalid for the rest of her life.[14] By July, Arthur wrote that caring for her even kept him out of church on Sundays. Arthur then used this opportunity to exhort Bill to attend church regularly while in Washington, and to ask about his chaplain. He continued:

> It is a sad day when a person divorces himself from the Christian viewpoint and Christian influences. You are surrounded by paganism rampant and bawdy. If you neglect to seek a periodic cleansing of the spirit you become spiritually—and morally sooner or later—like the person does physically who neglects to bathe. Won't you let me know how "goes" the contacts with the best way of life?[15]

It is worth noting that in 1946, Pursell was only twenty years old. Having attended a year and a half of higher education and enrolled in the military, he was already an independent adult, earning a salary, purchasing a car, and renting an apartment. In spite of his father's hopes, he was not attending church at this time. These paternal exhortations were typical of the upright Arthur Pursell, who regularly railed against the dangers of alcohol and tobacco. But they are couched in a loving tone, and it is clear from the letters that Arthur sent him not only moral advice, but love and support.

Pursell's parents, especially his father, wrote to him faithfully during his first tour of duty, encouraging and advising him. Some of Arthur's letters even correct Bill's spelling in his own letters, and all of them ask Bill to write more often. The letters from this time also mention the financial difficulties his parents faced, with his mother's increasing medical bills, and encourage Bill to be frugal with his own funds. A Christmas card from Delia Pursell mentions a new watch and some clothes as Christmas gifts, and a trip by Bill to Chicago, about which Delia writes: "I understand it is 'wicked in spots' so be careful that you are not ensnared by evil while there."[16]

Most of Pursell's own letters from this time do not survive, but he saved all or most of Arthur's letters to him. They give him advice on finances, roommate trouble, and other troubles that are only referred to in a very general way. Although Pursell's letters home as a young soldier were infrequent, it appears that he wrote his parents for advice when facing the sort of problems a young man newly on his own might face. Frequently, writing from Tulare, Arthur talks about the "screwballs" or "pagans" in Washington,[17] and one letter in particular exhorts his son to find good company. In this letter he also makes a reference to Pursell's origins, presumably in response to one of Pursell's letters to him. Perhaps Pursell had expressed some self-doubts to his father because of his status as an adopted child. Even far away from home, as a young adult, Pursell was still coming to terms with the fact of his adoption. This awareness continued to be a part of his sense of self throughout his life and would culminate, as discussed earlier, with a search for his birth father in the 1980s. Sometimes this awareness would manifest in a sense of not belonging, or feelings of uncertainty. All Pursell knew at this point was that his father had been in jail, and perhaps Pursell faced doubts about his own moral character. His father wrote:

> Don't grieve over your origin, Son. So far as you are concerned, your entry into this world was by the only route any of us took. We had no choice. It is what you do with your life that is important, not how you got here. You are not responsible for your origin but eternally responsible for what use you make of your life. We took you early and have tried to set your feet on the right path. So far as you are concerned you have no other origin.[18]

The majority of Arthur's letters to Bill are not of this soul-seeking manner and mostly contain local happenings, reflections on the weather, and news on the progress of his mother's health. But the occasional letter reveals the nature of their relationship—Bill asked his father for advice on big matters, and his father gently, without pushing, gave his opinions, which were usually morally grounded and firm. Arthur always clearly expressed support for Bill and confidence in the choices that he would make. As a young man, this moral support and love sent from the opposite coast surely helped Bill feel grounded and secure.

At the end of his eighteen-month tour of duty, Pursell faced an important decision, one that would determine the direction of his life as a musician. Should he return to Peabody and continue his music studies, or sign up for another eighteen months of service and continue to arrange for the orchestra? His scholarship was waiting for him, and conductor Reginald Stewart was ready to resume his mentorship. This was the path that had been laid out for him, to pursue a career as a concert pianist.

Pursell decided to stay with the Air Force. He wanted to continue his experience as an arranger, to keep honing his skills in orchestration and composition in an environment where he had to write quickly and then would immediately be able to hear the results of his work. And he was out on his own, making a salary, living in his own apartment, and driving his own car around Washington, D.C. But when it came down to a final decision, Pursell says, it was ultimately the weather that kept him out of Baltimore. It was too cold there. He did not want to live in a small room, ride the streetcar to school, and try to find a practice room, all in a very cold city: "I didn't want to live out in Rolling Park again, freezing, getting on the Sparrow's Point streetcar to go down to the city. Or live at Park Avenue in Mrs. LeCompte's room, try to find a piano, that kind of stuff. I didn't want that." He had gotten very ill his second winter in Baltimore, and he did not want to go back.[19]

He traveled to Baltimore to tell Reginald Stewart personally. The conductor said, "Well, you're coming back, aren't you?" Pursell replied, "No, I've extended my enlistment." Pursell relates that Maestro Stewart just shook his head sadly: "I feel, since he was the conductor there, that if I had come back, that I would probably have ended up playing with the orchestra there, and going back to Sklarevski. I've often wondered to this day, did I do the wrong thing? You know, when you're a kid, nobody's there to advise you, nobody's there to tell you what to do. And I look back on that many times, and I think to myself, did I close the door? I don't know. But I know that I was playing very, very well in those days, I really was."

Pursell's decision to enroll for a second term was not a complete rejection of his potential as a concert pianist, but it was a choice that sent him in a different direction and prevented him from continuing his piano studies with Sklarevski. Pursell would later return to music school, though not at the Peabody Conservatory, to finish his education, but the eighteen-month delay in this and the additional experience with the orchestra doubtlessly affected his future choices. His musical identity had expanded beyond that of a pianist and student composer to that of professional orchestra arranger, and that changed him irrevocably. His musical world was wider, bigger, and though he did not consciously shut the door forever on a possible concert career, this decision to re-enlist was a turning point, another major bend in the crooked river of his musical life.

Pursell now looks back on this time with more than a little wistfulness, and wonders what might have been. Some of his friends from the Air Force orchestra did go on to have successful careers in classical music. Bob Marcellus ended up with George Szell, in Cleveland, and Edgar Muenzer ended up in Chicago for forty-three years. Muenzer played with the Chicago Symphony from 1956 to 2003 under Fritz Reiner, Jean Martinon, Sir Georg Solti, and Daniel Barenboim. After his retirement, he founded his own orchestra in the Chicago suburbs, called the Park Ridge Civic Orchestra.

> I went up [to Chicago] one time when Edgar was conducting my second symphony with his orchestra. We were coming out of the artist's entrance of Orchestra Hall in Chicago after a Chicago Symphony Orchestra concert. We were going to meet [my wife] Julie and his wife, and he just up and said, "You know Bill, you could have been a world-class performer if you had wanted to." I'll never forget how I felt. This was a guy who had played under Fritz Reiner, Daniel Barenboim, everybody, all the big conductors, who had also played behind all of the big pianists who had come in there. Edgar said that, and he knows me better than just about anybody, because we were buddies back in the service. And so that's that, you wonder. Sklarevski did so much for me when I was studying with him. I'll never know; I've often wondered about it.

During his second tour, Pursell continued his arranging and composing duties, and eventually gained full responsibility over the music when Fred Kepner, the senior arranger, retired. Pursell also experienced his first lesson on the potential pitfalls of life in commercial music, an encounter with an aspiring songwriter who wanted Pursell to write music to his songs. Pursell was twenty-one at the time, and living in his own apartment off-base. As Pursell remembers it, a captain from the Naval Bethesda Hospital called him, and said that there was a paraplegic veteran by the name of Standard James who had written some song lyrics, and that he wanted to get them set to music.

> He read them through the phone to me, and the lyrics were this: "Powder your face with sunshine, bring on that sunny smile; powder your face with sunshine, everything will seem worthwhile. Walk down the path with laughter, with songs that we've never heard of; so powder your face hereafter with a sunshine powder puff."
> And I thought, "Well, that's the cheesiest thing I ever heard." He said, "What do you think of it?" I said, "The guy who wrote it has some kind of an optimistic attitude."

Later, Standard James himself called Pursell. He explained that he was a paraplegic at the Bethesda Naval Hospital and had heard Pursell's name announced on one of the *Air Force Radio Hour* broadcasts on WOL Mutual. He thanked Pursell for setting his lyrics to music and asked if they could continue to work together. For some time they collaborated over the phone.

Pursell decided to visit James at the Bethesda Hospital, but when he suggested a visit, James said not to come, that he was going to stay with his sister for some time and would not be there. Later, James called Bill and told him that he had gotten a contract with an orchestra but that the music he had set to "Powder Your Face with Sunshine" was not quite right, and that Pursell needed to rewrite it. He asked Pursell to send the music to a hotel in New York City, as he was going to visit ASCAP there to promote the songs. Pursell agreed and rewrote the songs, but at this point, he began to worry, and decided to call the hotel to see if the scores had arrived.

> So I checked with the hotel and they said, "Oh yes, Mr. James just walked in and picked them up." And I said, "Walked in? This paraplegic vet walked in?"
> So then I called the paper in Washington that had run the story on Stan, and the night editor said, "I looked up the phone number, and this phone number is for a guy named Stanley Rochinski. We ran an article on him about six months ago—his wife disappeared." So I said, "Holy smoke, this guy has really been pulling something here, we didn't know it." So he came back from New York and he called me up and said, "They didn't like what you did with it; it was

in a waltz time, they wanted it in 2/4." I said, "Listen Rochinski, let's cut this out, just get the music back to me. Otherwise, I'm going to look up a cop and we're going to go up there and get it." And then I heard him say, "Well how do you like that." And then he sent it back with everything marked out that he didn't think of, and it was just really weird, even some of the words that I changed in the work that we did over the phone, he remembered every damn word down to the "the" and the articles, and he would cross those things out.

Not long after that, Pursell's girlfriend called him and said that there was a song by Guy Lombardo called "Powder Your Face with Sunshine" on jukeboxes in the Washington, D.C. area. The music had been written by Lombardo's brother, Carmen Lombardo. Pursell remembers a newspaper article around that time with a picture of Rochinski in a hospital bed, but I have been unable to locate this article.[20]

The tune would later be recorded by countless musicians, including Doris Day, Frank Sinatra, Sammy Kaye, Dean Martin, and others. Rochinski's entry in the Internet Movie Database remarks that he was recovering from spinal injuries, and it is entirely possible that he *was* able to walk into his hotel in New York. It is difficult to tell whether Rochinski perpetuated real fraud, or whether this was a misunderstanding. He did use a different name during the songwriting process.

Pursell was deeply offended at the apparent deception. He could not stomach the dishonesty. This was Arthur Pursell's legacy to him—a firm insistence on honest work and above-board dealings. Pursell was highly sensitive to these situations, perhaps more so than the average person, because he knew from childhood that his birth father had been in jail and perhaps feared similar moral failings in himself. His strong reaction to Rochinski's claim of paraplegia and his refusal to work with him may have lost him a hit song; one can never know. Perhaps for Rochinski, claiming a medical condition was just a gimmick, a harmless deception. But for Pursell, it was unforgivable.

Pursell served out his second term in the Air Force and then decided to accept an honorable discharge rather than continuing in the military. He had left the Peabody Conservatory behind, having closed that door when he enlisted for his second tour of duty. He did, however, want to complete his education. Near the end of his second tour, his friends Sam Krashmalnik and Bob Marcellus encouraged him to contact Howard Hanson at the Eastman School of Music in Rochester, New York. In early

1949, Pursell took the train up to Rochester and applied to the school, but was told that there were no spaces available for him at the time. His meeting with Howard Hanson, however, won him immediate acceptance into the program.

> I ended up in Hanson's office, and I brought along an arrangement I had done of "Blue Skies," which I had done for symphony orchestra for one of the [Air Force] broadcasts. I played it for Hanson, and he said,
> "Well, you're going to enjoy it here."
> I said, "I can't seem to get in because you're full up."
> And he said, "Well just put down 'at the request of the Director.'"
> So that's how I got in. I ended up studying with him; I went there for six years and four summer schools, and it was a great life. All I had to do was study. I was on the G.I. Bill, and in those days the G.I. Bill was marvelous. And then when that wore off, I had fellowships. What a wonderful thing; I just decided to become a scholar. I just decided, well, why not? I'll just keep going. So that's what I did. And nobody was in the way, so I kept on going. That was the best. The only other time that I think I was happier, or that happy, was when I was in Berkeley High School, oddly enough, living with the Berger family, studying concert piano.[21]

Pursell's service in the military ended in February 1949, and after his visit with Dr. Hanson, he returned home to Tulare for a short stay before the summer term at Eastman began. His father wrote to him on January 30, expressing his pride for his only son and letting Pursell know he was looking forward to his visit: "We feel content, that our boy has won the respect and admiration of those who have long wished him well. We look forward to having you with us again, son."[22]

Pursell was afforded a brief rest after his three years of military service, surrounded by friends and family who loved and encouraged him. Another letter from his father mentions a concert that he played in Tulare during this time, and letters from his Air Force pal and former roommate Edgar Muenzer kept him up to date on what was happening out East. After this brief respite, he headed to Rochester to begin life as a music student at the Eastman School of Music.

4. A STUDENT AGAIN, AND THEN, NOT

Pursell's student years at Eastman were happy and fruitful ones. As he had done at Peabody, Pursell entered Eastman as a composition major with a minor in piano. He would receive his Bachelor of Music degree in 1952, his Master of Music degree in 1953, and complete all work but his comprehensive exams and dissertation for his doctorate by 1956. Pursell attended Eastman for six years and four summers, then later would return to complete his doctorate in 1995.

Howard Hanson's intervention in Pursell's acceptance to the Eastman School of Music was extraordinary. The Eastman School was, and still is, one of the most prestigious schools of music in the United States. Its faculty were all accomplished artists, and its students were the best of the best. When Pursell applied for composition study in 1949, he was granted a personal interview with Hanson and on the basis of his past accomplishments (previous study at the Peabody Conservatory and years of arranging experience in the Air Force) and his scores, was granted an exception and was allowed to enroll as a full-time student.

Pursell funded his education through the G.I. Bill, and then through fellowships and assistantships. He tutored for the theory department and served as accompanist in the opera department. He began his graduate work in music before he received his bachelor's degree; he remembers that he had finished all coursework for the bachelor's degree by his senior year, so his advisor agreed to allow him to begin his master's degree early.

Pursell remembers that as a theory assistant, he would be assigned students who had failed the regular theory classes. The chair of the theory department, Dr. Allen McHose, was conducting a research study on aural skills pedagogy. Pursell's job was to help them understand the concepts, and then report to his professor how he did it.[1] As a pianist, in addition to his work with the theory and opera departments, Pursell performed many modern piano concertos with the Eastman-Rochester Orchestra:

You know, those days at Eastman were so long ago. I was there during what we call the "Halcyon Hanson days," when the Eastman-Rochester Symphony Orchestra was constantly playing [composition] theses of master's and doctoral students. And the first run-through was always recorded because with that orchestra it was really a take. It was marvelous that they could sight read that well. Everybody contacted me to do their piano concertos. So here I was, jamming two weeks into learning these things so I could play with Dr. Hanson and the Eastman-Rochester Symphony, and I enjoyed it.

Pursell's piano teachers at Eastman were Cecile Genhart (1949–51) and Orazio Frugoni (1951–56).[2] When at Peabody, Pursell had spent most of his energy and time on his piano study with Sklarevski. At Eastman, however, his focus began to turn to composition, while he remained active as a pianist.

Pursell recalls that he was carefully nurtured and protected as an Eastman student. One summer he had forgotten to re-apply for his fellowship, and he received a letter from Howard Hanson stating that his fellowship had been approved. The faculty were also watching his grades. Pursell recalled that Flora Burton summoned him into his office and expressed concern that some of his grades were Bs. He remembers: "I think there was a lot more attention in that school then. When I went back for my doctoral degree [in the 1990s], it was an entirely different school. It seemed to be a little more, not indifferent, but a little more objective than it was before. So when I was there during that earlier time, really, there was a great deal of faculty interest in the students."

Study at any music school, then and now, creates a strong sense of camaraderie. Music schools are both nurturing and competitive places, and students develop special bonds, both with each other and their teachers. The nature of academic music study, which requires regular one-on-one private lessons and constant criticism and praise for one's creative efforts, is an intense experience. The long hours of practice, the constant pressure to perform, and the competition with fellow students can be exhausting but also exhilarating. Pursell's enthusiasm when he talks about his "halcyon Hanson days" at the Eastman School is palpable.

Pursell owns a copy of a picture drawn by one of his fellow students, Glen Morley, "The Eastman Comp Works," that presents Eastman as a factory, and the professors as the machines that process the raw material.

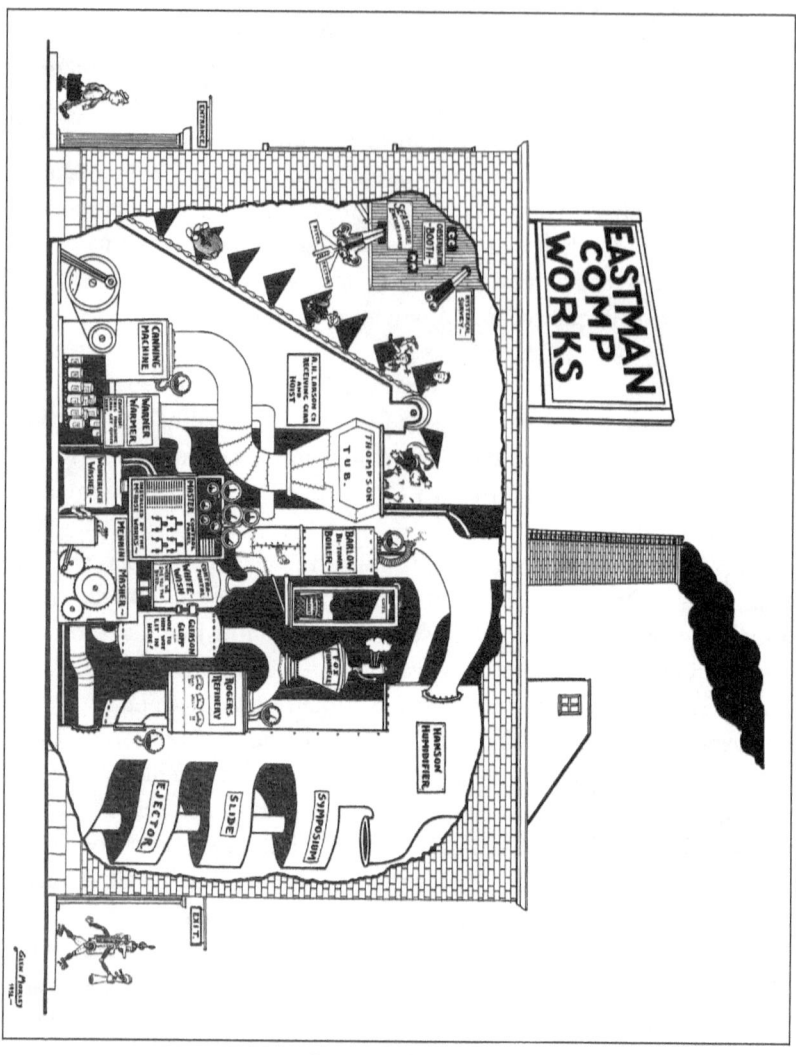

Eastman Comp Works

A student enters Thomson's tub (Thomson was a theory professor), goes through Thomas Canning's machine (composition), through the Warner Warmer, the Wonderlich Washer, the Mennini Masher, the Barlow Bitonal Boiler, other various machines, and finally exits the school holding his diploma, looking like a robot, with a keyboard on his back, a treble clef on his head, and a bass clef on his belt.

Pursell's fondness for the instructors at Eastman is clear when he talks about them. He remembers eavesdropping on lessons with the famous vocal teacher Lucy Lee Call: "And you'd go by her studio, you'd hear her yell, 'Drop your goddamn jaw!' You could hear her through the door. It was one of the calls that we used to use, you know. She would be working with a student, and they would not get the jaw open enough, and you'd hear her yell." He remembers this with fond nostalgia now; student years are often seen as the "good old days." But it's entirely possible the voice student behind that door left the lesson in tears. Often the most demanding professors are the ones who are remembered the most fondly.

Another of Pursell's favorite professors, Dr. Harold Gleason, was the head of the graduate department at Eastman while Pursell was a student there. He recalls with amazement that Dr. Gleason would bring original manuscripts from the Sibley Library into a graduate seminar for the students to examine. The acquisition of original manuscripts was a special project of Dr. Hanson. He worked with the musicologist Ruth Watanabe to locate and purchase things like the original four-stave sketches by Claude Debussy of *La Mer*. Pursell remembers: "I was allowed to take that score, the original sketches, go up into the stacks, and just sit there and look through all the pages. I always wanted to get a cassette tape and put it on and listen to it while examining the scores, never had a chance to do that" (Perone 1993, 145).

Howard Hanson was a dominant figure at the Eastman School and had a profound influence on Pursell's development as a composer and musician. Allen Cohen notes that Hanson helped transform music education at Eastman from a certificate-oriented, conservatory model of students taking chiefly private lessons to a comprehensive music school that included courses in music theory, aural skills, music history, and a broad liberal arts background. Hanson convinced the president of the university to hire more academic faculty, and by the end of his tenure, the Eastman School was (and remains) one of the top music schools in the United States (Cohen 2004, 11–13). Pursell came to Eastman in the years following this transformation of curricula and benefited from a strong faculty and also from Hanson's presence as a strong leader.

As a conductor who recorded music regularly, Hanson did not hesitate to change scores when he thought necessary. Pursell remembers that Hanson once called him up to his office to help with some copying of scores.

He was going to do a recording of the [Roy] Harris Third Symphony, and there is a part in the middle of it where he crosses strings in large intervals back and forth, and he gets a very floating effect. They were all crossing at different times, but there's a kind of a glistening, almost rosin-type sound that you get from that type of thing. And Hanson was re-orchestrating that whole middle section. And I remember walking into his study, where he had this big cigar in his mouth, and he said, "Aah, you know, old Roy just never really knew how to write for strings, and I'm just going to re-orchestrate this before I do it."

Hanson was infamous for his short temper when conducting (Cohen 2004, 10). He had built a large ensemble program at the Eastman School, and held the orchestra to high standards. Pursell remembers witnessing Dr. Hanson losing his temper during a rehearsal of "Christ Looking Over Jerusalem," when his friend Ron Phillips, the bassoon player, began playing scales, inexplicably, while rehearsing Pursell's piece.

And I heard Hanson go "ARRRR" like that at the top of his voice, really scream. And Mrs. Hanson said, "Oh dear, I thought this was going to happen," because he was going through a bout of sciatica at that time, and he was in a lot of pain. He got to the very end of the thing, he stopped and put his arms down, and then he shrieked, ten times, "NEVER, NEVER, NEVER, NEVER," and it went on like that, and I could feel my stomach coming up into my throat; it was just like the wrath of God! The judgment of God, and poor Ron was just sitting there. It was stupid for the kid to do, but at the same time, Hanson went off, like I've never seen any man.

Pursell's memory of Hanson was of a very strict teacher. He remembers that one time, a fellow student, Lindell Mitchell, was talking during one of Hanson's lessons, with all of the other students gathered around the piano, as Hanson liked them to be. Hanson realized that someone wasn't paying attention to the lesson. "All of a sudden, his big arm when whoosh-bang, like that at the top of the keys, and he looked around with this smile, and said, 'OUT,' to everybody. Everybody quietly went out. He was scary, in some ways . . . but he was very kind to me."

Pursell's composition teachers at Eastman were, in this order, Herbert Elwell, Wayne Barlow, Louis Mennini, Bernard Rogers, and Howard Hanson. He spent his last three years at Eastman studying with Dr. Hanson,

1953–56. His orchestration studies with Bernard Rogers were an unofficial audit. Pursell's curiosity was piqued because he had observed Rogers at work, experimenting with getting different sounds from timpani, and he knew that Rogers had written a book on orchestration. Dr. Hanson told Pursell that he did not need the orchestration course, so Pursell audited the course with Rogers, unofficially, without telling Dr. Hanson.

During Pursell's time at Eastman, he began work on a PhD in composition. However, Hanson was developing a new type of degree, a doctorate for performers and composers, the Doctor of Musical Arts. The Eastman School awarded its first DMA in 1955, and Pursell's program was changed to this new degree (Cohen, 14). Although he did not finish his DMA until much later, in 1991, he was one of the first DMA students at the Eastman School (Latimer 2010, 21).[3]

Pursell composed some of his most important classical works while a student at Eastman. He wrote a set of piano character pieces, called "Felis Domesticus" (1950). The movements were "Siamese" and "Lost Kitten." A third planned piece was never completed. Under the supervision of Howard Hanson, Pursell also wrote his first significant classical work for orchestra, *Three Biblical Scenes for Orchestra* (1953), the first movement of which later would be played on television after President Kennedy's assassination.

> It ["Christ Looking over Jerusalem" from *Three Biblical Scenes*] was a young piece. I wrote it in six hours. I remember that I started a kind of a chaconne-like figure, and I just repeated that figure over and over again and added instruments to it as I went along, and got them to weave in and out, sort of like a tapestry. It had one area towards the end that builds up to a big point and then comes back down again. The second movement was called "Suffer the Little Children to Come to Me," to describe Christ in a setting with children running around, and the last movement was "Calvary." In the last movement I had Christ musically depicted as stumbling under the cross, a very Cecil B. DeMille production in mind. I would never write it that way today.

Pursell remembers that Ralph Vaughan Williams had looked at the score during a visit to New York, and his response was that the whole piece was in the first movement, which, as Pursell agrees today, was an astute observation.

Manuscript page of "Christ Looking over Jerusalem"

The first movement, "Christ Looking over Jerusalem," won the first Benjamin Award for Quiet Music at Eastman. This was established by Edward B. Benjamin to reward a new composition of peaceful, relaxing music. Just before the first performance of his piece, Professor Mennini told him that he would be surprised at the concert, and he was, as the award was announced there. There was even an article in the *New York Times*.[4] The *Times* article noted that the composition faculty of Eastman chose the prize, which was awarded for "a work essentially in the nature of calm, uplifting music." An odd criterion for a composition prize, to be sure, but perhaps Benjamin was tired of atonal modernism in classical music and wanted to encourage work in a new direction. "Christ Looking over Jerusalem" was recorded by Dr. Hanson and the Eastman-Rochester Symphony and published on an album of Benjamin Award winners entitled *Music for Quiet Listening* (1959).

"Christ Looking over Jerusalem" begins with the chaconne chords, set as a pulsing, meditative foundation that gives structure and unity to the entire work. Their quarter-half-quarter rhythm continues throughout. The stacked thirds, giving sometimes a ninth chord, sometimes a half-diminished seventh, give the tone poem a tinge of Debussy, and sometimes of Stravinsky, a whole tone feel that is not quite whole tone. Over the chords, a flute solo rises, alternating with echoing strings, and then an English horn, which dominates the rest of the piece. The B section enharmonically shifts from the opening C Sharp Minor to D Flat Minor. The ending is signaled by a return to the opening pulsing chords and key of C Sharp Minor, and ends with only cellos playing a low C sharp. The tone poem is muted, lyrical, and haunting, breaking away from the quietness for one brief peak, then fading again to peaceful contemplation.

Other serious compositions by Pursell while he was at student at Eastman include an Introduction and Toccata for Piano, based on a nine-tone scale; his Symphony No. 1; and "Bluebeard," an unfinished tone poem for orchestra. Many of his compositions were performed at the regular symposiums that Eastman shared with other area music schools, including Juilliard and Yale. This was an opportunity to have his compositions heard and to meet other composition students.

At one symposium at Juilliard, Pursell played his Introduction and Toccata, *Felis Domesticus*, and Litany for Sunday. He had written the Introduction and Toccata with the famous pianist Vladimir Horowitz in mind, and to his surprise, after his performance of the piece at the Juilliard symposium, fellow student Lee Hoiby came up to him and said, "You're a regular Horowitz, aren't you?" and told Pursell that he should send the piece to Horowitz himself. Hoiby was a composition student at the Curtis School of Music with Gian Carlo Menotti, who was Samuel Barber's partner, and both of the composers had a close working relationship with Horowitz, because the pianist had been involved in the composition and promotion of Barber's piano sonata.

On Hoiby's advice, then, Pursell packed up the score of the Introduction and Toccata with a recording of himself playing it, and sent it to Mount Kisco, New York, where Barber and Menotti were living at the time. Pursell remembers this as the closest he ever got to "Sam Barber." He requested a trace by the U.S. Mail on his package, and they confirmed that Barber had signed for it in Mount Kisco. Later, Hoiby told Pursell that Menotti had indeed shown the Toccata to Horowitz, but his response was "No I have a Toccata, I don't need another one." Pursell tells this story with palpable irritation and says it was kind of like Horowitz saying, "I already have a Mercedes, why do I need another car?"

One thing I have learned in our years of interviews and phone calls is that Pursell is a person who takes things seriously. When you say "let's have lunch," he pulls out his calendar and finds a date. And he expects others to take him seriously, too. He remembers Hoiby telling him that Horowitz had listened to the Toccata, and that the rejection came from a reluctance to add another piece to his concert repertoire. Perhaps Horowitz really did listen to the Toccata. Or perhaps he did not pay much attention to the Toccata sent to him from an aspiring young composer. He probably received countless such submissions. And in one comment, Pursell's earnest work was reduced to "another Toccata."

GOING ON THE ROAD: THE JERRY JAYE TRIO AND THE INTERLUDES

During his time as a graduate student at Eastman, Pursell began to play weekends with rhythm and blues group the Jerry Jaye Trio, at a restaurant on the outskirts of Rochester called El Rancho. Pursell had come under some pressure to make a living, even though he was still a student. In 1955 Pursell married Susan Phillips, and they had a son, William "Sky" Schuyler Pursell, the same year. Susan was eighteen, and Pursell was twenty-eight. Pursell's marriage to Susan was a significant turning point in his life, because it turned his attention toward the adult responsibilities of supporting a wife and child, just near the end of his doctoral studies.

As a result, he wouldn't finish his DMA in composition until 1991. His decision to marry also meant that he increasingly spent more time in the commercial musical world than he did in the classical world. And so the river of his musical career swept around another bend.

Pursell is very forthright about his practical reasons for joining the Jerry Jaye Trio: he needed to earn money. He had enjoyed R&B music as a kid, so it was not too great a leap for him to join an R&B band, especially as it ensured a paycheck, and many adventures on the road. Not many composition majors at the Eastman School of Music would be capable of making such a switch. Pursell's skills at improvisation and his musical versatility, perhaps enhanced by his years in the Air Force as an arranger, served him well during this stage of his professional life.

The Jerry Jaye Trio was enjoying some success, and soon the McConkey Agency (from New York) suggested that they sign with them and begin to tour the Eastern states. Pursell, under some pressure to earn a living, "parked my doctoral work" and decided to go on the road with Jerry and the band. Pursell moved his wife and infant son to Schenectady, New York, and began life on the road.

Pursell describes his adventures on the road with a rhythm and blues band as "a vacation from my doctoral degree." He had completed all of the course work and written exams. All that remained to finish the Doctor of Musical Arts degree was two oral exams and a thesis. "Meanwhile," he says, "my dad is throwing up his hands and thinking, 'He's never going to finish that doctoral degree.'" I can only imagine what the upright Arthur Pursell, sitting at home in Tulare, caring for his invalid wife Delia, thought when he got the news that his talented son had married someone ten years younger and left school to tour with a band.

Pursell did intend to finish the degree, but needed to support his wife and child. He describes it as a nomadic life, going on the road and hoping to finish his degree someday in the not too distant future, but in the meantime, earning money. Pursell would eventually complete the degree, but not until almost forty years later. In between, he would tour, become a studio recording pianist, and eventually, college faculty.

The members of the Jerry Jaye Trio were Jerry Jaye (Allogio), a bass player; Bill Porter, the drummer; and Bill Pursell on keyboards. The first thing Pursell had to do after joining up with the Jerry Jaye Trio was change his name. Bill Porter did not want there to be two Bills in the group, so Pursell came up with a stage name, Stan Williams. "I knew Stan Kenton, so I figured well, I'll take my first name and put it last, and then put Stan.

Publicity photo of Bill in the late 1950s

Stan Williams sounds like a good R&B handle. So that was what I was known as; I went as Stan Williams. If I went to Hagerstown, Maryland, today, to Beck's Restaurant, they would call me Stan Williams."

Jerry Jaye was the leader of the group and would sing while he played his bass. Jerry wore a white coat and Bill and "Stan" would wear "town craft" coats. Part of their act was that Pursell, as Stan, would carry Jerry around on his shoulders while he played the bass, then they would both jump from the bar back to the stage. Pursell had been lifting weights, so he said it was no problem for him to carry Jerry around. Pursell describes Jerry as an incredibly talented musician and a fine performer. "I remember when we did a tune like 'Twenty-Four Hours a Day.' At each one of those rhythms, he would take the bass, hop over this way and that way fast. Very agile. And the girls would just go nuts over him." The band was very successful and had a good following, according to Pursell.

The Trio spent most of their time in Hagerstown and also toured up and down the East Coast, playing in restaurants, clubs, and bars. Pursell remembers that all three members of the group had convertibles; he had a 1956 green and white Pontiac and then a 1957 red and white one. Often their agent would call them at the last minute and they would have to drive madly to get to the next gig, sometimes in another state. One such night included a brush with the law.

They had just finished performing on a Sunday night in Massena, New York, which is near the Canadian border, when their agent called at 1:00 a.m. and said they had to be back in Hagerstown on Monday night. This would be a long drive. So they jumped into their convertibles, and drove as fast as they could. Pursell knew he wouldn't have enough time to shave and change into his uniform, so he was driving 90 miles an hour, trying to shave, his face covered with shaving cream. Then he saw flashing lights and a cop pulled him over.

> He pulls me over, and I forgot all about the suds, and so he walks over to the side of the car and looks down at me and said, "What the heck is this?" Well immediately, I knew what he was looking at, so I wiped off the suds and got out of the car and I explained to him about insane agents and so on. He said "You'd better come back with me," so we went back to the town. There was a justice of the peace there, a little old guy, and I guess they looked me as a nut because they only fined me something like twenty dollars. He said, "Now just watch out, take care of yourself," and so I said, "Listen, you guys are great, if you come into Hagerstown, I'll buy you a drink." So we went down, and I got on the stage, and about two days later the cop comes in, in plain clothes, so I bought him a drink. We sat at the bar, he looked at me, and he said, "I'll tell you one thing, when I pulled you over and looked at you I thought you were some kind of a nut." I said, "Well, that was exactly what I thought you thought."

Life on the road was hectic, and sometimes lonely. Both Bill and Jerry had dogs, boxers, as traveling companions. Pursell's dog was named Saltz, and she saved him one night, on the road. "I was traveling on the New York State freeway in the middle of the night, and I was tired. She never came over to my side of the car. But I nodded off and started to go off the road, to the left, and suddenly I realized she was licking my face. I woke up and saw what I was doing, and came back on the road."[5] He did not keep Saltz very long, though, as she tended to escape from his hotel room and run into the street. The touring life was not healthy for a dog. He sold her to a friend, and was sad when he drove away to look back and see the dog ignoring him completely.

Pursell remembers that his bandmate, Bill Porter, wanted to become a club owner and a millionaire. Pursell describes him as being very "thing-conscious." One of his favorite stories from his touring days is the destruction of Bill Porter's car. Porter loved that car and would spend hours polishing and detailing it. Pursell remembers that one day he came out of Beck's restaurant to see a truck drive too close to Bill Porter's convertible, catch onto it, and drag it down the street.

> The guy slammed his brakes on and backed up and took Bill's car, and banged it back against the rear car this way, and then it banged against another car. At the same time, I saw Bill [Porter] coming out of Beck's restaurant, and when he saw what had happened, he yelled, 'Oh no!' He put his hands in front of his head and started crying. I went up to the guy in the truck and I said, what in the heck, blankety blank blank this and that, and the guy was drunk, and he said [in a slur], "Well, I didn't see where we were going." Bill, bless his heart, he comes up and says, "Why did you do that?" It was almost tame, not like I'm going to beat out your eyeballs, but "why did you do that?" And it was so defenseless, and so he stuck by the car and then they called the tow truck. I saw this vanishing picture of the tow truck going back up the alley, pulling the car, and Bill sitting in the front seat of his car with his arms crossed. He looked like a sad teddy bear. I had to go back to where I lived and shut the door and put my head in the pillow and laugh my head off so that no one would hear me.

Bill (Pursell) laughs and laughs when he tells this story and describes the helpless expression on his bandmate's face. When Pursell talks about his time on the road in the late 1950s, he does not talk about the music he played, or hours spent rehearsing. Rather, he tells stories about his bandmates and people he met along the way. The music he was playing at this stage of his life, unlike the music he had been studying so earnestly at Eastman, was for him a vehicle to earn a living. He was merely the pianist for the star, Jerry Jaye. The music was entertainment, and he spent many more hours behind the wheel of his convertible than he did on stage as a band member. And what he remembers best are the people, his friends from this time, and the hours spent on the road between jobs.

Life on the road could be unpredictable. Pursell remembers that one night he drove into Toronto, only to find that his agent had told the band to go to the wrong place. He was inside the club, talking to Bill Porter about this, when someone told him that the top to his convertible had been slashed.

> I had all my uniforms hanging in the car, in the back, and at the same time he's giving me this bad news, someone said to me, "Do you own a red convertible with a white top?" And I said, "Yes." He said, "You'd better go look at it, it's been slashed." I went out, and I found that someone had slashed the top and had taken all my uniforms out. So I spent a good part of the rest of the night going up and down the streets, hoping that they threw them out. No luck there, so we went back into the United States, and went back to Harry Specter's place in New Jersey, and it was lousy luck.

Pursell remembers that he didn't like that car as much as his first convertible, because it didn't have power steering. When his estranged wife in Schenectady asked him to send more money, the only choice he had was to get rid of his car (and thus his car payments). He signed the car over to the bank and didn't look back.

The Jerry Jaye Trio played at a variety of venues, even the Apollo Theater in Harlem. Pursell felt out of place: "We were at the Apollo on a Saturday afternoon, and I couldn't wait to get off that stage because here was this beautiful black band, all these black guys, and they're trying to make some sense out of these three white kids up there playing blues in the Apollo Theater. It didn't make sense." There is more than a little irony in the phenomenon of the all-white Jerry Jaye Trio playing the blues, a style developed by African Americans, on the quintessential African American popular music stage, the Apollo Theater. However, that is precisely the kind of musical diversity that Pursell would champion all of his life. He was a musician, not a classical or popular musician. And later in Nashville he would play with African Americans on stage at a time when that wasn't done in the South. Pursell was aware of race issues; they just never seemed to bother him overmuch, personally.

The Jerry Jaye Trio would end badly, and fairly dramatically. Jerry Jaye was, Pursell remembers, a very ambitious musician. The group's demise came about in part because of this ambition. The trio was playing in Atlantic City one night, and afterward an agent came up to Jerry and told him that if he had met him six months earlier, he could have created the next Elvis. This simple comment struck Jerry hard, and Pursell thinks that he began to consider himself a failure.

Jerry became more and more erratic and unstable, until one night in Hagerstown, Bill Porter came up to Pursell and told him that they couldn't play that night. Jerry was having a breakdown upstairs. "All of a sudden he started screaming, he started running around, pounding walls with his fist and everything else. Dolores [Jerry's wife, who traveled with the group] had to take him back home up to Pennsylvania. Evidently this had been working on him; he felt he had missed out. And you know, those of us who were standing on the sidelines looking at that would say, 'Jerry, you just took it too seriously. Somebody made a statement in New Jersey, and you believed it.' He felt like he never got his chance. And those of us would say, 'No, Jerry, that had nothing to do with it.'"

After Jerry returned home, Bill Porter and "Stan" went on the road by themselves, and eventually hired a saxophonist to replace Jerry. But things were never the same, and after a short time, the group broke up for good. Bill Porter returned to his home in Rochester, and Bill Pursell (still as Stan Williams) continued on the road for a while as a solo piano act, still with the McConkey Agency. His marriage was not working out (his wife and he had been separated for some time, and she had no interest in reuniting), so he had no home to return to, and he continued to tour.

Pursell played as a single act for several months. During that time, he began to experience severe pain when he sat down. He visited a doctor in Cumberland, Maryland, who diagnosed him with a pylonidal cyst, and told him that it had to be removed.[6] Pursell, however, was dependent on playing regularly to earn his income, and he could not afford to take the days off that recovery from surgery would require; he would lose his job. He said goodbye, and turned to leave the doctor's office. But the doctor called him back and told him to return on Monday morning, and he would remove the cyst as outpatient surgery and not require a hospital stay, something that is common today but was not common in the late 1950s.

Pursell remembers: "I went into his office Monday morning. He put me out on the table, he gave me a cigarette to smoke, he froze my tail up, he

The Interludes

dug out this pynonital cyst and put gauze in there, and that night I went to work as a single. And the way I cured it was sitz baths. It was draining, but I would take sitz baths, and it finally healed. On a Monday or Tuesday night, he came into the bar, this doctor, he got a little tipsy; he came over and says to me, 'You're a stupid freak!' It was painful, but I did it. You would ordinarily go to the hospital with it. It was out of desperation; I had to keep working, because I wanted to send money home to Susan."

Pursell sees this story as an important example of the kinds of things working musicians do in order to keep working. He was especially vulnerable as a solo act, and as the saying goes, "the show must go on" regardless of, well, just about anything. He was still supporting his estranged wife and child. Eventually, he heard of a group that was looking for a pianist, and moved to Troy, New York.

The group was called the Interludes, and for a short time they played in clubs in Troy. The members were two brothers, Mickey and Johnny Milanese, and Jerry Benoit. Jerry was a comedian, and would sing and do skits. Mickey played the bass, and Johnny played the drums. The Interludes were not an R&B band like the Jerry Jaye Trio had been; their act was closer to a Las Vegas–style act, with middle-of-the-road pop tunes and comedy skits. As a member of the Interludes, Pursell changed his name again, taking his middle name as his last name, and became Bill Whitney.[7]

In 1958 the Interludes moved to Fort Lauderdale, Florida, and began to work there. They played regular jobs at Bea Morley's Supper Club, then Jimmy Fazio's club, then the Boca Key Hotel. Their routine was to begin with Mickey singing a Sinatra tune like "I'm a Fool to Want You," then they would do a comedy routine, and they would finish with more music and a silent movie sketch. Jerry would play all of the silent movie characters, and Pursell would improvise music on the piano behind him. Their audience was typically people in their fifties and sixties, or people in town for a convention. Pursell remained with this group in Florida for about two years.

During his stay in Florida, Pursell was able to obtain a divorce from his first wife, Susan. They had endured a long legal separation, indeed, had only lived together for a very short portion of their two-year marriage. While playing at the Boca Key Hotel in Fort Lauderdale, Pursell met another woman, Marion Lumpkin, and would marry her in 1960. Marion was from a well-respected family in the Athens, Georgia, area. She had won a trip to Fort Lauderdale from a local radio station, and had brought her parents with her.

Eventually, Pursell discovered that he was not being paid fairly for his work in the Interludes. Johnny Milanese, who was the leader of the group, had broken his foot, and so he asked Pursell to pick up a check at Jimmy Fazio's club.

> And so I did, and the girl told me, "Okay, this makes it complete. I gave a check to Johnny about three or four days ago, and this makes the other check." Then I started totaling up this in my mind and realized there was a heck of a lot more money coming in here than we knew about. So I went up to deliver the check, and Johnny was lying in bed and he had his cast on. I said, "Okay, here's the check. And the girl told me that this makes up the balance of what you were supposed to get, which was a total of," and I gave him the total. He looked at me, and he said, "Well, that's none of your business now, is it?" And I said to him, "Johnny, you see that cast right there on your foot? I could kick that right now and break it, and you'd be in a great deal of pain, wouldn't you?" He said, "Yeah," and I said, "Well, that's how I feel right now, but I'm not going to do it." And I walked out. And that was the beginning of the end, and that was when I finally took Eddy up on his offer to come to Nashville.

Pursell had met Eddy Arnold during his time in Florida. In the late 1950s, Arnold was working with Chet Atkins to reclaim some of his successes from earlier years after a dry spell (Streissguth 1997, 167–69). Arnold was well connected with musical life in Nashville, and he told Pursell that if he would move to Nashville, Eddy would find him work as a musician. The Interludes were falling apart; not only had Pursell discovered that Johnny was cheating the rest of the band, but the two Milanese brothers were beginning to fight. "Mickey and Johnny would get into it every now and then, and Jerry and I would break them up, and we didn't understand what was going on. And finally I said, 'Look, I can't do this. We get into rehearsals, and Johnny says something and then you pile in on him, and then Jerry grabs you and I grab Mickey.'" As these problems grew worse, Pursell decided to follow Eddy Arnold's advice, and he and his new wife Marion moved to Nashville in 1960. Pursell would remain in Nashville for the rest of his life. After four years of touring with two different bands and as a solo act, Pursell was ready for a change. The change he chose would prove to be a fruitful one for his career, and another bend in his personal crooked river.

5. NASHVILLE SESSIONS

In 1960, when Pursell arrived in Nashville, the thriving recording industry there employed increasing numbers of studio musicians, live music venues downtown provided regular gigs for many, and stars would hire band members for tours that left from Nashville. Then, as now, having a good contact was invaluable in finding work, and Pursell's connection to Eddy Arnold (who had invited him to Nashville) ensured that he would get attention as a new pianist in town.

Eddy Arnold was a Tennessee native who had made his name in the 1940s and 1950s as the "Tennessee Plowboy," a country musician. When Pursell met him in Florida in the late 1950s, Arnold was trying to broaden his image and gain some success on the popular music charts (Streissguth 1997). Although Arnold did not achieve the success he had hoped for in the New York recording studios, by the time he returned to Nashville in the late 1950s he had developed a new take on the country music style that has become known as the Nashville Sound. Arnold became part of an effort in the Nashville music industry to make the country sound more palatable to a wider audience, removing the steel guitar and fiddle and replacing it with strings, piano, and rhythm guitar, and featuring a less "hillbilly" vocal style.[1] Albin Zak (2011), a recording industry scholar, calls the Nashville Sound "country music's flirtation with pop" and "a smooth blend orchestrated in large part by the efforts of such producers as Chet Atkins and Owen Bradley" (122).

Arnold's invitation to Pursell was timely and shrewd—he brought the highly educated pianist to Nashville at a time when his skills could best be put to use in the new commercialized style of country music that was emerging. As his circle of musical contacts widened, Pursell's musical experiences in Nashville in the 1960s began to reflect his own musical versatility, from playing jazz downtown to becoming an A-list studio keyboardist for Columbia to performing concertos with the Nashville Symphony.

Right after he moved to Nashville, Pursell went on the road a few times with Eddy Arnold, and worked with him in the recording studios as well.

Pursell also worked with Eddy's coach, Gene Nash, to produce a show called *Stock and Trade* in the Circle Theater. Pursell played all of the music on piano, serving in the role of the orchestra. It was through these jobs that Nashville musicians came to know Pursell, and soon he was getting phone calls to come to the studio to record as a keyboard player.

Pursell also spent a lot of time during his early months in Nashville playing jazz downtown at the Carousel, also known as Jimmy Hyde's Supper Club. The Carousel was a gathering place for many of the musicians central to the development of the Nashville Sound, and it was there that Pursell made many valuable connections to Nashville royalty, including Chet Atkins, Hank Garland, Boots Randolph, and Harold Bradley. At the Carousel, these musicians played mostly jazz, but also some pop and country tunes.[2]

The state of Tennessee was dry when Pursell first came to Nashville, and the Carousel was a typical "inside" club. Pursell notes that the presence of liquor in all of the clubs downtown was an open secret, and that the local sheriff had a friendly relationship with the owner of the Carousel:

> Here we are, down at Jimmy Hyde's Supper Club and it was somewhat like working in New Orleans, very exciting, looking at all these drinks that were setups, and everyone having their own particular bottle in there. We were in two raids under Sheriff Leslie Jett. It was all very political. He would be in there having a drink, but then two weeks later, Jimmy would say, "Now boys, get up there and play one set, because Leslie's going to hit the front door, they're going to have a raid tonight." Jimmy was paying the cops off, and Leslie had been in there having a drink. Yet there was Leslie at the front door, serving Jimmy papers. It was sort of like *Thunder Road* if you ever saw that movie. During the raid, I would sort of bob and weave to get outside; I didn't want to get in the television lights, and I would see all these people coming out of all the other clubs in the alley, girls with their coats over their heads, fur coats.

Pursell remembers that the sheriff and Jimmy would have a friendly conversation outside in the sheriff's car, then they would drive downtown for a short time. Soon Jimmy would be back, the liquor would come back out, and the club would once again be swinging. The Carousel was clearly the place to be. Through his gigs there, Pursell was able to expand his connections and eventually began to be asked to record in the famous Nashville studios.

Pursell's first recording session was with the country music comedy act, Homer and Jethro.[3] Chet Atkins was Jethro's brother-in-law, and Homer and Jethro recorded for RCA. Pursell had not played much country before, but Chet assured Homer and Jethro that he could do it. Pursell remembers that his fellow musicians were encouraging him to study the playing style of country pianist Floyd Cramer. Floyd was self-taught, and played very simply. Pursell, however, on his first session, thought they would want to see what he could do. He remembers: "So I played all over the place. And I'll never forget, Jethro looked at me and said, 'Well, sure good to see you again Bill,' and then I knew I had flunked out. It was very condescending. It was like, 'You didn't play simple enough for us.' So I started watching Floyd, playing those little licks. And then you start doing that kind of thing and well, yeah, you're playing exactly what they want in these Nashville country records."[4]

As a classically trained musician, Pursell was both at an advantage and a disadvantage in the Nashville recording world. His training and excellent musicianship meant that he was an incredibly versatile pianist, understood harmony and theory, and could improvise just about anything. However, in Nashville, when someone asked a musician if he could read music, the correct answer was "Not enough to hurt my playing." Both Chet Atkins and Harold Bradley were famous for saying this. It was almost bad manners to reveal advanced musical knowledge, but Pursell did not understand this, and in some ways still doesn't. He could read music very well, and made no effort to hide his skills. This alienated him somewhat from the local musicians, who are described by Paul Hemphill (2015) as "a small clique of extremely talented musicians who had similar small-town Southern backgrounds" (62). Pursell certainly measured up in terms of talent and may have had a small-town background, but he was from California, not Tennessee or Mississippi or Kentucky. This made him an outsider from the very beginning. A more shrewd, less honest person might have found ways to fit in, but Pursell just could not hide his musical training, nor did he want to do so.

Coming into a Nashville culture of mostly self-taught musicians, Pursell felt that he was somewhat of an anomaly. He says that he never experienced any direct discrimination, but he sensed the attitude, all the same, and he believes that his fellow musicians certainly weren't inclined to give him any breaks. He says, "I can tell you, coming in as a classically trained musician and jazz player, I felt a little out of place." It didn't help that he was moonlighting nights with the Nashville Symphony, playing piano concertos at their summer concerts in Centennial Park.[5]

THE NASHVILLE SYMPHONY

Not too long after Pursell moved to Nashville, he was playing piano for a Ralph Emery show at the local radio station WSM.[6] Willis Page, who was the music director of the Nashville Symphony at that time, was present. Pursell decided to introduce himself, so to speak, by playing something unusual (for country music–oriented WSM) on the piano. He remembers:

> I very coyly started playing the theme from the Rachmaninoff Third Piano Concerto on this little spinet piano, and immediately got Willis Page's attention. He immediately came over and said, "How do you know that?" And I said, "Well, I've played it." "Where?" I said, "I played it in Baltimore; I studied it with Alexander Sklarevski." And he said, "No!" That led to a park concert, outdoors with the Nashville Symphony, when I played the Grieg Piano Concerto.

This encounter marked the beginning of a long relationship with the Nashville Symphony for Pursell. He would go on to perform many times with the symphony as a solo pianist and arrange and compose various commissions for them as well. All of this was happening simultaneously with his sessions with Hank Garland, Chet Atkins, Johnny Cash, and others. Pursell moved seamlessly between the musical worlds of the recording studio and symphony concert hall stage. Country music scholar Travis Stimeling (2016) notes that string players in Nashville were doing much the same thing—recording country music in the studios by day and performing classical music at night. However, string players were not considered part of the core group of session musicians. As a pianist, Pursell was part of the rhythm section, and thus more of a regular in the eyes of other session players.[7]

Some of his performances with the Nashville Symphony reflected his stylistic versatility; he played Gershwin's *Rhapsody in Blue* and Concerto in F with them many times, pieces known for their popular music influence. And many of these concerts were part of the symphony's Pops Series. He also made arrangements of country songs for the symphony to play, perhaps the best example of the blending of his musical worlds. But his commissions were straightforward classical works, an overture and a symphony, pieces no typical Nashville studio musician would compose. Pursell's collaborations with the Nashville Symphony are evidence of the effortlessness with which he moved from one musical world to another, country to classical, and did both, as Harold Bradley said, extremely well. Pursell's musical life in Nashville, thus, wound around all of the major music venues in town, just like the crooked Cumberland River that curved around downtown.

Pursell's first performance with the Nashville Symphony took place on May 14, 1961, outside at Centennial Park, the city park in Nashville most famous for its full-scale replica of the Parthenon, and home to many outdoor concerts, then and now. The symphony concert was the grand opening to a weeklong arts festival. First up was the Nashville Youth Symphony at 4:00 p.m. with several short pieces, then the Nashville Symphony at 5:00 p.m. with the *Tam O'Shanter Overture* by Malcolm Arnold, the Piano Concerto in A minor by Edward Grieg (with Pursell featured as pianist), and the *Marche Slave* by Tchaikovsky. Later events that week included chamber music concerts, lectures, plays, films, ballet, modern dance, and art exhibitions.[8]

Pursell received high praise for his performance of the Grieg concerto. Both reviewers, Sydney Dalton and Louis Nicholas, noted Pursell's experience making music recordings in a variety of musical styles. Nicholas wrote, "Pursell has been recording and playing in the popular field for some time, but we would welcome more appearances by him like yesterday's." Dalton also expressed hopes for more performances by Pursell, perhaps even a recital. Dalton wrote: "This work [the Grieg Concerto] may be dated and too obvious and sweetly melodic for some of the ultra-modern ears, but it somehow always sounds fresh and appealing when it is well played. And it was very well played by Pursell, who always had it completely under control, technically and musically." Nicholas wrote of the excellent rapport between conductor, soloist, and orchestra.[9]

Pursell's first performance with the Nashville Symphony was a triumph. For Pursell it was a welcome return to a life he had left behind for some years, and an affirmation that yes, he could function successfully in both the commercial and classical fields, even simultaneously. However, Pursell's success in the classical world did not earn him extra goodwill in the recording studio, and indeed only exacerbated his feeling of being an outsider in a Southern world. He notes that his calls for session work

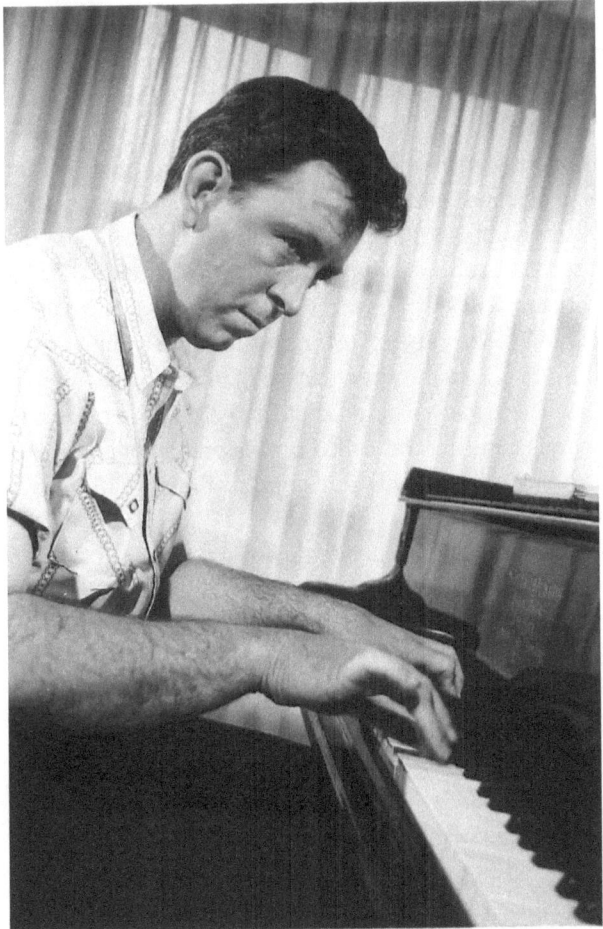

Publicity photo of William Pursell at the piano in the early 1960s

would drop about five percent every time he played with or composed for the Nashville Symphony. "Because they figured I was too uptown, that kind of thing. I'm certainly sure that's not my imagination."

Pursell would go on to play Gershwin on a regular basis with the Nashville Symphony. In 1962 Pursell played both the Concerto in F and *Rhapsody in Blue* with the Nashville Symphony in War Memorial Auditorium. Reviewer Louis Nicholas notes that the concert ended with an impromptu jam session on "I Got Rhythm" with Pursell and members of the orchestra, featuring improvisation by Sam Hollingsworth on bass, Steve Sefsik on clarinet, and Karl Garvin on trumpet. Nicholas noted that the applause during this encore was so loud that he could hardly hear the music. Then Willis Page, the conductor, grabbed Hollingsworth's bass, and he and Pursell began to jam together.[10] Even a symphony concert could close with a jam in Nashville.

Pursell's strongest memory of this concert, however, is that he lost a contact lens on the stage when he bowed. He had to play the Concerto without his contacts, but stagehands later found his lens. This concert was repeated that summer (June 12, 1962) in Centennial Park as a farewell concert for Willis Page, who was leaving for Japan to spend a year conducting in Tokyo.[11] The review notes that the benches were full, and hundreds more listeners sat on picnic blankets or lawn chairs to hear the concert. The reviewer noted that Pursell's playing was equal to that of the previous concert, and called him "a pianist of broad attainments, equally at home with serious and popular music, with a well-rounded technique and rich tone."[12]

Pursell had arrived in Nashville during a time when the hard work of the local musicians had begun to pay off, but their success was bringing about changes in their beloved country music. The Nashville country sound was shifting from fiddle and steel guitar–dominated recordings to a smoother string- and piano-based sound. Some of the country musicians were less comfortable with this pop-influenced sound, but Pursell's skills fit perfectly into this new idiom. Part of their discomfort with Pursell's education and his "foreign" upbringing may have been connected to some resentment of the new, more commercialized sound that had won country music its success but that also meant a goodbye to some much-loved traditions. The gregarious and outgoing Pursell, who too obviously was not a country musician, may have been oblivious to these undertones. At the time, country music was traveling from Nashville to California (Bakersfield), not from California to Nashville (Bomar et al. 2012). Even today Pursell is largely unaware of his central role in the rise of what later would be called the Nashville Sound.

Eddy Arnold, of course, probably brought in Pursell precisely for his skills. In the 1960s, Arnold was part of a group of singers, musicians, and producers (including Chet Atkins) who were transforming the sound of country music coming from Nashville into something more polished, a little more urban. Paul Hemphill's book *The Nashville Sound: Bright Lights and Country Music* (2015) traces these changes and discusses the divide in the early 1960s between the country musicians who had built the Grand Ole Opry and the new players coming to town who were changing the sound of country music.[13] Pursell's piano stylings (and later, his string arrangements) were part of this shift toward a more polished, commercial sound, but he was unaware of these bigger trends. All that he knew was that he was an outsider.

Much later, in the mid-2010s, commenting on some of his old friends' induction into the Country Music Hall of Fame, he expressed no small resentment that he was not included. "But you're not a country musician," his colleague argued, "You're a composer, a pianist, and you were a session player. You did so much more than that." Pursell is aware of this but the exclusion still rankles.

Years after "Our Winter Love" (1962) had been a hit, Pursell heard that some of the session musicians that he had worked with on a daily basis resented him for getting a hit only two years after coming to Nashville. After all, Floyd Cramer, who was a Southerner if not a native of Nashville, had worked in town for at least five years before he made his first big hit. Cramer, along with Chet Atkins, Hank Garland, the Bradley brothers, and others, formed a tight-knit group that had worked hard to bring the Nashville music scene to prominence.[14] Pursell didn't arrive until 1960, and arrived during a shift away from the traditional country music sound that had put Nashville on the map.

Pursell, who in some ways is still only vaguely aware that he was part of the transformation in country music called the Nashville Sound, thought the attitude of the established Nashville musicians was childish. After all, he had the skills. "Everybody I was working with had been working here since the 1950s, and here I come in 1960. I play in the Alley, and suddenly I'm on sessions. These people had come off the road, had worked for Roy Acuff and for Hank Williams Sr., and worked themselves gradually into the sessions. And what right did I have to just suddenly sail into town and get into sessions like this? But that's precisely what happened."

His skill at playing jazz was one of the first things that gave Pursell an entrée into the recording business. Pursell played fast jazz in the style of Oscar Peterson at the Carousel, and so people began to associate him with Hank Garland, who was doing the same thing on guitar, often sharing a stage with Pursell. "And so," he says, "immediately I'm in." But even though Pursell got plenty of session work, he always felt like he was an outsider, like his fellow musicians did not quite trust him. His thoughts on this reveal that perhaps there was a subconscious feeling of superiority to these earthy musicians. Maybe they sensed this, and that's why Pursell never felt quite part of the good old boys' club.

When I first came here, I sort of popped in out of the blue and was working with Eddy Arnold, but at the same time I came in with a background. I ran into a kind of a regional mentality, and it's a sort of inherent distrust for anybody who has any "larnin'" in the background. Now, you can be just as versed as anybody, but have gone further in your education in terms of studying music in conservatory, whereas a lot of these people that were on these sessions came from parts of the South that were quite deprived. The biggest thing for them was of course the Grand Ole Opry on Saturday night. And so you have a sort of a general distrust. Consequently when it comes to advancement, you might be on all of these different records, but at the same time, you're not going to advance yourself economically, because they're afraid that you're going to walk off with the whole ball of wax underneath their nose.

If you know that ahead of time, there's nothing you can do about it. You're not going to change their minds. You can be on the biggest records in the world, like Johnny Cash's *Ring of Fire* or Burl Ives [as Pursell was], but at the same time you're not ever going to crack through that, it's just impossible.

Pursell has a sensitive spirit, and it is entirely possible that his sense of alienation also came from his own insecurities, his self-knowledge as an adopted son (see ch. 2), and his struggles to make a success for himself in a highly competitive industry. However, Nashville is a bastion of the South, a place with a strong sense of heritage and family connections, and anyone who moves there might experience a similar feeling of being an outsider. Almost all of the regular session musicians had deep Southern roots. Pursell's California roots, his extensive classical training, and his willingness to reveal it may have exacerbated the situation. And the local musicians were experiencing a growing identity crisis with the rise of the new style of country music.

This clubby attitude came out in little jokes while they were working. Pursell remembers that in the studio, his fellow musicians would play a chord and ask him to play it on the piano, and he would, to their amazement, and then another chord, the same way. Pursell has an incredible musical ear. He says it was odd to them that he could do that on the spot, and that he felt like a trick dog. Hovie Lister, the pianist for the gospel group the Stamps, played on sessions with Pursell. He used to joke, "I've taught him all he knows," when it was clear that Pursell could play circles around him.

These kinds of jokes are more funny to the people who tell them than they are to their objects, of course. Pursell would simply laugh and move on and try not to let it get to him. "The one thing you have to do is to keep yourself from mentally beating up all these people in your mind. You have to just simply resist all of that. You simply say to yourself, well, that's the way that it is. If I worked in a brewery, loading trucks, right away they'd pick me out as being the educated guy. You see that in the industry."[15] A more reserved person might have been reluctant to demonstrate these skills and might have been more welcome. Pursell's outgoing personality and his showmanship got the better of him, though, and he could not resist showing off from time to time.

People in any career are cliquish and can be protective of their local culture. The good old boy network that Pursell experienced is certainly not unique to the music recording industry. In his case, the result was not so much lost jobs as it was a sense of not completely belonging. Pursell, the adopted son of Arthur and Delia Pursell, was especially sensitive to this. And, as Pursell asserts, "They don't give you any plums." If there was a big break, they were first loyal to their own, meaning, those from the South.

Pursell remembers one night having a drink with Chet Atkins. Floyd Cramer, the pianist who worked with Chet, had recently found his signature lick, and had used it on a session with him. Chet, raising his drink, said to Pursell that Floyd had just cut a hit that day ("Last Date," 1961). He continued, "Well Bill, you could have been my boy, but Floyd's my boy."

Pursell, who was normally not terribly bothered by the occasional reference to his position as an outsider, was furious. Even today he gets angry, remembering that night: "I thought to myself, you lousy, stupid, arrogant, mountain crap! That you would even load that kind of crap on me. Shame on you! I'm in here, and I'm working with you, and you treat me like a servant hand over here, to go and pick up your little trash for you? What did you bring all that with you for? Why are you bothering my time with that for? I thought, well, I'm never going to trust these guys, they're too ignorant." It reminded him of the time during his military service at Keesler Field when one of his fellow soldiers made fun of him for using big words like "analyze" and nicknamed him "Fesser." Atkins, in a very un-Southern way, was telling Pursell rather directly that he was not part of the club.

In spite of encounters like that, he figured out what he had to do, studied Floyd Cramer's style, and learned to play simply. He worked hard in the studio, showed up on time, and played his best, and in the end, earned the respect of many Nashville musicians. Hank Garland brought Pursell in for many country recording sessions, as did Eddy Arnold. Pursell spent his early years in Nashville recording mostly at the two major studios in the Nashville area: RCA Victor (between 16th and 17th Avenues) and Owen Bradley's studio (the famous Quonset Hut on 16th Avenue, which would later become the Columbia studio).[16]

Having his musicians' union card helped. Pursell had joined the American Federation of Musicians in 1949.[17] Sessions in Nashville, at least by the 1960s, were closely regulated by the union, and Pursell was diligent in following the rules. Harold Bradley, a guitarist who with his brother Owen was greatly responsible for the unparalleled growth of the Nashville music industry in the 1950s, was president of the Nashville chapter of the American Federation of Musicians for many years. He describes the life of a studio musician in Nashville as busy but fun. The union controlled the scheduling of sessions, which were three hours at a time. A typical working day would be three sessions for a musician, sometimes four. Bradley remembers that one might play in one studio from 10:00 a.m. to 1:00 p.m., then drive across town for another session from 2:00 p.m. to 5:00 p.m., go to a different studio for a 6:00 p.m. to 9:00 p.m. session, and finish the day with a 10:00 p.m. to 1:00 a.m. session.

Bradley describes this life as "like being on a merry go round. But we didn't really think of it that way, because it was an adrenaline rush. It was the greatest fun in the world; it was to me like going to a party. You go to a party at 10:00 and then you go to a different party at 2:00 and you go to a different party at 6:00, and sometimes you go to a different party at 10:00, because they're all different people, different music, because Nashville is very capable of doing all kinds of music."

Bradley remembers Pursell as being a lot of fun in sessions.

> He had a great personality, he fit in just great, because we were always kidding, cutting up and telling stories. Then when it came time to work, we were all serious. We were really into it. Bill can play any style; I don't know of anybody that could play jazz, pop, rock and roll, and classical like he can. Some of them can touch parts of them, and fake part of them; I can fake parts of stuff too, but he can really do them all. And not only can he do them all, but he can do it effortlessly, and I admire that.

Most of the musicians with whom Pursell worked in the recording studios could not read music. They would have to learn the song by ear before they recorded it, and they had developed a system to identify the different chords that was called Nashville numbers. Pursell would watch the other session musicians with curiosity as they would gather around, listen to a demo, and write down the chords in numbers, 1141, 1151, etc. He realized that they were doing the same thing a music major in college might do today, but with Arabic instead of Roman numerals. 1 is really I, or tonic, 5 is V, dominant, and so on. It is a simple way of notating harmony, an adaptation for non–music readers now known around the world as Nashville numbers.

The Nashville number system was a way of learning a great deal of music very quickly. It was an efficient process, as time in the studio equals money spent. Pursell recalls:

In the early days, when everybody was working demo sessions for publishers here, the publishers would like to get in there and get eight or nine tunes in three hours. All they had was a tape. The engineer would play the tape through the loudspeakers, and everybody would gather round the tape, and simply take the numbers down. Then they would go ahead and sit down and just record the demo, and it would take something like fifteen minutes to do it. That's how you broke into master sessions, by doing a lot of demos. And in those days, you were supposed to get four tunes in three hours. It would just amaze me, years later, to see two sessions on one song. I thought it was a waste of money.

Pursell quickly learned the simple keyboard style that was required for country and pop sessions, and soon was in demand as a session player. His recording sessions in the early 1960s were with the primary figures of the emerging Nashville Sound: Chet Atkins, Boots Randolph, Hank Garland, Patsy Cline, Eddy Arnold, Johnny Cash, and many others. Harold Bradley remembers first hearing Pursell play at the Carousel, and was soon, along with Eddy Arnold and Chet Atkins, inviting him to record at sessions that he led. Pursell and Harold Bradley would become lifelong friends.

Another friend that Pursell made playing at the Carousel was W. O. Smith, an African American bass player. This was the early 1960s, and in the South racially mixed groups normally did not play on stage together; the jazz group at the Carousel was an exception. Still, tensions were running high as the civil rights movement gathered steam.

Pursell remembers one rude customer at the Carousel who came in and asked them to play some "nigger blues." Dr. Smith laid his bass down

William Pursell, far left; Chet Atkins, far right; President John F. Kennedy, center

and left the stage. It was left to Pursell to explain that the bass player was a very distinguished person, who had a Ph.D. from the University of Iowa, and was on many important recordings. The man apologized and said he thought that's just how they said things around there. "Anyway, Smitty came back up, and it turned out this guy was a guitar player, and we told him to come up, he played very well, and Smitty turned to me and said, he's got some black in him." Pursell's good nature defused what could have easily turned into an ugly scene.

"Smitty" and Pursell would become close friends. Pursell would later receive an academic job offer from Smith, at the Tennessee Agricultural and Industrial Normal School (where he would be the first white instructor; now Tennessee State University), and also would be asked to join Smith's Wednesday Night Club, a group of white and black men who would gather to discuss the racial issues of the day.[18]

In 1961 Pursell was invited by Chet Atkins to go to Washington, D.C., and play for the White House News Photographers' Association annual dinner at the Sheraton-Park Hotel.[19] Atkins's decision to invite Pursell rather than his regular pianist, Floyd Cramer, may have been due to Pursell's background; as a highly educated musician, Pursell could add an air of sophistication to the group of musicians from Nashville in this most exalted of venues. The dinner was on May 19; Pursell wrote a detailed letter to his parents on May 23, describing his impressions of the event. Pursell had already experienced many brushes with greatness in his life, meeting the great conductor Arturo Toscanini, studying with the dean of American music Howard Hanson, playing for the famed pianist Rudolph Serkin, but he had never met a political leader like the president of the United States. Clearly he was moved.

In his letter, he writes of his awe at meeting someone who had the same job Abraham Lincoln had held. He describes the scene of his encounter with President Kennedy in detail. Pursell was standing in a room with many people, and the President had entered without him even noticing. His impression of President Kennedy: "He's a magnificent appearing person, healthy looking, poised, intelligent, completely at ease, and he gives the impression that he's capable of handling any situation. He looks much better than his pictures indicate, and in fact, he looks like something of a movie star." Pursell wrote to his parents that the music was well-received and that Chet Atkins even gave Pursell and the other musicians credit for the music coming out of Nashville. "It was a very kind thing for him to do, but Chet is that way."[20] Perhaps Chet had brought Pursell to D.C. instead of Floyd Cramer because of Pursell's educated background. Maybe this time, his outsider status was an advantage.

Pursell was not a prolific letter writer (as his father's constant pleas for more letters attests), but this experience was significant enough to him that he took the time to write a detailed reflection on it to his parents. His encounter with Kennedy took place after the disastrous Bay of Pigs invasion but before the Cuban Missile Crisis, two key events of President Kennedy's tenure. And even though he was not Chet Atkins's "boy," he was the pianist who was invited to the White House.

Pursell would remember this visit two years later, when on a quiet Saturday evening he heard his own music coming out of the television. President John Kennedy had just been assassinated, and the television networks were broadcasting live from the Capitol rotunda, where the President's body lay in state. He recalls that the television networks cancelled all of their programming and played music for days. That Saturday night, he was writing a letter, and he heard "Christ Looking over Jerusalem," his Benjamin Award piece, coming out of the television. He heard it again on Sunday. The next day, Frances Preston from BMI called Pursell and told him that he should ask for performance royalties for the use of his piece. Pursell remembers: "And the first thing I said, was, 'It seems a little weird, Frances, to be paid off on something like this.' She said, 'Well,

Pursell working in the studio

let me talk to Richard Burton of ASCAP and we'll work this out.' It turned out that they decided not to log anything those days, neither ASCAP nor BMI. Possibly I could have been assassinated by writers! Maybe a few of the others voiced the same opinion or the same kind of reaction." Thus Pursell received no compensation for the use of his music on television during the time of national mourning for President Kennedy.

COLUMBIA RECORDS

By 1962 Pursell had played on many sessions and had won a good reputation for himself among recording musicians in Nashville, and was getting regular work. Two record labels approached him for a recording contract: Columbia, with producer Don Law, and Monument Records, with producer Fred Foster. Pursell, who had grown up listening to Columbia records, considered a bid by Columbia to be a sign of success, and so he signed with Columbia, a contract that lasted from 1962 to 1967. Pursell became Columbia's A-list studio pianist, and he recorded with most of the musicians who made albums with Columbia in the mid 1960s.

Some of his most interesting stories from this time are about his sessions with Johnny Cash. Cash had left Sun Records in 1958 to sign with

Pursell with Buddy Harmon, Craig Nelson, and an unidentified musician during a studio session

Columbia, and recorded most of his music in Nashville in the 1960s and 1970s. As the A-list Columbia pianist, Pursell was the pianist on most of Cash's Columbia albums. His appointment books from the mid-1960s show several sessions with Cash at the Columbia studios. Pursell was working with Cash on the song "The Legend of John Henry's Hammer," a single that appeared on Cash's Columbia album *Blood, Sweat, and Tears* (1963). Pursell remembers that recording this song took two days, and that there was a real anvil in the studio to create the sound of the hammer. Cash did something very strange during one of the sessions. He had sent the studio go-fer person out for a liverwurst sandwich, which was delivered and laid on the floor next to Cash.

> Johnny was trying to tune his banjo, and I was standing around like everyone else waiting to see what was going on. John was sitting there, he looked at this liverwurst. It was a beautiful sandwich; I love liverwurst, I just love liverwurst, and this liverwurst was so thick. I'm sitting there looking at it thinking, oh God, I wish I had one. I could probably have had Ed go out and get me one.
>
> Then John looked at that and then he looked up at the Telefunken microphone that was over his head, a very expensive microphone, about $5,000, and he looks down at the sandwich, and he looks up

at the mike. He gets up, takes all of the liverwurst off the sandwich and proceeds to work the liverwurst into the mesh of the microphone, this beautiful microphone, just to do it. I just looked at him; it was like one of those Virgil Partch cartoons [with people frozen into static positions]. I'm sort of looking at him, and he's doing this bizarre thing. I looked over at the booth and Frank and Don were kind of laughing at it. Everybody else was doing something else, and I'm the only one that's seeing him do this. So finally, without a word, Mort [Mort Tomlinson] opens the door, comes out with a brand new Telefunken microphone, goes over there, unscrews the thing, puts the new one in, takes it back into the control booth, and that was the end of it. And that was that.

This was a very expensive microphone. Pursell suspects Cash's behavior may have had something to do with drug use.

Pursell remembers Cash as easy to work with, if a bit unpredictable. He played with Cash on the famous Nashville Fan Fair shows, and he remembers looking out into the audience, which was "transfixed by him up there." Pursell also recorded "Ring of Fire" with Cash. To this day, Pursell remains somewhat awed by the image Cash projected of "the man in black" and his magnetism as a performer.[21]

Back home, Pursell's California family, who mostly lived in rural areas, was much more impressed with his efforts in the Nashville recording scene than they had ever been with his classical piano successes of the 1940s and 1950s. Pursell recalled: "And when they found out I was recording with Eddy Arnold and Jean Shepard, my lord, I was a celebrity. Because I was on the Grand Ole Opry."

Pursell's first solo album with Columbia was *Our Winter Love*, recorded from August to November 1962. The title single, released in November, broke into the *Billboard* Top 100 chart by February 1963, and the album, released in April 1963, made the *Billboard* Top LPs list. Pursell would go on to record two further solo albums with Columbia, but neither of those achieved the success that "Our Winter Love" did. Why this happened is a case study in Nashville recording studio politics.

6. OUR WINTER LOVE

The genesis of Pursell's first solo album with Columbia, *Our Winter Love*, is a lesson in the inner workings of the recording industry. It's the story of how a song is discovered, how an album is recorded and produced, how a hit is made, and what role the record label plays. It's the story of Nashville politics, competing egos, and the many forces that combine to make a hit.

The logistics of making an album are more complicated than a musician renting out a studio and playing for a few hours. First, songs must be selected, and that usually requires a publisher. The songs must be arranged, and that requires of course, an arranger, work that Pursell had no small experience in from his time in the Air Force. Arranging a popular album to be released by Columbia, though, was a bit different from making string orchestra arrangements for the military, so Pursell enlisted the help of some of his friends.

In many recording sessions Pursell's friend Bill Justis was serving as both session leader and arranger, thus getting paid double on sessions that he worked. Pursell told Justis that he wanted him to be the arranger for his first solo album. "And I said, Bill [Justis], listen, why don't you get involved in this thing with me? You're doing a lot of arranging around here for a lot of different people; I'm an arranger too, but let's do it this way. I'll be the artist, you be the arranger, but I'll tell you what I want." The two agreed to work together.

Justis and Pursell founded their own publishing company, called Omni Music, to publish Pursell's compositions. They had a small office on 17th Avenue in Nashville. Pursell chose the name because he was flying a lot at that time as a private pilot, and he used Omni radio as a navigational tool and thought it was a good name for a publishing company. Any of Pursell's own compositions that appeared on his solo albums would be owned by Omni Music and produced under the Columbia label.

Pursell began to look for material to use on his first solo album. Grady Martin, Hank Garland, and Floyd Cramer, all musicians with whom Pursell worked in various studio sessions, had founded a music publishing company called Cramart. Grady Martin, an electric guitarist who along

Album cover of *Our Winter Love*, Courtesy of Sony Music Entertainment

with Atkins, Cramer, and Garland was a central player in the development of the Nashville Sound, served as the session leader on many of the recording sessions that Bill Pursell was doing.

One day, Martin brought to him a Cramart demo by Canadian trumpeter Johnny Cowell called "Long Island Sound." Grady told Pursell he had had one beer too many, and had played the album at the speed of 45 rpm instead of 78 rpm. He suggested to Pursell that he listen to the record at that speed. They were in the Columbia Studio B, and using the record machine in the control booth, they played it at the slower speed. The pitch dropped, the trumpet sounded like a trombone, and the fast "slapback" on the piano slowed to a meditative "short-long" motive. Pursell had found an idea for his first tune. He remembers the slapback as "a slower very attractive figure that I could emulate by shifting the weight of my hands, making the second chord softer than the first, creating my own kind of echo 'slapback' as a kind of piano gimmick above the rest of the arrangement." Pursell took his ideas on "Long Island Sound" to the Omni office, and Justis agreed that they should record the tune with the slower speed.

The other distinctive sound on "Our Winter Love" was the fuzz bass sound, which comes in at the second chorus. The fuzz sound had originated as the result of a bad circuit, but would go on to become a hallmark characteristic of rock music, known as distortion.

Pursell had been present when this sound was first discovered. He was playing piano on a recording session in 1961 with Marty Robbins, in the Columbia Studio B, the same studio where he would later record his own solo album. Just before they began recording Robbins's own tune, "Don't Worry," Robbins plugged his guitar into the amplifier and strummed a chord. Out came a distorted static sound "that literally threw him backwards," Pursell remembers.

> He looked towards the control booth where Don Law was sitting and said, "What in the hell was that?" Don, in his English accent, responded, "I don't know, old boy, but we're looking into it." Long story short, it turned out that the Bradley brothers [Owen and Harold] had just bought a new stereo board and installed it in the control room, but there happened to be a short in it. After fooling around for some time, the engineers didn't know what to do about it, and Grady said, "Hell, when I kick in my pedal, let's use it on my guitar solo when it comes in the middle of the tune." I myself had been generally unaware all this was going on (I was talking to Bob Moore, the bass player all through this) and when we started the recording and came to Grady's solo, I almost fell out of my chair!

Engineers at Columbia decided to figure out how to reproduce this sound, and eventually came up with a "fuzz box," a device that could be attached to any amplifier, to be activated by a pedal.[1] Thus was born the guitar distortion that would eventually become ubiquitous in rock and roll. Pursell's tune "Our Winter Love" was, according to Pursell, the second single in music history to use this effect. Harold Bradley was Pursell's bass player, and he used it on his bass guitar solo, with Boots Randolph simultaneously playing the same melody on the saxophone an octave higher.

The first recording session of "Our Winter Love" was done in Columbia Studio B, following Pursell's preference for using all the instruments at once, rather than recording each part separately. The session players were Nashville stalwarts: Buddy Harman on drums, Grady Martin on electric guitar, Ray Edenton on rhythm guitar, Bob Moore on bass, Ray Stevens on electric sustained organ, Boots Randolph on tenor sax, the Anita Kerr Singers, several unnamed string players, and Pursell on solo piano. Selby Coffeen served as head engineer, and Pursell remembers that Coffeen did a "marvelous job putting baffles up all around the studio to absorb and still deflect the sound." Coffeen also added reverb, which made the "short-long" motto really sound like a slapback, and later, Pursell was told by Jerry Kennedy (an Artist and Repertoire rep at Mercury Records) that several people called to ask how they got a slapback machine to go that slow. Pursell said he never told anyone that he simply played it that way to get the effect.

The recording process was typical of the laid-back approach that characterized the rise of the Nashville Sound—loose arrangements, decisions on the fly, and an overall mellow approach, resulting in a laid-back, almost easy-listening sound.[2] Pursell's description of the relaxed atmosphere in the studio is similar to stories told in other accounts of Nashville studios in the 1960s.

> We went into the session, and Bill [Justis] puts this chart in front of me, and all it has is me just playing the chords of the tune. I'm playing this lick on top at the start of the record. Bill had gotten the idea, since we had done that record for Marty Robbins, in which that fuzz sound appeared for the first time, of using a bass fuzz [distortion] in this record, on the second chorus, with Harold Bradley playing that on the bass guitar, and Boots playing the same melody an octave higher, and me doing the lick on top of it. So I looked, and I said, "Is this it, is this the only thing you've got?" 'Just play the chart, Vlad" [from Justis], so that was it.[3] So I started off with the lick, with just the slow slapback sound, with a rhythm section, and then started playing the melody. Then on the second chorus, when the strings started, we had Anita Kerr on the session as vocalist, doing aaah's, and that's how we built the record. It was in three choruses, and I played the first chorus with the introductory lick, and then for the second one, I kept the lick going on top while the arrangement was building. It turned out to be an orchestra record, basically, around that particular gimmick that we used. I regarded the thing just as an album cut, I didn't think it was really that important.[4]

The tune begins a few iterations of the slow "slapback" sound, short-long, short-long, then a brief lyrical phrase in the piano, echoed by strings.

Throughout the first chorus, the piano is prominent, backed up by strings, wordless vocals, and brushes on a drum set. It is meditative, calm, simple. The fuzz bass sound enters in the second chorus, playing the melody under Pursell's "slapbacks," and it is a bit jarring at first, but this distinctive sound is memorable and gives the song a unique flavor. The second chorus also brings up the strings and the wordless vocals, with Pursell filling in the spaces, and then fades back to the slow slapbacks and lyrical phrases from the opening. "Long Island Sound/Our Winter Love" was not a typical Nashville country song; it was an instrumental easy listening tune. But it had many of the characteristics of the hits coming out of Nashville studios at the time: the strings, the fuzz bass, and the general laid-back atmosphere.

When the recording reached the Columbia offices in New York, two Artist and Repertoire reps at Columbia, Mort Hoffman and Bob Thompson, heard the song and loved it, but wanted to find a different name for it. They decided it sounded wintry, and came up with the name "Our Winter Love," and that's how it came back to Nashville.

The single "Our Winter Love" had a release date of November 16, 1962. Pursell remembers a meeting that winter, sometime before Christmas, in the Columbia offices of Don Law. Bill Justis was there, and he said that he knew the tune would be a hit, but that sales had not taken off yet. Frank Jones, Don Law's assistant, told them that they were in the midst of Christmas sales, but that he thought sales would begin to climb sometime in January.

Sure enough, one cold winter night in Nashville, Bill Pursell was driving home from the recording studio after a long day of work. It was well after midnight, and all of the Nashville radio stations had gone off the air. He twisted the dial, trying to find some music, and found a station out of Alabama. He listened to a few songs, musing about the day's work. Then he heard a slow slapback motive on the piano, and a plaintive melody rising above it. It was "Our Winter Love." He leaned back in the driver's seat and listened to the fuzz bass of Harold Bradley in the second chorus, and thought, "Well, it's a regional breakout." Within a few days, the song was being played on radio stations in New Orleans, St. Louis, and beyond. Bill Pursell had a hit.

The tune was becoming a regional breakout, which means it was beginning to be popular in certain areas of the nation. In the January 5 edition of *Billboard*, "Our Winter Love" is noted in the "Radio and T.V. Programming" column as a strong regional seller in St. Louis, Nashville,

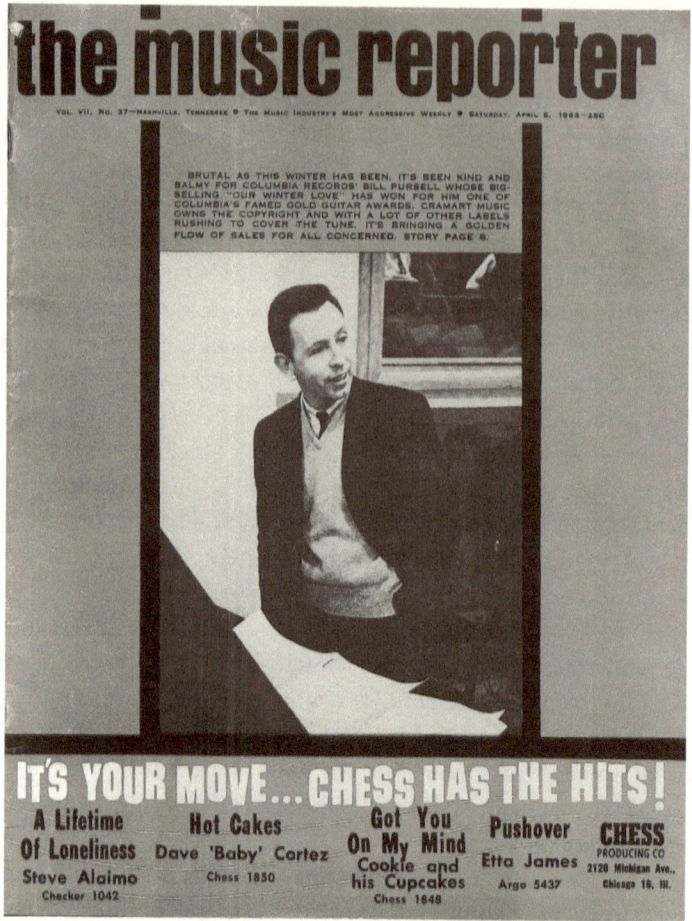

William Pursell, featured on the cover of *Music Reporter*, April 6, 1963

and Chattanooga. The columnist Bill Gavin noted that "Our Winter Love" had won a listener contest for the most popular tune several nights in a row at the St. Louis radio station WIL, and that such contest wins were an indicator of a future hit.[5] By January 19, *Billboard* listed "Our Winter Love" as a regional breakout, and the January 26 issue designated the tune as number 105 in the "Bubbling Under the Hot 100" list, a list designed to sniff out future hits.

"Our Winter Love" made *Billboard*'s Hot 100 list by February 2, at #88, and continued to climb until the end of March. The single remained on the Hot 100 list for fourteen weeks. It broke into the Top Ten on March

30, at #9 on the Hot 100 list. It was also listed as high as #8 on *Billboard*'s "Honor Roll of Hits" (determined by record sales and radio plays).[6]

"Our Winter Love," however, was still a single without an album. By October 1962, before the single was even released, all of the tunes had been recorded, so the music was ready. The album was mostly made up of covers of tunes by Nashville recording artists, such as Johnny Cash's "I Walk the Line" and Hank Williams's "I Can't Help It If I'm Still in Love with You."[7] Most of these were country tunes, with an easy listening instrumental style, not exactly country, but closer to the new Nashville Sound than anything else. Pursell had one original on the album, "Dark Alley," a funky jazz number.

Although the music was complete, producer Don Law, according to Pursell, could not decide on an album cover, and this resulted in a three-month delay of the album's release. In the meantime, Felix Slatkin in California released a cover of the tune, and, as Pursell says, "killed all the sales, took a lot of the sales away from what we had." Pursell remembers that he got several calls that spring from New York, asking what was taking Don Law so long to release the full album, and Pursell himself called the Columbia offices frequently, asking for action on his album, but the album *Our Winter Love* was not released until late March. By then, the single was beginning to descend, listed as #15 on the *Billboard* Hot 100 chart. The album did get national attention and would be listed in the "Top LPs" chart in *Billboard*, but it never broke into the Top Ten sellers.

The cover of the April 6, 1963, *Music Reporter* magazine features a picture of a dapper young Pursell, with open music in front of him, looking off to the side. The caption read: "Brutal as this winter has been, it's been kind and balmy for Columbia Records' Bill Pursell, whose big-selling 'Our Winter Love' has won for him one of Columbia's famed Gold Guitar awards. Cramart Music owns the copyright and with a lot of other labels rushing to cover the tune, it's bringing a golden flow of sales for all concerned." The story notes that the artists who covered the tune included Felix Slatkin, Lawrence Welk, Clebanoff, Hugo Winterhalter, and Andre Kostelanetz. The rise of sales for "Our Winter Love" is characterized as "one of the most exciting hit record success stories of a long brutal winter season."[8] This article makes clear that the success of this album was not only good for Pursell and Columbia, but also for the publisher (and copyright holder) Cramart, its president Grady Martin, and the composer of the tune Johnny Cowell. Pursell's first solo album had the attention of the entire record industry.

Pursell's father sent a letter in mid-April. He had heard from various relatives and friends about Pursell's success:

> It has been most interesting to me to hear the apparently almost universal comments of pleasure from people who have heard your record. Evidently you have something here that makes a wide appeal. Uncle Frank has been quite enthusiastic about the new album among so many others. He remarked in his last letter that you have "fans!" Evidently Mark fairly revels in listening to the record. Of course, we are duly pleased and complimented by it all. What we hope most is that it will also be a financial success.[9]

Pursell's father, whose tastes ran to classical music, seemed a bit puzzled that his son's career had taken this direction, but was pleased for his success, of course. Arthur also enclosed a letter from his cousin Linda Peterson, telling the story that she had heard Pursell's tune in a record store. This letter too, is worth quoting at length.

> A few days ago Bert, Jeannette's husband, said to her, "I was passing in front of the stereo and Music Shop and I heard an album with piano and orchestra that sounded very good, and I went in and asked who was this artist and he told me it was a Bill Pursell, and Jeannette [yelled] Bill Pursell, why I know who he is and of course told her husband all about him and she said I will buy this album, and she told me and I said, I'll buy it. Well today, Easter Sunday, Bert surprised us with it. The name of the album is Our Winter Love and I just got through playing it. We love it and think he will go far. Anyway, I wish you would tell him how we enjoy it, and wish him all kinds of luck and success with it, it's such a thrill to hear him. I remember how he used to go to the piano in Tulare and compose little pieces when he was only a little tot.[10]

It was an instrumental album of country music covers that made Pursell a hometown hero, instead of his classical piano recitals or his prize-winning classical compositions. The irony is that, in spite of its genesis in Nashville, *Our Winter Love* is essentially easy listening instrumental music. Although it contains covers of country tunes, the style is generic and peaceful. Pursell, the classically trained pianist from California who came in a very roundabout way to the famed Columbia Studio B in Nashville, Tennessee and worked with the likes of Johnny Cash and Patsy Cline, had released a solo album that was mild, instrumental, and appealing to a wide audience. No Rachmaninoff here, just a bit of a jazzy tune in "Dark Alley" to spice things up a little.

Pursell did tell me that at one point he did receive a letter from his father expressing sincere disappointment that he had not pursued a classical concert career, as both his parents had hoped he would do. Pursell carried that letter around for years, but finally destroyed it, because he did not want his father to be remembered for his conservative attitudes. Straight-laced Arthur Pursell had a difficult time coming to terms with his son's success in popular music. But this never became a divisive issue in their relationship and they remained very close.

"Our Winter Love" touched a lot of people. Years later, Pursell would receive emails from fans, telling him how much they loved his tune and that they had played it at their wedding, or at their spouse's funeral. Comments on a copy of the song posted on YouTube by DrinkingStar tell stories of young love, of childhood, of fond memories:

This song was on the radio when I was in second grade 1965, it was snowing hard and school let out early, very rare in those days. Mom came to get me from her job at the telephone company and hand in hand we slipped and slid the 12 blocks toward home but first we stopped at the Genuine Cafe soda fountain downtown for a cherry coke. No one else was in the place. I felt so secure and happy. It was one of the sweetest memories of my childhood. (Trellis2, 2014)

I remember hearing this beautiful song on some cold winter mornings on our bus ride into school, back in the 60's. WBZ 1030 Boston, Carl DeSuze their classy morning DJ, played it a lot. A very warm, nice, memory now.... and so long ago. (K Jen, 2010)

Always a favorite last hour spin on the Terry Lee Show on WMCK in Pittsburgh. Elaine and I always knew it was near midnight (she had to be home) when this beautiful song was playing. Windows in the car all steamy, never wanting the nite to end. What a beautiful, romantic song. Thanks for bringing back some wonderful memories of young love. (pennridgeboy, 2009)

The FABULOUS PIANO ARTISTRY OF BILL PURSELL
POSITIVELY KALEIDOSCOPIC

WHO IS BILL PURSELL?

BILL PURSELL is the PIANIST, COMPOSER, ARRANGER, whose every performance is a HAPPENING!

BILL PURSELL is the ARTIST who is so excited about what is occurring in today's music world, he immediately radiates this excitement to his audiences.

BILL PURSELL, whether performing in the commercial or serious field of today's music, reflects the brilliant spectrum of experiences in his educational background.

BILL PURSELL:

- started playing piano at age three and composing at age four.
- studied Harmony and Species Counterpoint before age fifteen.
- won a National Composers' Contest in high school for two serious compositions.
- performed in concert and studied with concert coaches in California, Maryland, and New York.
- attended the Peabody Conservatory on the Boise Composition Scholarship.
- was Composer-Arranger for the Air Force Radio Show in Washington, D.C., while serving in the armed forces.
- attended the Eastman School of Music at the University of Rochester on Fellowships, earning the Bachelor's and Master's Degrees in Composition.
- won the first Edward B. Benjamin Award for Composition at Eastman.
- has appeared as guest soloist with symphony orchestras.
- has toured the nation as a Rhythm and Blues and a Pop entertainer.
- has had his serious orchestral works recorded and performed, both in concert and on radio and television, throughout the country.

BILL PURSELL, in the past few years, has concentrated on the recording and television fields, and worked closely with many of the biggest names in the entertainment industry, such as: BURL IVES, JOHNNY CASH, MARTY ROBBINS, BOOTS RANDOLPH, EDDIE ARNOLD, BOBBY VINTON, BRENDA LEE, ANITA BRYANT, CHET ATKINS, TERESA BREWER, VIC DAMONE, TOMMY LEONETTI, FRANKIE RANDALL, FREDDIE CANNON, BOBBY VEE, DIANA TRASK, and many others.

BILL PURSELL is best known internationally for his TOP 40 hit single and album, OUR WINTER LOVE, which has since become a standard.

BILL PURSELL was named MOST-PROMISING INSTRUMENTALIST and MOST-PROGRAMMED ARTIST in the National Cashbox Magazine DeeJay Poll.

BILL PURSELL is the multi-faceted musical talent with a provocative new way with music who can turn your next concert into a HAPPENING!

Meet BILL PURSELL

Publicity brochure for Pursell in 1963.

Publicity brochure for Pursell in 1963.

I have a different take on this all time favorite. I was a young Marine at Camp Pendleton, CA in 1963, and since it doesn't snow there I never had that as an image of this song. Instead I'll always picture a winter afternoon at Laguna Beach with low grey clouds, a light rain falling and the waves crashing on the shore every time I hear "Our Winter Love." (threefour66, 2009)

Great song. I hear this a lot on KCEE, KGVY and KTUC in Tucson, Arizona, and KOY in Phoenix. Also heard this on The Yule Log during Christmas time. (frank d, 2008)

Every time I hear this—I still have my original '45—I too just fall into a whirlpool of memories. I was 15 y/o—10th grade, & in the midst of my 1st real crush on an impossibly pretty girl. Her name was Gayle,

& though she too was a sophomore, she dated a senior—& I didn't stand a chance. Worst of all, she "liked me for a friend"——well, whenever "Our Winter Love" came on KTLN, 1250 AM in Denver, I dreamed of her. I still do today Wolfsky9, 67 y/o Now. (Wolfsky 9, 2013)

I was 14 when this song came out. I'm 62 now. It brings back feelings of a place and time I had forgotten. While I was listening, I caught myself whispering the name of someone that I knew, so very long ago. Somehow, I believe she heard me. I still love you, Annie. (EdD, 2012)

"Our Winter Love" was more than a several-weeks' hit; it became one of those songs that people remember the rest of their lives. Hits are like that—they are born without much attention, grow, and then suddenly they are everywhere. With some luck, they last beyond their decade. "Our Winter Love" could have been for Pursell the beginning of a series of hit albums, but circumstances would eventually send him in a different direction.

DON LAW AND SID BERNSTEIN

Although Pursell's contract with Columbia gave him the opportunity to work with many major artists like Johnny Cash, the story of his relationship with Columbia Records is an unhappy one, as can easily happen with artists and major record labels. Even though "Our Winter Love" as a single went as high as #9 on the *Billboard* Hot 100 and as an album remained on the Top LPs list for several weeks, Pursell says that he never made money on the album. It is typical for artists to record under a recoupment clause in their contract, which means that the label deducts studio costs from the performers' advance payment and royalties.[11] Pursell's royalty rate was three percent. As he explains it, as soon as his hit album earned him enough royalties, Don Law would call him back into the studio to make more recordings. In this way, Columbia could avoid paying royalties to its artists. If an artist made multiple hit records, he might be in a better position to find a lawyer and demand that Columbia revoke the recoupment clause, but Pursell's second and third albums did not receive the attention from Columbia that his first one had. He wrote a letter to Columbia in January 1966 asserting that he had never made a penny from his work with Columbia and protesting their treatment of him. A new contract was issued in August 1966 that stated that "advances pursuant to our agreement with you dated June 29, 1962 shall not be charged against your royalties under the current recording agreement."[12]

If Pursell had signed with an agent, the story would have been very different indeed. An agent would have shepherded the first album and future albums, insisting on publicity efforts from the label, and he would have protected Pursell's financial interests. Sid Bernstein, a prominent agent who worked with General Artists Corporation, approached Pursell in 1963 and wanted to sign with him as his agent. The next year, Bernstein would succeed in bringing the Beatles to the United States.

Pursell was not terribly excited about this bid from such an important agent, because he remembered an earlier time when he had tried to get Bernstein's attention and failed. It was in the late 1950s, when Pursell had been touring the Eastern seaboard with the Jerry Jaye Trio. They had gone up to New York City to get some pictures taken (this was also the time they played the Apollo Theater), and they went to Sid Bernstein's office to see if they could pitch their group to him. Pursell remembers that they sat in Bernstein's office for almost three hours, and never got to see him. Thus, he was not terribly impressed in 1963 when he went up to New York to record a vocal cover of his instrumental "Our Winter Love," and Bernstein called over to Columbia's offices and asked to meet with him. This time, Bernstein was ready to deal, but Pursell was suspicious. He decided to agree with conditions:

> So I go across town to Sid's office, and this time, I'm inside. Sid is sitting there, and I'm looking at him and he's looking at me. I don't say anything to him about the fact that three years or four years before I was sitting outside and I couldn't get in to see him. I'm sitting there very cautiously thinking, okay, and he has this little flunky going in and out of the office saying, "Oh it's a great record, it's a marvelous record," hyping the whole thing. He didn't even know what the record sounded like. He just saw it on the charts. I'm sitting there saying to myself, Sid, you don't even know what the record sounds like, but you want to sign me! Sid said, "I'd like to sign you, it's a great record." He said, "I'm a soft sell." I remember him saying that, "I'm a soft sell." So I said to Sid, "Look, I'll tell you what. If you can put me on two or three TV shows, syndicated or whatever, if you can do that, then let's talk about it." Then I left the office.

This decision not to sign with Bernstein would cost Pursell dearly—he never did hear from Sid, and he never got the television spots he requested. He did not have an agent to shepherd his second solo album or his third, and neither made any significant mark in terms of sales or radio play. His producer Don Law was managing many artists, Columbia was a large company, and Pursell's work simply did not get any attention. Without significant publicity and support, his career as a solo artist never took off after his hit album.

Three years after "Our Winter Love" hit the charts, Pursell discovered the reason he never heard from Bernstein. Bob Thompson (a former Columbia employee), who was producing some recordings for Arthur Godfrey, asked Pursell to come up to New York to discuss this work. "I'm sitting there with Bob, and we start talking about my old record. I said to him, 'I just couldn't understand it, I never got any nibbles on the thing for any shows.'"

> He said, "Oh you got nibbles."
>
> And I said, "What are you talking about?"
>
> He said, "Well, it was coming through to Columbia, and then to Don Law's office in Nashville. Because Don was one year from retirement, we had to respect everything he said, and all those people said, he's the 'old man of the sea.'"
>
> I said, "What's that got to do with anything?"
>
> He said, "Well, you got nibbles."
>
> And I said, "Who was trying to get ahold of me?"
>
> He said, "Well, the William Morris Agency tried several times. And we were told by Don Law in his office that you weren't interested, that you were busy in the studio."
>
> I said, "Who else?"
>
> And he said, "The Ed Sullivan Show tried three times to get ahold of you. And the third time, they said, pay him the maximum."
>
> I never heard it. Never heard of it.

Pursell recalls that it took him years to get over that discovery. Sid Bernstein had made good on his offer, and had even gotten Pursell offers to play on *The Ed Sullivan Show*. This was just a few months before the Beatles made their famous splash on that show (thanks in great part to Bernstein), and it was an important venue for rising artists. An appearance on that show would have likely made a difference in Pursell's career, and furthermore, he would have signed with Sid Bernstein as an agent, and he would have had someone looking out for his interests for the remainder of his career. But Don Law blocked the "nibbles," and Pursell never heard of them, and so his promise as a solo pianist with Columbia faded away gradually.

This was another bend in the crooked river of Pursell's career, and not a beneficial one.

Pursell is philosophical about this today. He says that perhaps he would have gotten some appearances; perhaps he would have had a spot on Ed Sullivan and nothing more. There is no way to know what might have been. At the time, Pursell was also going through divorce proceedings, and he was taking care of his young daughter Shari full time.[13] If he had begun getting a lot of work, he would not have been able to keep Shari at home in Nashville with him. But Pursell often felt sorely the lack of an agent, and this fact shaped his career. This crooked bend in his musical career would change his direction from a hit solo artist to a studio keyboardist and arranger.

There was no certainty that signing with Bernstein would have guaranteed him a fabulous career, or that Don Law was the sole reason that his solo career never took off. This decision was one of a series of choices begun when he signed with Columbia Records. Talking about what would have happened if he had signed with Monument instead of Columbia, he says,

> It's hard to say. Looking back never solves any of your problems. I call it the "What If" club. And if you do this, what do you gain? You just fool away all your time, saying "What if?" You play the game, you play the scenes, and you get this thing going in your mind, oh you can see this and that sort of thing happening, it might have been this. And then when it's all over with, you're still sitting there, and you haven't gotten anywhere.

Pursell has puzzled over Law's behavior; surely it would have been in Law's best interest to promote his own artist. Pursell suspects that it may have been a personal issue with him, and he recalls one incident during 1963 that might have influenced Law's actions. Law had recommended that Pursell and other Columbia artists use the accountant Bill Wilkins to do their taxes. Pursell thought that was a good idea, but when he went to see Wilkins, he was informed that it would cost him $500, a great deal of money in the 1960s.

Pursell thought this was a high charge, and so he decided to call Don Law's office to talk about it and see if he could negotiate a lower fee. Law's secretary, Irene Stanton, answered the phone, and Pursell could hear "a ruckus" in the background. Stanton said she would tell Law and then hung up rather abruptly. She soon called Pursell back and told him not to answer the phone when Law called, that he was "on the warpath." When the phone rang, though, Pursell did answer the phone, and Pursell says that Law was yelling and swearing at him, saying "You can take your record and . . ."

The next morning, Stanton called Pursell and told him to act completely normal, that Law had completely forgotten about the incident. Sure enough, when Pursell showed up to the studio, Law said, "Hello Bill," in a friendly tone, and Pursell was baffled. "I then thought he had to be crazy."

Pursell suspects that this incident influenced Law's opinion of him, but he has no way of knowing for sure. It's quite possible that Law forgot all about that phone call. It is also possible that Law was angry because Pursell protested that amount being charged by his accountant (Pursell did use that accountant, once). Whatever the reason, Law did not pass along to Pursell requests from William Morris and *The Ed Sullivan Show*, requests that would have likely furthered Pursell's career.

CHASING A DREAM

Pursell's second solo album with Columbia, *Chasing a Dream*, was released in 1963 on the heels of *Our Winter Love*. Pursell describes this album as mostly middle of the road, popular-style tunes, rather than the country flavor of his first album. Originals by Pursell on this album included "Chasing a Dream," "Never and Forever," and "Farewell to Adra." The album did get some attention: the Wimbledon tennis tournament picked up the title song "Chasing a Dream," as their theme song on their broadcasts in England. Royalty reports from BMI show a foreign royalty earning for "Chasing a Dream" in 1966, so it is likely that it was that year's broadcast that used Pursell's song.[14] However, without an agent to hold the fire to the toes of Columbia marketers, "Chasing a Dream" was not promoted heavily and so did not make it to hit status as "Our Winter Love" had.

PROFESSOR PURSELL

In 1963 Willis Page (music director of the Nashville Symphony) took a year-long residency as a conductor in Japan. He asked Pursell a favor: would he teach his music appreciation class at Vanderbilt University? And so Pursell returned to his academic roots, for a very short time. The paycheck, however small, was welcome as a guaranteed source of income for this otherwise freelancing musician. It also gave him a taste for college teaching, which would later serve him well.

Upon Page's return to Nashville in 1963, a celebratory concert in the park was given, this time with Pursell's arrangement for the Nashville Symphony of his hit, "Our Winter Love."[15] During Page's time out of the States, Pursell had graduated from a very talented session musician to a hit solo artist. With this concert, his two worlds would join, as the Nashville Symphony played his hit for an outdoor audience. Further, Pursell made his own arrangement for the symphony to play, something he could do easily because of his years of experience arranging for the Air Force Orchestra. This was a foreshadowing of his future years as an arranger for countless recordings, in Nashville and beyond.

Pursell would enjoy one further short stint as a college instructor. In 1964 his friend W. O. Smith (his bassist friend with whom he played in Printer's Alley) asked him to teach at the Tennessee Agricultural and Industrial Normal School for a semester as a maternity leave replacement. There, he taught form and analysis and piano, the only time the pianist ever taught piano lessons.

Tennessee A&I (now Tennessee State) is a historically black college, and in the early 1960s, the civil rights movement was in full swing. Pursell remembers running into his students at sit-ins in downtown Nashville, but they never told him what they had been planning. Many of his students joined the famous protest march with Martin Luther King from Selma to Montgomery, Alabama. When Pursell left Tennessee A&I, he heard that the students wished he had stayed there. He felt this to be a high compliment, as the only white teacher in a historically black school.

After his brief teaching stints at Vanderbilt and Tennessee A&I, it would be many years before Pursell found his next teaching job. In between, he was recording for Columbia as a featured artist, developing a reputation as an arranger, and beginning to travel to London for recording sessions there. He would also occasionally play some Gershwin with the Nashville Symphony, arrange a song for them to play, or even compose new music for them on commission.

Album cover of *A Remembered Love*, Courtesy of Sony Music Entertainment

A REMEMBERED LOVE

A Remembered Love (1965) was Pursell's third and final solo album with Columbia. The title song was something that had been sent to Pursell by one of his fans, Susan Hoffman from North Carolina. He liked the music, and so he decided to use it. The genesis of his song "Madrilena," also on *A Remembered Love*, is a story of unexpected connections. Pursell's attorney at the time, Jack Norman, was married to a former circus performer, Duana Zacchini Norman, of the famous circus troupe, The Flying Zacchinis. Pursell remembers that he and his wife were at the Normans' house one night for dinner when Duana brought out the music of a tune that they had played when she was shot out of a cannon. The tune was written by Alfred Longo. Pursell liked the tune, and arranged it, and it became

"Madrilena," or "Lady of Madrid," in his third solo album. "Madrilena" was a fast, virtuosic showpiece for the piano, betraying his classical roots and showcasing his tremendous technique. Again, though, without an agent to encourage promotion of the album, and with Columbia's growing lack of interest in Pursell as a solo artist, the album did not reach hit status.

Pursell's contract with Columbia lasted from 1962 to 1967. During that time, he was the first-call pianist for any studio recordings made in Nashville on Columbia Records. He recorded with almost every artist who recorded for Columbia in those years, including Carl Smith, Billy Walker, Anita Bryant, Ray Price, Marty Robbins, and Johnny Cash. He was not limited to the Columbia roster, either, and recorded with Decca artist Patsy Cline and many others. Floyd Cramer was the first call pianist for Decca, but when he was unavailable, the next person they called was Pursell. Harold Bradley remembers that when he wanted to cut an album, his first choice for a pianist was Bill Pursell.[16]

7. NASHVILLE AND BEYOND

In the years following the release of his third solo album, the crooked river of Pursell's career began to resemble the wide Missouri much more than the winding Cumberland. His circle of influence was expanding beyond Nashville, and his musical projects were incredibly diverse. By the late 1960s he was beginning to get calls to work as a producer or arranger. Pursell also began to take many of his projects to London for recording, because musicians' wages there were significantly lower, thanks to union rules. Pursell collaborated for several years with Word Records, a Christian music label that specialized in hymn arrangements and gospel tunes. He also made three albums for *National Geographic*, and began to write jingles and commercials for the advertising firm McDonald and Little. Pursell's comfort with writing for a variety of combinations of instruments, his instinct for what would sound good on a recording, and his hardworking nature all made him well-suited for these kinds of musical jobs. In the 1970s, his diverse musical life bore fruit in a great number of unique and interesting commercial projects. He also continued to perform with and write for the Nashville Symphony.

NASHVILLE SYMPHONY

His last performance with the Nashville Symphony under Willis Page took place in 1966, when the Fisk University Choir, soprano Phyllis Bash, and baritone Andrew Frierson joined Pursell and the symphony for a concert conducted by Page. Pursell played Gershwin's *Rhapsody in Blue*, which was followed after the intermission by selections from *Porgy and Bess*.[1] Sometime after this concert, Pursell and Page had a minor falling out. As Pursell tells it, he was playing a session, and Page called to ask him to do another concert with *Rhapsody in Blue*. Grady Martin, the session leader, called Pursell away from the phone to continue recording, so Pursell had to hang up quickly. He told Page that he was on a session and that he would call him back. But Page never took any of his calls, and Pursell did not play any more concerts with the Nashville Symphony under Page. Pursell remembers: "I tried to figure out, what's the matter with this man? I was in a session; I had to go back and play it; we were on call. But Willis took it very personally; he thought I was fluffing him off. And later on, I heard stories that he got into a little bit of problem with other people over that sort of thing." Here was a clash of Pursell's two musical worlds, and a lack of understanding on the symphony conductor's part of the professionalism that was required of studio musicians. Studio time was paid by the hour, and although the atmosphere in the studio was (and is) at times casual, the musicians were on the clock and were expected to give their full attention to the session.

This was not the end of Pursell's career with the Nashville Symphony, however. Thor Johnson replaced Willis Page as artistic director and conductor in 1967. Perhaps this was the reason that Page never returned Pursell's calls; maybe he knew he was on the way out and was reluctant to make an effort. Although not all of the summer concerts are documented, Pursell remembers playing Gershwin's *Rhapsody in Blue* and Concerto in F several times with the Nashville Symphony throughout the late 1960s. His collaboration with the symphony would also extend to creating arrangements of works and, eventually, commissions for newly composed works as well.

In a piece that brought together the disparate parts of Pursell's musical life in the studio and on the concert hall stage, he made an arrangement for the Nashville Symphony called *Two Orchestral Impressions on Country Tunes*, "I Can't Help It If I'm Still in Love with You" and "Wabash Cannon Ball." It was performed on a pops concert May 17 and 18, 1968, alongside Broadway tunes sung by baritone Earl Wrightson and soprano Lois Hunt.[2] For his arrangement of the "Wabash Cannon Ball," Pursell remembers that he asked the French horns to blow through their mouthpieces to imitate the steam sound of the train.

Pursell explained it this way in his letter to Joe Habig of the RCA Record Division: "The 'steam,' by the way, or rather the sound of it, I got by having the brass players blowing through their trombones and trumpets consecutively; while the 'whistle' was reproduced around an augmented chord by winds in various positions, and the horns also simulated escaping steam with the whistle. If this sounds confusing, it will be clearer when you hear it."[3] The distinctive sound of a steam whistle on a train was a sound from Pursell's California boyhood in Tulare, a sound that to him signified faraway places and the glamor of San Francisco. He had to get it just right for this arrangement.

He also asked for a train bell. An article in the *Tennessean* dated the day before the performance informed the public that Pursell and the symphony were seeking a solid brass bell to use in the performance, also to depict the train sound for "Wabash Cannon Ball."[4] Apparently they found a bell, because Louis Nicholas's review remarked that the orchestra used a bell from the last Tennessee Central locomotive to use one.[5] Music critics Louis Nicholas and Werner Zepernick both commented on Pursell's orchestration and his ability to combine instruments to create a rich and varied sound. Pursell's days of intense labor as a young arranger in the Air Force Symphony bore wonderful fruit for him in his years as a professional composer and arranger. *Two Orchestral Impressions* was revived in September 1971 on another pops concert for the Nashville Symphony.[6]

MAUREEN REAGAN

Pursell first met Maureen Reagan, the daughter of Ronald Reagan, in a Nashville studio. She had hired him to do arrangements for an album for her, and they developed a friendship. Reagan even came to Pursell's house for dinner a couple of times. In 1968 Reagan called Pursell with another job. She asked him to arrange nine songs for a small band and herself as vocalist. It was a rush job, and Pursell would have to work long hours to complete it by the deadline. Reagan wanted to use the tunes on campaign stops for her father Ronald Reagan, who was campaigning for governor of California. Pursell remembers that when he finished, Reagan's staff had an airplane waiting at the airport, in order to deliver his arrangements straight to the campaign bus.

However, when Pursell sent his invoice for the work, $900 in all, including the copyist's fee, he ran into trouble. He waited for several weeks, and no payment came. He called her and spoke briefly with her, and was reassured that the payment would be sent soon, but still no payment came.

Pursell was finally contacted by Mike Casey, Reagan's manager, and was told that Reagan had overextended herself, that she intended to make the payment but was having a difficult time raising the money. Pursell was angry that Reagan had delegated a manager to avoid personal communication, and replied with an indignant letter: "I've done jobs before where the money was slow in coming in afterwards, but the amount of effort expended on this particular job, with the complications and the first eventual problem of getting paid from a client who refuses to settle it directly, . . . all of this just floors me! George Tidwell [the copyist] and I were sitting here, and beginning to wonder, think, or feel that we might have been 'had.' For what it's worth, the name Reagan isn't very impressive from here."[7] Subsequent letters from Casey state that Reagan was getting small jobs but not generating enough income yet to pay Pursell's invoice.[8] She did send a payment of thirty dollars, but that was all.

Eventually, Pursell wrote a lengthy letter to Stanley Ballard, secretary-treasurer of the American Federation of Musicians, in order to involve the union in the matter.[9] His letter mentions that he had heard several of his arrangements being used on syndicated television shows, including *The Merv Griffin Show*. Finally, after no progress toward getting payment from Reagan, Pursell decided to play hardball. The musicians' union newsletter featured on the back page a list of defaulting clients who had not paid for musicians' work. Pursell threatened to have Reagan listed on this defaults page. He gave her thirty days to pay. Ronald Reagan was campaigning for governor, and the family could not afford bad publicity. On the final day, Pursell received full payment for services rendered.

Pursell's troubles with Maureen Reagan are a cautionary tale for those working in the recording business. In the 1960s, a lot of work was done on a verbal agreement, a handshake, and the reputations of the persons involved. Pursell remembers that he asked Reagan very pointedly whether she could afford to commission these arrangements before he began the project, and that she had agreed to pay him. There was no written contract. Pursell's letter to the union describes several long-distance phone calls that he made at his own expense to consult with her while making the arrangements, something that was not normally done by an arranger, but that he did for the "sake of friendship." Normally these kinds of friendly arrangements worked out, but in this particular case, Pursell was stung. He is still incredulous at this experience—that the daughter of the governor of California could (or would) not gather up $900 to pay him and his copyist he finds simply astounding.

HEARTBEAT

One day in Nashville in 1969, Pursell visited Bill Beasley's basement recording studio and recorded some songs on an old spinet piano, one of which would make waves in England. Beasley was the owner of Spar Records, and he had made a habit of watching the *Billboard* Bubbling Under lists for future Top 100 hits. He would select a song and make a cover of it, so that when the record broke into the Top 100, there was a Spar Records cover of the tune sitting in the record store next to the original, at a fraction of the price. This is similar to what Felix Slatkin had done to Pursell with "Our Winter Love," rushing a cover to market before the full album came out to steal sales from the original artist. Beasley built Spar Records by creating these quick covers. Pursell's tune with Spar, recorded for a lark on that spinet piano, was "Heartbeat," and he describes it this way: "It was just a piece of junk, just a piece of junk that we did one afternoon. It sounds horrible, but it's got a lot of funky stuff on it. I've listened to that record, and I think it's a travesty. We just hammered it out in one afternoon, and the mix is terrible."[10]

"Heartbeat" begins with solemn chords played by Pursell on the piano; then a strong beat emerges, with a repeating motto in the piano, tambourine beats, and an electric guitar picks up the funky motto. It's a combination of boogie-woogie and the blues, and Bill is right, the recording quality is terrible, but there is something catchy about the tune. It's repetitive, rhythmic, and funky, perfect for dancing.

In 2011, Pursell received an email from a music fan in Australia asking him if he was the Bill Pursell who had recorded "Heartbeat." Joe Kirby informed Pursell that the song was one of the most popular records in the Northern Soul dance scene in England, and that he had bought a bootleg copy himself in 1978. Northern Soul was a youth movement that began in small clubs in the late 1960s and continues in the twenty-first century. It is characterized by a love of all-night dancing and hard-to-find soul music imported from the United States.[11] "Heartbeat" somehow made its way to Northern England and into these clubs. It is one of the many things that Pursell made that had significant impact on the musical life of many people, yet few know about it.

HAUSGEISTS

Many of Pursell's collaborations with the Nashville Symphony involved new music with a local theme. When the Nashville Symphony Guild decided to commission a work by Tupper Saussy, a prominent local businessman and composer, the piano part was written with Pursell in mind.[12] Pursell says that when Saussy approached First American National Bank for commissioning funds, Bill Greenwood, "second in line" at the bank, said he would give the funds "under one condition, that Bill Pursell plays the piano." Pursell remembers that Saussy then approached him and said that he had written a piano concerto just for him. The two then worked together on the piece until its premiere as "*Hausgeists*: Piano Concerto No. 1" in January 1969.

The premiere of this work received a lot of press attention. The *Tennessean*'s gossip columns mentioned the concerto and its upcoming performance at least three times, describing an open house held by Pursell and his wife Julie and the reception planned (and then held) by Saussy's mother-in-law Julia Fay Haun, in her Belle Meade home.[13] These articles seemed more concerned with the flower arrangements at the parties and the names of those attending than with the music. Pursell, having lived in Nashville for almost nine years by this time, and having married Julie Hollobaugh, a *Tennessean* reporter from a highly placed Nashville family, was making the society pages.[14]

More serious announcements of the concert also appeared in columns in the *Tennessean* (by Louis Nicholas, "The Music Scene") and the *Banner* (by Werner Zepernick, "The Music Score"), both describing Saussy as "a versatile musician, artist and composer" who recently left his job as an advertising executive with McDonald-Saussy Agency to devote himself to composing full time. They also refer to Pursell as a "well-known figure in the local recording industry as pianist, arranger, composer, and producer" who had attended the Peabody Conservatory and the Eastman School of Music.[15] In this sentence, we find the musical worlds that Pursell inhabited, classical and commercial, joining almost effortlessly.

An extended feature article in the *Tennessean*'s Sunday Showcase of January 12 described Saussy's compositional process and Pursell's impressions of the piece: "The composition is very hard to play. He has the piano doing everything, technically, a piano can do. You have to literally fold yourself over double to do it." *Hausgeists* ("House Ghosts" or "House Spirits") is three movements, each portraying the "spirit" of a historic home in Nashville. The first movement is a depiction of the Acklen House, now known as the Belmont mansion, which is even today said to be haunted. Saussy set it to waltzes, in conflict with more modernist music, to depict the intrusion of contemporary life on the old house. The second movement is set in a haunted house in Lawrenceburg and includes the breaking of real glass, as its ghosts were said to break windows.[16]

Pursell remembers Saussy bringing an antique door from his own house to a rehearsal, to break the glass in that movement. Pursell says that "after the first rehearsal, Thor [Johnson, the conductor] was left sitting on the stage in the first violin section. He said, 'I just don't get this movement, I can't understand it.' I thought that was the most honest thing I ever heard any conductor say. He was right there, right in front of me."

The lyric third movement of the concerto is set in the house of Saussy's late friend Rogers Caldwell, who had weekly Saturday lunches with area businessmen. Throughout, Saussy says in the program notes, the pianist plays the role of a composer observing, not necessarily talking to the house but developing an impression of it. The piano as composer is often in conflict with the orchestra, which plays the role of the house.

After the premiere, pictures of Pursell and Saussy with their wives at the Belle Meade reception were placed prominently at the top of the page in the *Banner*.[17] And reviews by Nicholas and Zepernick refer to a full house at the concert and an enthusiastic reception of the new piano concerto. Of Pursell, Nicholas wrote: "The piano part is by turns proclamatory, rhapsodic and decorative, and practically always demanding. William Pursell has just the facile technique it demands, and was completely in sympathy with its style which owes something to the big Gershwin piano works and their descendants." And from Zepernick: "Pursell played the difficult piano part with sure fingers and a beautifully graded tone. No matter how furious the passage, it was always well controlled."[18]

A further review in the *Banner* dated January 17, 1969, lists prominent society attendees and guests at the reception following the concert.[19] From the large amount of attention this concert received in the Nashville press, it is clear that it was at least equally as important as a society event as a musical event. No other concert that Pursell played with the Nashville Symphony received this amount of attention, but most of the attention was on the post-concert receptions, and who attended the concert. This was a different sort of society from the one Pursell enjoyed during his day job as a session musician.

Pursell's solid piano technique enabled him to traverse smoothly between the disparate musical worlds of the recording studio and the symphonic stage. And though this might not have seemed unusual in a city like Los Angeles or New York, most session musicians in 1960s Nashville, with the notable exception of the string players, were unable or unwilling to cross these lines.[20] Pursell's moonlighting with the Nashville Symphony was surely yet another reminder to the native Nashville session musicians that things were changing in Nashville. His arrival in 1960 may have been one of the signs of change from the old hillbilly country sound to the commercialized, polished Nashville Sound. His performances with the Nashville Symphony further underscored his differences from the Nashville regulars.

Although symphony performances led to a slight reduction in session calls, Pursell did not let it bother him overmuch. Pursell's relationship with the Nashville Symphony would continue to be fruitful into the late 1980s. His activities in the classical music world would also increase, with a concert at Trevecca Nazarene College and a performance of *Rhapsody in Blue* with the Nashville Youth Symphony. The Trevecca performance (November 15, 1969) itself walked the line between musical styles, including a classical first half and popular second half, complete with a combo to back up Pursell.[21]

LONDON AND DENHAM

In 1969 Joel Habig at *Reader's Digest* contacted Pursell and told him that they planned to compile an album of piano hits, *Cocktail Piano Time*, performed by their original pianists.[22] The album would include Pursell's 1963 hit, "Our Winter Love." The plan was to take the original pianists to London and record there. However, the London musicians' union refused to allow them to bring musicians from the United States and insisted that they hire local pianists. Clearly they did not understand the album's concept of having the tunes played by the original artists. If they wanted to record in London, *Reader's Digest* would have to hire English pianists to make the recording, and Pursell would not be able to perform his own hit.

Habig still wanted Pursell to help with the project, so *Reader's Digest* hired him to serve as arranger and conductor. This became Pursell's first trip to London. The English pianist Ronald Price played the piano part

Pursell working in the studio in the 1970s

in "Our Winter Love," which Pursell admits he did mind a little, but as he says, "it was so nice to be in London, and record at Decca Electric."

Pursell remembers that one day Leopold Stokowski pulled up outside the London studio in a limousine: "Here we are out on a coffee break, and somebody says, 'There's the Maestro,' and the Maestro is getting out of the car with his secretary. So he comes in and everybody is talking to him. I talked to him and said, 'I met you when I was 14, when you were conducting the All-American Youth Symphony Orchestra in San Francisco,' and he says, 'Oh you were a little goat then, weren't you?'"

When Pursell returned to Nashville, he told some of his friends in the record business, Rick Powell and Ron Huff, that one could record over there for twenty-five to fifty pounds a session, and before long, it became fairly common for some labels, especially Christian music labels, to take their recording projects overseas. Pursell remembers predicting that this trend would grow, telling his friend Harold Bradley that when (Nashville) union rates topped ninety dollars a session, the "gospel billies" would all go overseas, and many of them did. Pursell began to work with Kurt Kaiser and the religious label Word Records, and arranged and conducted several of their albums at Anvil Studio in Denham, a town just outside of London.

John Williams was recording his *Star Wars* soundtracks at the same time, and he too went to England, where he could afford to hire a ninety-piece orchestra. Often Pursell would arrive for a project just after Williams had left. Throughout the 1970s and into the 1980s, Pursell recorded several projects in England, many of them at Anvil Studio and some at the famous Abbey Road Studio in London, where the Beatles recorded. When Pursell later met Williams at a Grammy Awards event, they laughed together that they had kept missing each other in the studio.

One afternoon at Anvil, the engineer Eric Tomlinson, who supervised many of Word's records, called Pursell over to listen to something. For the recording of *The Empire Strikes Back* (1980), Tomlinson had placed three microphones around the studio and recorded on separate tracks. He told Pursell, "I hung three mikes over the entire orchestra, about ninety-five people." He showed Pursell that he could adjust the levels using the different microphones, for example, if one wanted more viola, one could raise this track a little. Tomlinson was in the process of mixing the sound for John Williams. Pursell remembers: "That was something he invented. And probably one of the reasons why, when you went to the movies to see any of these Steven Spielberg things, that you would get this bigger-than-life sound that was coming out of these speakers, was because of all this experimenting around that Eric was doing. And he used it on our stuff, for Word. And finally, Eric got a Grammy. He certainly deserved one." Tomlinson had a particular skill in finding just the right balance for the orchestra, to Pursell's and Word's benefit.[23]

WORD RECORDS

Pursell's first album with Word was *Nostalgia*, a collection of hymn arrangements. Word had just acquired the Rodeheaver catalog and wanted to do an album of their hymns. Pursell was given a free hand in selecting and arranging the hymns. Pursell went to London to record the instrumentals, and Charlie Brown, who worked for Word, recorded

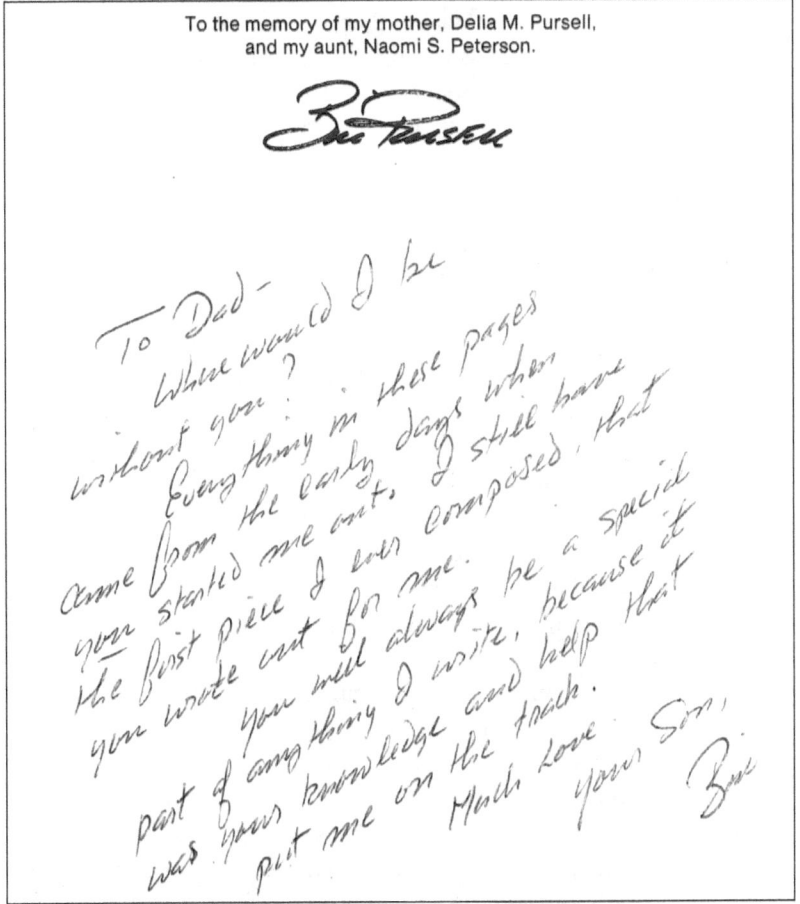

Dedication and note to Pursell's father inside the printed score of *Nostalgia*

the vocals in Waco with students from Baylor University. The album was recorded in late 1973 and issued in spring 1974.

A letter from Pursell to Kurt Kaiser, an A&R rep at Word, about the liner notes of *Nostalgia* explains the reasons for some of Pursell's artistic choices:

> There are some things that I very definitely had in mind when I did the album. First of all, it was a people oriented album in terms of people and their faith. For instance, on "Unclouded Day," I was thinking of a farmer, maybe 175 years ago, living in the Middle West

of the United States who had a faith that dealt with such things as cities with streets paved with gold, because he worked with the dirt, and his life and his whole means of supporting his family was governed by weather, by drought, by storms and good weather, or anything else that came his way. So, after a certain period of time it would be normal to wonder where his friends had gone and what the beyond was going to be like because there must be some sort of solace for the things he had gone through. I was thinking of him, toward the end of his life, looking bleakly at life like this.

Another thing that was on my mind at the time was that my Mother was extremely ill and, toward the middle of the project, I received word that my aunt was terminally ill. And so, the two of them passed away shortly before Thanksgiving. Without going into all this, if you consider it not out of taste, I still would like some mention made in the liner notes that this album, my first with Word Records, is dedicated in my mind to the memory of my Mother, Delia M. Pursell, and my aunt, Naomi Peterson. "Rock of Ages" was my Mother's favorite hymn, and it was with her in mind that I did this arrangement.

Also, the main thing was that the tunes, along with those I have already mentioned, such as "In the Sweet By and By," "Beyond the Sunset," "The Old Rugged Cross," and "Amazing Grace" were tunes that I grew up listening to, as everyone else has, and it is normal to think of the people whom you knew in a small town of Tulare in the middle of the San Joaquin Valley in California—then years later go back and pull these hymns literally out of the wall and fit them into the memories that you have had with these people.[24]

The title *Nostalgia* not only signaled to Word's customers that the album was a collection of old favorite hymns; it took on a deep personal meaning for Pursell.

In November 1973, between recording sessions for *Nostalgia*, Pursell received the call from his family. He immediately flew home to California to play for his Aunt Naomi's funeral. Naomi Peterson had been very special to him; he calls her his "musical mother." When Pursell was young, Naomi would sing Brahms Lieder at meetings of her ladies' club, while Pursell played the accompaniment on the piano; their love of music formed a special bond between them. Naomi died on a Friday, and Pursell flew out on Sunday so that he could be with the family and then play the piano for her funeral, a piece by Debussy, "The Girl with the Flaxen Hair," one of Naomi's favorites.

When Pursell arrived at home, his Uncle Frank told him that he should go right away to the nursing home to visit his mother Delia. Pursell found his father, and the two of them left immediately. When they arrived, the staff told them that they had been trying to find them all day; Pursell's mother was in her last hours. She had been ill for a long time, with tuberculosis of the spine, and her spine had become soft. She had been in a cast for over a year. Delia was also suffering from pulmonary edema. She was, as Pursell says, ready to go, and she died on that Sunday, not long after Pursell and his father had arrived in her room. Thus, Pursell attended two funerals that week (on Monday and Tuesday), funerals for the two women who were at the center of his life, his being, and his sense of self. The liner notes of *Nostalgia* did include his dedication of the album to his mother, whose favorite hymn, "Rock of Ages," was on this album, and his aunt, his musical mother.

Nostalgia was a great success. By August 1974, the album was getting good reviews in *Christian Life* and *Christian Review*.[25] The following year, Douglas Childress, the director of the Wesleyan Hour Radio Choir, sent a glowing letter to Pursell via Word, praising "the beauty and quality" of his arrangements and asking for more. Word responded with thanks and told Childress that there was indeed another album of Pursell's arrangements, *Listen . . . the Music of Ken Medema* (1974).[26]

Listen won Pursell his first Grammy nomination. *Listen* was a collection of Medema's own songs, but they were less religious in nature, more generic, so that the album could be used in a school setting, for a show choir or the like. Medema said that Pursell used a "very unique orchestration, full of life and color."

Pursell arranged two albums for Word with Ken Medema, a blind singer-songwriter whose career, like Pursell's, continued well into the twenty-first century.[27] Their second album together was *Through the Eyes of Love* (1977). Medema remembers Pursell as a last-minute arranger. He describes all-night arranging sessions, furious chart writing on the train to Anvil Studio, where they would record, and then a quick copying of parts at the studio while the orchestra, engineers, and Medema waited. When the orchestra got their parts, though, and began to play them, Medema said that they played "with a delight and enthusiasm that was palpable, they loved it!" They had expected, according to Medema, a typical religious music arrangement, replete with whole notes in the string

Album cover of *Listen: The Music of Ken Medema*

parts and unimaginative writing, but they got instead Pursell's colorful, rich orchestration, full of interesting lines for the violins. Medema said: "The strings are doing things that (Dmitri) Shostakovich would have us doing, or Ralph Vaughan Williams, but this is not Christian music, this is something else, and Pursell is running around, fixing this note and that note. Pursell is always running around, always doing these fixes. The players are delighted, the engineer is delighted, I'm thrilled out of my mind, because the orchestrations are way more than I had imagined."

The album was recorded at Anvil Studio with all instrumentalists playing and Medema singing simultaneously rather than laying down tracks separately (rhythm, strings, winds, vocals, each in their turn, a method which had become the norm at that time in recording studios). Medema recalls having to make special accommodations, such as covering his microphone with foam to prevent bleed-through with the orchestra. This approach, which Pursell insisted upon, resulted in a special "live" sound to the album, and Medema and Kaiser were extremely pleased.

Most of the time, recording in London put musicians like Pursell at an advantage, because of the cheaper musicians' union rates. But at times, the rigidity of the union rules could cause problems. On one session with Medema, Pursell remembers, they ran into a significant problem, and a five-minute over-run resulted in having to pay for an entire second session.

He was recording the instrumental background for a medley of songs at the Abbey Road studio in London, and as usual, Pursell was writing out the orchestral parts at the last minute and handing them off to the copyist as quickly as he could. He remembers: "We went in to Studio No. 2, and I was getting ready, and all the orchestra was there, and I put the earphones on and heard this buzz. I looked at the concertmaster and said, 'Are you getting a buzz in your earphone?' He said, "Yes," and I looked at Kurt [Kaiser, of Word Records] and said, 'We're getting a buzz down here,' and he said, 'Well, we're trying to find it.' The session was from 2:00 to 5:00. That was the allotted time. And so, it was 2:40 by the time that they found it." The source of the buzz was just a loose jack, but they had lost forty minutes of the session in finding it.

At five minutes until 5:00, when the session was supposed to end, Pursell raised his baton, dropped it, and "all of a sudden, everything hit the fan, big discord." It took him several minutes to find the source of the problem—he had forgotten to write in a key change. By this time, they had gone past the 5:00 deadline. After the session was over, his friend Raymond Mosely informed him that it was unfortunate that they would have to charge him double for the session musicians, because they had run over time. Pursell says, "This is the English union for you then, this is the reason we went to war against England back in 1812, because you can't reason with them, they're impossible. I thought well, they're probably going to charge us fifty minutes for overtime, usually they do it in quarters like that, or in short fifty-minute-increments, and the studio will have to make up that time."[28]

However, the union rules stated that if the recording was an overdub, the technique Pursell was using, they had to charge for an entire new session, which Pursell hadn't known. He says that he was very angry about the situation, but there was nothing to be done; he had to pay for the extra session. The studio did pay for the extra forty minutes of studio time, but they refused to pay the musicians' fee. Pursell remembers that he would not return to the studio for several months because he was so angry at the outcome.

Raymond Moseley and Pursell became close friends during the years that Pursell was traveling back and forth to London to make recordings. Raymond would arrange for studio time and would hire the musicians. Pursell would wire the money into an English account, and Raymond would pay the musicians and the studios. It was a mutually beneficial business arrangement, and in spite of that one extra session charge, one that continued for some years.

In 1978 Moseley sponsored Pursell for membership in the Savage Club, an elite gentleman's club in London with a centuries-old tradition. It was created to support intellectual and artistic life, and activities are based mainly on participation in shows, good conversation, food, and drink. The Savage Club was founded (with the help of Queen Victoria) in 1857, in a part of London known as Bohemia, by a group of writers, artists, and thespians.[29] The club cultivates a deliberate atmosphere of informality and levity, along with various dinners and shows, and copious alcohol consumption. A sharp wit is greatly valued, and life within the society is unequivocally egalitarian, in spite of its many famous members.

It is the tradition at the Savage Club that the Prince of Wales is an honorary member, and they also have welcomed literary lights such as Charles Dickens, Dylan Thomas, and Mark Twain. The pianist Benno Moiseiwitsch, a friend of Pursell's teacher Alexander Sklarevski, was a popular member there who often provided musical entertainment. Sergei Rachmaninoff twice attended the club as a guest. Many orchestral players in London were members of the Savage Club, including the principal horn player of the BBC Symphony Orchestra, Alan Civil (Norgate and Wykes 1976, 27). Most of the members were British. Pursell claims that he was one of only three American members when he joined, along with Jascha Heifetz and Frederik Prausnitz.[30]

The Savage Club maintains facilities in London, rooms that include a bar, dining halls, and hotel-like rooms. The clubhouse at Carleton Terrace was hit by a bomb during World War II, but was rebuilt within months in order to host the annual dinner. The club later moved to rooms at the top of Lansdowne Hotel, off Berkeley Square, and then to One Whitehall Place. Its furnishings are historical, of course, including a chair with a plaque that reads, "Here Old Odell sat," in honor of an irascible club member who once shooed His Royal Highness the Prince of Wales himself out of his customary chair (Norgate and Wykes 1976, 43). Pursell remembers being offered cigars out of a beautiful sterling silver cigar box that was the gift of the Prince of Wales to the club. Pursell and his wife and daughter stayed at the Savage Club occasionally when he was in London for his recording sessions.[31] He has attended Savage Club dinners and stayed at the Savage Club's rooms at the top of the Lansdowne Hotel, but his London travels ceased by the 1990s, and he has not been active in the Savage Club since, although he is still listed as a member.

NIBBLIES AND BOOZE

It was around this time that Pursell's friend W. O. "Smitty" Smith invited him to be a member of his Wednesday Night Club, a men's club of a very different nature from the Savage Club. The club was a continuation of a 1960s group of community leaders, black and white, who would gather on Wednesday nights at a member's house to discuss racial issues, or as Smitty called it, "the Issues." Pursell had first gotten to know Smith as a fellow band member when he first came to Nashville and played jazz at the Carousel, and Smith had also hired him to teach a semester at Tennessee A&I. Pursell is a social man who loves clubs, and he fit in instantly with this group of men concerned with civil rights issues.

Pursell remembers Smitty calling him up to remind him it was his night for the "nibblies and the booze," and he would procure the necessary refreshments, and host the meeting. Pursell remembers the editor of the local newspaper, the *Tennessean*, and the owner of a bookstore, Bernie Schweid, as members of the group. Smith writes in his memoir that the group that Pursell joined was the second iteration of the club. The Wednesday Night Club was a deliberate reorganization in the 1970s along "interracial lines," Smith writes, "an excellent forum in which to clear up a lot of the ignorance that existed between the races" (Smith 1991, 277). Many of the members joined the group before they became prominent in society, Smith notes, such as "Warren Moore, who became the executive director of the Tennessee Human Rights Commission; Del Sawyer, dean of the Blair School of Music at Vanderbilt; Frank Sutherland, now editor of *The Tennessean*; and Al Birch, now a Tennessee appeals court judge." Pursell was their "resident composer."[32] Smith says in his memoir that the idea of calling Nashville "Music City, U.S.A." (now the city's slogan) came out of these meetings.

Another perennial topic of discussion at the Wednesday Night Club was the unavailability of music lessons to low-income children. Smith remembered how music gave him, a poor child in Philadelphia, the means to lift himself out of poverty: "Music was my ticket out of the ghetto" (Smith 1991, 303). These discussions led to proposals for a school in Nashville, and finally sponsorship of the Nashville Symphony and support from powerful community leaders such as Buddy Killen, producer and music publisher, with whom Pursell would later work on the *Platinum* album with the Nashville Symphony. Pursell was present for the groundbreaking of the W. O. Smith Music School in 1984, and he remembers "Smitty" standing there with tears in his eyes, watching his dream become reality. Smith died of cancer in 1991, but his dream lives on in a thriving music school that offers music instruction to underprivileged children for fifty cents a lesson. All instruments and books are provided, and all of the instructors are volunteers. The school opened with forty-five students, and by 2014 had over 650 students. Pursell was present at its birth.

NASHVILLE SWEAT BAND (1976)

Meanwhile, back in the Nashville studios, Pursell made another series of singles that would achieve international fame. Under the name "Bill Pursell and the Nashville Sweat Band," Pursell put together several disco songs, which were published by Peer Records.[33] The band was not what one would expect for a disco band. In addition to four guitarists, two bass players, five percussionists, and Pursell on piano, there were seven vocalists (including Duane Clark as soloist), nine violinists, two violas, three cellos, harp, five trumpets, and five trombones. This shift in instrumentation, which was string-heavy, is reminiscent of the country sessions in Nashville in the 1960s, when strings played an important role in the development of the Nashville Sound. Once again, Pursell's experiences in the Army as an orchestrator and his session work in 1960s Nashville were affecting his music, this time in the realm of disco.

Union pay sheets show that the recording took place in four sessions, two on January 9 and two on January 13, 1976, with one additional working session for Pursell on February 2.[34] Pursell believes there may have been more sessions than this, especially with himself and Gene Nash for the mixing of the record. Pursell remembers flying a Cuban percussionist up from Florida to do an overdub after the initial sessions were over.

These recordings were later issued on an album called *Bill Pursell and the Nashville Sweat Band and Aides*, with the memorably-named tunes "Walk Right In," "Bump Me Baby (Cumbancherio)," "Cachita," "Every

Day of the Week," "Hold My Hand When We're Going Home," "Now," "Sandwich Spread," "Peter Piper Pumped His Pecks," and "Déjà Vu."

"Now" was issued as a single, with "Déjà vu" on the B side; they made quite a splash overseas. The description in *Music Week* (England) says it all:

> I mean, no amount of listening or dancing to a single like "Now (Hoy)" (Spark) by Bill Pursell and the Nashville Sweat Band would give you a clue to its identity. And its identity you'll really want to know because here's a disco smash. One of those purple, lush orchestrations which swell and blaze with piano arpeggios, flute solos, string ripples and brass bashes—the lot set against a funky unrelenting percussion chucka-chucka.
>
> Not to mention the breathy-girl choir ah-ahing and do-it-nowing to great effect. This particular number feels very pop-classic Rachmaninoffish. It's a find.[35]

"Now" is truly a strange and unique song. The strings and background vocals take you back to the instrumental style of "Our Winter Love," even if the genre, disco, is entirely different. Somehow Rachmaninoff even makes an appearance, as noticed by *Music Week*'s reviewer. The other side of the 45 was "Déjà Vu," with similarly odd combinations of string sweeps, disco-style electric guitar, and melodic piano solos, and semi-pornographic sighs and moans from the female singers. This 45 was released in Mexico, England, and Germany, and perhaps elsewhere. Memos to Peer executives show that "Now" was played widely on the radio in Germany and England.

"Now" was a big hit in England. A handwritten note from Mike Stuart in Cardiff exclaimed "Just received single by Bill Purcell [sic] and Nashville ... etc. ... YOU'VE GOT A DISCO HIT ON YOUR HANDS ..." And deejay Richard Spinks, in a letter from Havant discussing recent Peer releases, wrote, "Which brings me to the latest and Greatest of the Spark product the sensational 'Bill Pursell' single NOW (HOY), which has got to be the best piece of soul for months. Hissing Hi-Hats, Thumping beat and Driving Harmonies all add up to make one of the most promising records around. I really think this one's going to make it. One first playing I liked it and knew it was mover, this was reinforced after a few live plays, this one's a winner." A telegram from Richard Searling noted, "NOW THE NASHVILLE SWEAT BAND IS A NORTHERN DISCO SMASH."

A report from Pete Owen of the Pete Owen Record Show in Middlesex on records recently sent from Peer to be played on the radio said "Excellent—By far and away the best record from your stable this year. I still have 'Our Winter Love' from 1962 by Bill Pursell—He's a great pianist. LOVE IT LOVE IT LOVE IT." Owen remarked that the record was played on the "Pre-Match Spin" at the Chelsea Football Club and on his "mobile Disco—Saturday Nights." Another deejay, Dave Caff from Lancashire, wrote a note as well: "Now (Hoy) Bill Pursell is going down a storm only after I was playing my record of the week. Chart Cert. What more can I say only let's have more great sounds like these. p.s. Please let me know if Bill has an album out."[36]

According to these memos to Peer executives, British deejays were having great success with "Now." Pursell believes that some of this may have been music-business hype, and he admits that he knew nothing of the business side of this album at the time. Things like this happen in the music business all the time—a song gets a lot of attention, and then fades. Evidently Peer did not respond to the deejay requests for more albums from Bill Pursell and the Nashville Sweat Band. Whether they considered a hit overseas insignificant, or this was deejay hype, or whether Pursell was simply not interested, the band did not record another album. Once again Pursell had a project that made a brief, glorious splash in the popular music world, and then he moved on to something else. The workings of the music industry are indeed fickle, nonlinear, and unexplainable.

CIRCUS WORLD (1976)

Pursell almost ran into serious financial trouble on another project. In the spring of 1976, Pursell's friend Hank Levine asked him to arrange and produce a lengthy musical show for Circus World, a Ringling Brothers, Barnum and Bailey park in Haines City, Florida. Mariana Levine and Paul Crabtree, who had both worked at the Opryland theme park in Nashville, served as choreographer and composer, respectively. The show, called "The Day the Circus Came to Town," was supposed to be an opening number for the Circus World show, and was a show *about* a circus, before the actual circus began. It was a narrated celebration of the traditional circus figures, from the ringmaster to the trapeze artists and clowns. The biggest prop would be a scale model of a working circus train. The concept was that the recorded music (with a series of live acts by the circus performers) would open the show, and would be followed by the circus proper, complete with a live band. Crabtree's script lists a total of sixty-seven minutes for this opening sequence.[37] Pursell's job would be to arrange the music for orchestra and supervise the week of recording, then send a finished recording to Florida for use in their show.

Pursell agreed to produce this on a tight time schedule, and worked many late hours to ensure that the arrangements were completed and the studio work happened on schedule. He did not ask for money up front, a mistake he later regretted. Normally half the money would be deposited at the musicians' union, and half would be due upon completion of the job. Instead, all Pursell had was a two-page agreement from Ringling Brothers, outlining the following:

- $100 per minute of music
- $200 per day consulting fee for Pursell, plus travel expenses
- credit for arranging and conducting the orchestral music
- payment for recording services at the American Federation of Musicians rate, including Pursell's services as conductor
- an estimate of expenses to be made by Pursell and submitted to Ringling Brothers[38]

At the time, Pursell thought this would be sufficient.

Pursell coordinated the activities of a forty-three-piece orchestra. A chorus and tap dancers (to test the danceability of the music) were also brought into the studio. A timetable laid out by Paul Crabtree demonstrates the complexity of the process and the number of different people involved:

MARCH 1ST—REHEARSALS (of the circus actors) MOVE INTO THE THEATRE (a newly built structure made to look like a circus tent)

MARCH 6TH—BILL PURCELL [sic] ARRIVES WITH ARRANGEMENT SKETCHES INDICATING ORCHESTRAL ENTRANCE CUES AND MUSICAL CHARACTER THAT WILL BE SIGNIFICANT TO THE PERFORMANCE ACTION, CHOROGRAPHY [sic] AND CHORAL ARRANGEMENTS

MARCH 7TH—A REHEARSAL PERFORMANCE WILL BE GIVEN FOR BILL PURCELL FOR THE PURPOSE OF CHECKING HIS ARRANGEMENT SKETCHES AGAINST THE ACTUAL

TIMING AND PERFORMANCE, CHANGES AND ADJUSTMENTS WILL BE MADE TO COORDINATE PERFORMANCE WITH ARRANGEMENT

MARCH 8TH—PURCELL RETURNS TO NASHVILLE AND MAKES NEW REHEARSAL TAPE (2 PIANOS—DRUMS) TAPE WILL BE FLOWN TO CIRCUS WORLD IMMEDIATELY UPON COMPLETION

MARCH 9TH TO 15TH—PURCELL AND HOST WORK ON COMPLETING ORCHESTRA AND CHORAL ARRANGEMENTS

MARCH 15TH TO 19TH—ORCHESTRA AND CHORAL RECORDING AND MIXING

MARCH 20TH—FINISHED TAPES DELIVERED TO CIRCUS WORLD FOR FINAL REHEARSALS

MARCH 21—LIVE CIRCUS BAND COORDINATED WITH TAPES

MARCH 28TH TO APRIL 2—DRESS REHEARSALS

APRIL 2—DRESS REHEARSAL FOR AUDIENCE

APRIL 3—OPENING DAY[39]

Union timesheets show that the musicians recorded in Woodland Studios on March 15, 16, 19, and 26. Pursell's notes show that he mixed the recording on March 26, 27, and 28.[40]

Pursell did not particularly enjoy working with Paul Crabtree. He remembers being continually surrounded in a cloud of smoke from Crabtree's smoking. Crabtree was not an educated musician, and he would make up melodies and then write numbers on the keys of the piano with a pencil to notate the tunes. Pursell also remembers:

> It was idiotic; he [Crabtree] would stop the session on paid union time and want to put the boards down to see if the tap dancers could dance to the music we had just recorded. It sounded like a hailstorm out there. I mean, it was just ridiculous. Hank [Levine] was sitting back and these guys were loitering out in the hall there, waiting to get back in and record.

Perhaps someone should have reminded Crabtree that the billing was related to time spent in the studio. Recording the Circus World project really was a circus.

The *Tennessean* covered the recording session, noting that a bit of Nashville would come to Circus World in the form of twenty-eight minutes of recorded music. The article included two pictures, one of Pursell conducting the orchestra in the studio, and one of Paul Crabtree and Pursell conferring with the score. Crabtree said that Nashville was "the best place in the world to do music" and that Bill Pursell, as arranger and conductor, was the best available person to do the job.[41]

In April, after the dust settled, Pursell received a letter of thanks from entertainment manager Bud Davis, which said,

> Now that we have a couple of weeks behind us after our re-opening here at Circus World, I wanted to thank several people who I think contributed the most to our success. You are certainly among those who deserve the most credit. "The Day the Circus Comes to Town" is an even bigger success than we had hoped and although we are still ironing out some rough spots, in general everything looks really great. The hard work and terrific amount of talent you contributed to this project are appreciated not only by those of us in the Entertainment Department, but by everyone who works in the park, by those in management positions, and of course by several thousand people who have already enjoyed the show and are telling their friends to come see it.[42]

These were effusive thanks, but unfortunately, when the time came to pay the musicians, Pursell ran into serious trouble. He recalls that the bill for the whole production, including the musicians, singers, studio time, and his own services, ran just above $78,000. The cost for the musicians was a little more than half the total. He sent the bill to Circus World, and then Chuck Smith, the controller of finance for Irving Feld, the owner of Circus World, called Pursell. He told him that the total was too high and that he wouldn't pay it. Pursell told him that this was a union job, and that the musicians had to be paid. The matter unresolved, they ended the phone conversation. Pursell went up to Chicago to do a session, and when he returned, he called the union and talked to Johnny D. George, who told him that the union could not cover the full bill, because the union pay for the musicians was only $49,000.

And I said, "What am I going to do?"
He said, "I don't know, maybe you'll have to deal with them."

So here I go, and the phone rings again, and here is this fellow [Chuck Smith], and he says, "We're going to have to pay all these people," and so on and so forth. He thought that it would be $78 thousand for the musicians.

So he said, "Make me an offer." Well, then I began to get suspicious. And I put him on hold and I said to my wife, "What shall I do?" and she said, "Take 72,500 and stay out of the hospital." So I said, "Well, what about $73,000?" and he says, "Well, okay that's cool."

Then I realized that if I had said $75,000, he would have taken it. He was playing with me. So, I'd got $73,000 and I said, "Okay, I'll tell you what I'm going to do. I'll send you a telegram, making it, understood, $73,000 becomes public record." And he said "Okay," so the $73,000 came in.

I felt very lucky; I got everybody paid off. I worked for free on the sessions. I did get paid for the arrangements, but the rest of it I worked for free, but I got everybody paid off. And my tax attorney said, "I have never seen anybody come closer to the cliff and not fall off than you did." I said, "I'm never going to do this unless I get money up front."

Later Pursell heard that Circus World didn't even use the recording more than three or four times. All of that trouble was for very little. However, Pursell feels that he was very lucky, because he thinks that if Smith had known that the $78,000 was not all union pay, Pursell would have gotten significantly less money for the job. The singers were in a different union (AFTRA), and if Pursell had itemized the bill in detail, Smith would have seen that and would have refused to pay them. He later was told that the union did call Smith and told him that they would not allow any union musicians to play for Circus World unless he paid Pursell's bill.

As he says, this was a very close shave for Pursell; he could easily have been held personally liable for thousands of dollars. He remembers the Circus World project with distaste, and feels that he worked incredibly hard and was still taken advantage of, as he did not get paid himself for his week in the studio. But his music, after all, was appreciated. On the same day that Circus World issued Pursell a check for $73,000, Dick Kuegeman, general manager of Circus World, wrote Pursell a letter, explaining that he was resigning from his position but that he wanted to take a moment to thank Pursell for his hard work:

I simply want to express to you how very much those of us intimately involved with the show appreciate the fine quality work that you did on its behalf. I can't help but recall a comment that Bill Prine, the Musical Director of Ringling Bros. Barnum & Bailey Combined Shows, made to me after having heard the show for the first time. He said, "Whoever that person is who orchestrated that show (I then told him your name) is capable of taking music written by a six year old and turning it into a symphony." I couldn't have put it better![43]

Pursell shines as an orchestrator. His piano skills are formidable, his compositions well-crafted and emotionally fulfilling; but in his life as a professional musician, it was his orchestration skills that got him the most attention. As a musician he was the complete package, an excellent performer who could also create and mold music into whatever the needs of his clients were. And this is why he achieved such success in both the classical and commercial worlds—knowing how an orchestra works, what parts sound best in which instruments, and how to combine them most effectively, is a skill applicable in circus shows, films, and on the concert stage. Pursell's versatility as a musician assured him an incredible variety of projects during this period of his life. Further, his organizational skills and business sense led to leadership roles in most of these projects—assembling the musicians, reserving studio time, supervising the sessions, and sending out invoices when the work was done, and ensuring payment when necessary, as we have seen above.

Pursell wrote music for two other theme parks: Cypress Gardens and Six Flags Over Georgia. The music for Six Flags was specified in a contract (signed in November 1975) as two pieces of music, each three and a half to four minutes in length, to be played at the carousel, with rights to use the music in jingles and commercials for local publicity. The agreed-upon fee was eight thousand dollars, out of which Pursell had to pay the musicians, the studio fees, copying costs, and traveling costs. A breakdown of the costs shows not only what such a project might have cost in 1976, but also the different ways such costs were incurred in such a project.

The music was recorded in Woodland Sound Studios in Nashville. The union timesheet shows that for recording the two songs, one three and a half minutes, one four minutes seven seconds, the cost for five musicians and one copyist was just over a thousand dollars.[44] The studio invoice shows a cost of $480.50 for four hours of studio time (including one hundred dollars for the master tape). Synthesizing costs, invoiced by "My Place" (Sylvia Powell), were $975.00. This totals about $2,600; the remainder of the $8,000 fee, then, was for composing, arranging, and travel. Notes in the Six Flags folder also show that more music had been discussed, with an estimate of a total cost of around $45,000. But this project remained relatively small, about seven minutes of music, at just over a thousand dollars a minute to compose, record, and produce it.

The Cypress Gardens project was more complicated, as it was recorded in London with the Westminster Sinfonia Orchestra. No contract is extant for this project, but notes by Pursell and various invoices paint the picture of four recording sessions at Olympic Studios in November 1977. The total cost for the orchestra was UK£4,785.10. Notes written by Pursell show that he composed music for the entire show, fourteen numbers and an estimated total of forty minutes of music to accompany the water ski show. This included numbers like "Beach Barefoot," "Corky," "Tiger Act," "Jumping Act," "Ballet," "Flags Semaphore," "Kite Act," and more. Pursell's notes show a total estimated cost of the project of $24,500, with income for himself of around $8,000.[45]

Recording in England meant, once again, some adjustment for British musicians' union rules. A letter from Pursell's friend and "fixer" Raymond Moseley outlines some necessary finagling for the final overdub session. According to union rules, Moseley explained, overdub sessions were limited to four songs. Thus, if one wanted to record more than four songs on a three-hour session, he could string them together with piano music segues to create fewer separate songs. Moseley advised Pursell to do this (he could cut out the segues in the later mixing) but that he would have to limit the total amount of music recorded, regardless, to twenty minutes. Pursell followed his friend's advice, and all of the work on the sessions went smoothly.

These details of the inner workings of recording commercially oriented music show not only the influence of musicians' unions on the recording process, but also the keen mind for business that a working musician must cultivate. Pursell was every bit as much an entrepreneur as he was a composer, arranger, and performer.

Meanwhile, Pursell's collaborations with the Nashville Symphony were increasingly diverse. One such event was a pops concert at the Grand Ole Opry House on May 4, 1978, called "A Musical Odyssey into Outer Space." The concert included an arrangement of music from *Star Trek* by Pursell; music by Richard Strauss that was used in the film *2001: A Space Odyssey*; selections from Holst's *The Planets* and *Seven Moon Phases* by

Bill and his family in 1979

Matthias Bamert; and orchestral suites on the music from *Close Encounters of the Third Kind* and *Star Wars*. The Nashville Symphony performed this music, spectacularly, to a laser light show by Soleil Laser Fantasia. Although the laser show received much more attention in the press than the music, the review of the concert did mention that Pursell was called to the stage "for an enthusiastic ovation" for his *Star Trek* arrangement.[46]

Thus, the 1970s saw Pursell's musical career take many twists and turns all around the city of Nashville and beyond, just as the wide Cumberland sweeps in a loop around downtown. His collaborations in the studio for various types of commercial music, his forays into theme park music, and his continuing work with the Nashville Symphony took full advantage of his diverse and deep musical skills. He was at the apex of his career as a working musician: studio pianist, classical piano soloist, orchestra arranger, studio arranger and producer, composer, and even university instructor. What lay around the next bend would eventually give him a guaranteed regular paycheck and some financial security, something for which his wife would be most grateful.

8. HERITAGE

By the late 1970s, Pursell's musical horizons had spread even wider. His connections in London meant more recording projects there, but he also began to cement his ties to Nashville, working closely with the Nashville Symphony on various projects, both arrangements and new compositions, and even landing a secure academic job by 1980. He was fully transitioning from session musician to arranger and producer, and eventually, even professor.

Pursell made three albums for *National Geographic* in the late 1970s for their American Adventure series, serving as arranger and conductor. Once again it was his studio work that provided the connection—he had worked with Russ Miller at Audio Media, who knew John Lavery, the director of recordings at *National Geographic*. Miller told Lavery that Pursell was the man for the project, and Pursell was given complete control over the selection of songs and the arrangements.

The first album was called *Barbershop Days* (1977), and it featured the Park Pavilion Concert Band and various choruses and quartets. The Society for the Preservation and Encouragement of Barber Shop Quartet Singing in America (SPEBSQSA) helped sponsor the album, and it included such chestnuts as "Hello, Ma Baby," "My Wild Irish Rose," and "Meet Me in St. Louis, Louis."[1] *National Geographic* offered its audience more than just a collection of songs; the album was a miniature history lesson (and an exercise in utopian nostalgia).

The cover featured a picture of a reproduction of a turn-of-the-century barber's table, and its inside featured a lengthy essay by Michael J. Bernstein on America in the early twentieth century, replete with nostalgic photos, a trolley car, a rower in a boat, a baseball card, and pictures of old-fashioned bicycles. Bernstein's essay paints a portrait of an idyllic, simpler time, the World's Fair, the local barbershop, and the rise of Tin Pan Alley. It ends: "As our town bandsmen turn down Mulberry Street, another Fourth of July parade is over. Now it is time for the barbershop quartet to join in the festivities. So find a place out of the sun, settle back, and listen to songs that bring back delightful memories of the good old days."

Album cover of *Barbershop Days*

Pursell wanted to create a sense of flow to the album and created interludes between the songs. Pursell's arrangements sound like a traditional American park wind band (plus strings), with flutes, trombones, trumpets, cymbals, and of course, sandblocks. In addition to the individual songs, Pursell compiled two medleys, each with a few verses from three different songs, connected by brief interludes. Pursell's orchestration is light and comfortable, just right for a barbershop album. One of the great strengths of Pursell's musical style is that he always has a concept in his mind (a different idea for each song, such as auto horn effects on one) and has impeccable taste in orchestration, honed by his years serving in the Air Force. The orchestra stays in the background in this album; one listens to the singing and hardly notices it is there, yet its absence would be missed sorely.

John Lavery wrote to Pursell that the listener response to the album was so enthusiastic that they hoped to continue the American Adventure series. *Barbershop Days* had opened with a march by Sousa, "The Thunderer." One of Pursell's next albums with *National Geographic* would be *On Parade: The Music of John Philip Sousa*. He began to work with Sousa biographer Paul Bierley, and to select the tunes for this album Pursell made a trip to the Library of Congress. Librarian William Parsons acquainted him with the Sousa archive, in which Pursell found a song that Sousa had written when he was sixteen years old, called "Fall Tenderly Roses," and another unknown song, "Day and Night." "Fall Tenderly Roses" had been found in Sands Point in 1932, not long after Sousa died, and the manuscript had made its way into the Library of Congress. Pursell wanted to include these tunes in the album.

> I just decided that it would make good sense to start off this particular album with me doing a Brahmsian type of piano transcription of this piece of music ("Fall Tenderly Roses"), and then after I finish it with a roll-off, into Stars and Stripes Forever, so that you are coming from 15, 16 years old to 43 years of age. And then end the entire album with the same thing, only in this case, it would have Shelly Kurland playing the violin and I would accompany him. John Philip (Sousa) was a violinist, and when he sat at the table, he would have his left hand up in the air, fingering while he was writing. He was thinking, basically, from the violin keyboard. So now I understand where all this counterpoint is coming from in his marches; it comes from his string playing. He was a contrapuntal thinking guy.

However, *National Geographic* had trouble getting permission from Sousa's heir to use these early songs. Mary McPeak, secretary to John Lavery, told Pursell that she could not get a positive response from the Sousa family. So Pursell, in typical fearless fashion, took the matter into his own hands and called John Philip the Third, Sousa's grandson. He told Mr. Sousa III:

> "Well, here's what I have in mind. I want to do an album that isn't going to be the starched type of military album that it seems they all have done. I want to show him as a sort of cigar-chomping, normal kind of guy, who likes to box, which he did, and I want to start it off with this piece of music he wrote when he was 16."

He said, "You know, I like that idea, I like that approach."

And I said, "What can we do?"

"Well, you have to understand, I've got to go to my lawyers and everything."

I said, "What kind of money are we talking about here, Mr. Sousa?"

"Well, I don't know, um, maybe between zero and one thousand, I suppose."

I said, "Really?" because I thought it would be thirty thousand, forty thousand, and I said,

"How about $500?"

He said, "That's okay."

And I said, "Mr. Sousa, you've got a deal, if I have to send it to you myself."

I called Mary and said, I got the song; I got it for you for $500, so please send him a check. And then I said to Paul later, we got to referring to Sousa as the Old Man, and I said "I wonder what the Old Man would think if he knew we were using that tune he wrote when he was in his teens," and Paul said, "He'd never believe it. He's probably forgotten about it."

"Fall Tenderly Roses" was written by Sousa as a piano/vocal score. Pursell's arrangement for solo piano (performed by himself on the album) enhances Sousa's sweet melody with, as Pursell had planned, Brahmsian harmonies and a slightly richer texture. Pursell added a snare drum roll to the end of the song that leads right into Stars and Stripes Forever, perhaps Sousa's most famous march. "Fall Tenderly Roses" is reprised at the end of the album, with Pursell's violinist friend Sheldon Kurland playing the romantic melody, just as Pursell had planned.[2] The use of this tune at the beginning and end gives the album a cohesive shape and a sense of nostalgia, and provides an effective contrast to the rousing marches that comprise most of the music.

Like *Barbershop Days*, *On Parade* was recorded at Anvil Studio in London. During one session, a strange banging was heard, and Pursell thinks it might have been John Philip's ghost:

There was a little man sitting down in front of me, playing the cornet, and I asked who it was, and Raymond Moseley, who was the fixer over there, pointed out that this little man had played with John

Philip in his world tour one year before he died. He was sitting there with his little glass of whiskey, right in front of me. A very strange thing happened in that session.

I was on the podium, you can hear me talking, very quietly, and I think we were doing El Capitan. Here I am, and I'm going this way [snapping], and I said, I think that's the tempo that he liked. All of a sudden from the ceiling, bam, bam, bam, bam, bam, the sound comes from the ceiling right over my head, way up there in the rafters, and I picked up the phone and called Eric and said, "Do you have workmen up there doing any kind of construction or anything?" He said, "No, there's not supposed to be anybody up there. I'll send somebody up," and they sent somebody up, and they couldn't find anybody. It was the same tempo. But on the tape, you'll hear, bam, bam, bam, and then you'll hear an English voice saying "Oh, it's John Phillip!" I would love to think that's what happened. He might have been looking out at what we were doing.[3]

Pursell loves a good ghost story, and throughout the making of this album he felt a special connection to Sousa. From researching in the Library of Congress to corresponding with Sousa biographer Bierley, Pursell was actively seeking a unique approach to Sousa's music that would honor his memory in a way other collections had not done. Pursell does not say whether he thought the banging was approval or admonition from the afterlife, but he loves to tell this story to affirm his close connection to Sousa's music.

After the album was released in 1978, *National Geographic* received letters asking for sheet music of some of the tunes, especially "Fall Tenderly Roses," and forwarded them to Pursell. John Lavery replied to some of the letters, stating that the songs were produced by special arrangement with the Sousa family and were not commercially available. Other letters were forwarded to Pursell, and he remembers answering some of them, in 1995 even sending a copy of the piano score so it could be performed at a wedding. The bride, Judy Fernbach Simon, wrote to Pursell that her father-in-law's friend, Ned Battista, had made a string quartet arrangement of Pursell's arrangement of Sousa's tune, and enclosed a copy. Thus, "Fall Tenderly Roses" followed its own crooked river, from piano/vocal manuscript in the Library of Congress, to Pursell's piano/violin arrangement, to a string quartet arrangement used for a 1995 wedding. Simon wrote: "Ned Battista is a huge Sousa fan and was incredulous that I knew of a piece he had never heard of before. Thanks to you and the National Geographic recording I heard as a teenager, this piece has lived on."[4]

Another letter (and unsolicited review) came from Larry Wittkugle, producer and host of *Heritage of the March*, a radio show out of Columbus, Ohio. He appreciated the album but not so much the cornet player: "I very much enjoyed your arrangements of Sousa's lesser known but charming songs. It is about time that we begin to see this kind of recording available to the general public. I thought that the band lacked spirit and drive on several of the marches. You really should have a long talk to the cornet player who screwed up his part in 'Semper Fidelis.' The intonation was dreadful. I would take away his horn and turn it into a cymbal. I hope that you can persuade National Geographic to expand on this recording perhaps to include other American composer(s) of band music."

When reminded of this review, Pursell laughed. He said that Wittkugle was highly critical, as are many Sousa devotees: "You have these aficionados, these people who take possession of the tradition of Sousa, and they're very uptight about everything. Well sure, what Raymond put together with me was a typical English band that played smoothly. They certainly didn't play in the tradition of Sousa. They played 'Stars and Stripes' as if they were playing it out on some kind of English island or something." Pursell remembers being told by some of these aficionados that he should have used a band in Detroit, which was purported to produce the "authentic" Sousa sound. But of course it was much cheaper to record in London. For projects like this one, practical matters outweighed the artistic, especially where money was concerned. But *On Parade* was an artistic success on many levels, regardless of the band style. Pursell's use of "Fall Tenderly Roses" was a unique touch and the medleys and interludes gave the album a coherent shape.

Pursell arranged one more album for *National Geographic*, *An American Christmas* (1977). His arrangement of "We Three Kings" on this album won him his second Grammy nomination, for Best Arrangement Accompanying Vocalist, in 1978. All three albums with *National Geographic* were successful, but Pursell would not be asked to make any more arrangements. According to him, John Lavery told him that they were too much of a commercial success, and *National Geographic*, as a non-profit organization, did not want to get into the record business. Pursell points out that the *National Geographic* offices were right across the street from the IRS building, and thinks that this might have made them nervous.

MCDONALD AND LITTLE

Throughout the 1970s and into the 1980s, Pursell did several projects with the advertising firm McDonald and Little. He wrote and recorded the music for an industrial propaganda film for Coca-Cola called "A Decent Thing, Honestly Made." He wrote music for television commercials for Busch Gardens, Fresca, Golden Flake Chips, Busch beer, Coca-Cola, and Sabena Airlines.[5] In the 2000s, he would compose the music for a network television film, *A Time to Heal*. All of these projects provided necessary income to help support his family, and were undertaken at the same time as he was composing classical music, performing with the Nashville Symphony, and, by 1980, embarking on a new career as a college instructor.

BELMONT COLLEGE

In the late 1970s, one of Pursell's studio jobs was working as an arranger for the choral conductor Buryl Red. Two Belmont College faculty, Jerry Warren and Jay Collins, were on the same sessions. Jay Collins taught in the business school, and Jerry Warren was head of the Department of Fine Arts. As Pursell remembers it, Collins encouraged Warren to consider Pursell for a faculty position (Warren does not remember this). Warren had recently launched a new Bachelor of Music degree in Commercial Music and was on the lookout for new faculty, and Pursell was an obvious choice. He remembers that Pursell was "one of a kind, very unique. We were very fortunate to get him. And I think it's been good for him too."

Pursell began as full-time Belmont faculty in January 1980. He says that his wife "went out into the front yard and offered a silent prayer of thanks that I took the job." Finally he would have a steady paycheck, and medical insurance. Julie Pursell remembers: "I was so relieved he had a regular paycheck, because you're always dependent on the phone to ring. That's an uneasy feeling, when you have a family of seven people." Bill and Julie were raising five children, one from Pursell's second marriage (Shari), two from Julie's first marriage (Ellen and Margaret), and two of their own (Bill and Laura). This was a lot of mouths to feed, and they had bought a large home in the Berry Hill section of Nashville. To help support their large family, Julie worked full time as a reporter for the *Tennessean* and later as a speechwriter for the mayor of Nashville.

The home on Curtiswood Lane. Photograph by Showcase Photographers

The job offer from Belmont came at the right time for Pursell. He remembers that the decision seemed pretty clear to him: "The recording business in the late 1970s was a heck of a lot different than when I came here in the 1960s. I wasn't really working a lot in Nashville. I was going over to London about five times a year, just doing, coming in, and doing an album, for different people in the country, and then come home. It was sort of a gypsy life really. I loved working in London. I think I was getting a little tired of doing things over the phone, and waiting for the phone to ring for the next job. I figured then, why not start teaching, why not get into using the degrees that I had?"

Pursell was hired as an associate professor and was given a tiny office in the basement of the fine arts building. He taught the History of Commercial Music his first semester at Belmont, and taught it every semester until his retirement in May 2017. He also taught music theory, commercial music theory, composition, counterpoint, and orchestration. At the time, Belmont was a small school with a growing music program, nothing like the powerhouse schools that Pursell had attended as a student, but it was a return to the academic music life, and a welcome one. Over the years, Pursell would enjoy a period of incredible growth for the Belmont School of Music. When Pursell was hired in 1980, there were 155 music majors.

By the fall of 2014, Belmont College had become Belmont University and there were over 700 music majors (Shadinger 2016).

Pursell's presence on the music faculty was a key part of the development and growth of the new degree in commercial music. Belmont had offered a Bachelor of Business Administration in Music Business since the early 1970s, but Warren began to notice that many of the students who entered that program wanted to be performers. So in 1977, planning began for a music major in commercial music, and the new program was launched in 1978. Pursell was one of a crucial cohort hired in the early 1980s, along with John Pell, Jay Collins, Roy Vogt, Michael Harrington, Rachel Lebon, John Arnn, and Jeannine Walker (Shadinger 2016, 102). Many other commercial faculty were hired on a part-time, adjunct basis, but the above were all full-time positions. And where it was the norm at the time for a commercial music program at a university to focus on jazz, Belmont offered study in a range of styles, from pop to country to jazz to bluegrass. Belmont was, and remains, a unique place that embraces a diversity of musical styles, an ideal match for Pursell, whose musical life made that a regular practice.

Taking the job at Belmont did not mean that Pursell completely abandoned his life as an arranger and producer. He continued to record in London, traveling there several times a year for various projects. He would find someone to cover his classes while he was gone. After some years, this got to be more trouble than it was worth, and Pursell decided to discontinue his London work sometime in the 1990s. He did occasionally take on arranging and composing jobs that he could do from Nashville, such as advertising jingles, film and television music, and orchestral arrangements for various albums.

The Belmont job (and perhaps the steady paycheck that came with it) renewed in Pursell a desire to compose classical music. Pursell remembers: "One of the good things about teaching at Belmont was that it got me back into composition again." He had been working with the Nashville Symphony on an occasional basis since his arrival in Nashville, as recounted in chapter 7, and the 1980s saw the birth of many of Pursell's mature classical compositions, including his Piano Sonata No. 2, the *Homecoming Overture*, and his Symphony No. 2.

MEMPHIS MEDLEY

In 1982, not long after he was hired at Belmont, Pursell received an unusual request from the governor of Tennessee, Lamar Alexander. The governor asked Pursell to help him arrange some popular works for piano that Alexander himself would then perform in Memphis for a Sunset Symphony Concert as the "Memphis Medley." He even helped him choreograph his performance. As the review of the concert said, "When the end came to a Jerry Lee Lewis medley, Lamar Alexander's music was scattered on the stage, his bowtie was hanging from his neck, the piano stool was on its side and the audience was screaming for more. If only the election could have been held last night."[6] After his performance and return to Nashville, Alexander was effusive with his praise. In a thank you letter dated June 14, he writes: "I know you spent a great deal of time on it when you could have been doing other things, but I want you to know that your hard work helped provide me with one of the most extraordinary experiences of my life. The arrangement is perfect. I can't imagine anything that could have been received in a more spectacular fashion. Thank you for all you did."[7] Pursell had the gratitude and goodwill of the governor (and future senator) of Tennessee. Perhaps Alexander was familiar with Pursell's work with the Nashville Symphony; Pursell does not know why or how the governor came to him to make these arrangements. But surely his reputation as a hard worker and skilled and versatile musician served him well here. Pursell had become the go-to guy, even for the governor.

TMTA COMPOSER OF THE YEAR

In 1985 the Tennessee Music Teachers Association named Pursell Composer of the Year. The award came with a commission for a new piece (he composed a Piano Sonata) and the chance at the national Composer of the Year award, which he did not receive. Pursell's Piano Sonata No. 2 was performed at the state convention in June 1985. He received letters of congratulations from Tennessee state senator Douglas Henry Jr.; Nashville mayor Richard Fulton; and Belmont chancellor (and future president) Herbert Gabhart.[8]

Not long after he began teaching at Belmont, Pursell also received a commission to cowrite the incidental music for a play, *The Towers of the*

Brazos, written to celebrate Baylor University's history. His co-composers were Kurt Kaiser, with whom he had done so much work for Word Records, and Ted Nichols, who taught at the Western Conservative Baptist Theological Seminary in Oregon. Pursell wrote the Overture, an Entr'acte, and nineteen cues for the play.[9] It was performed at Waco Hall on Baylor's campus on February 2, 4, 5, and 6, 1982, with Pursell as featured pianist. The review of the play in the *Waco Tribune-Herald* singled out Pursell's overture as one of the most memorable musical moments of the performance.[10]

At Belmont, Pursell also began to compose and arrange works for his fellow faculty members. *The Duel* (1985) is a miniature opera for two voices, written for Linda Ford and Sherry Kelly. The opera is based on a poem by Eugene Field, also titled "The Duel" but commonly known as "The Gingham Dog and the Calico Cat." The sung melodies are tuneful and the voices often cross and move in thirds and sixths, while the accompaniment is angular and sporadic. The marked contrast between the vocal lines and the accompaniment highlights the absurdity of the poem, which Pursell edited slightly for effect:

> The gingham dog and the calico cat
> Side by side on the table sat.
> 'Twas half past twelve and (what do you think!)
> Nor one nor t'other had slept a wink!
>   The old Dutch clock and the Chinese plate
>   Appeared to know as sure as fate
> There was going to be a terrible spat.

Pursell says that this mini-opera was never performed.

Today the opera exists as a piano/vocal manuscript in the Pursell archive. The piano part is sparse, with stacked third chords and leaping gestures, not atonal necessarily, but not terribly tonal either, in the post-tonal style of a Samuel Barber or Ned Rorem. The meter changes frequently, from 4/4 to 3/4 to 2/4, depending on the demands of the vocal part. Pursell kept closely to the spoken rhythm of the poem and set the voices with repeated-note phrases and some passages of spoken text, mostly when the poem turns to narration. The phrases chiefly ascend and end with rests, giving the entire work a disjunct, uneven feel, as befitting Field's poem. The two sopranos tend to begin their phrases in dialogue and end them singing together, as in:

Voice 1: The old Dutch clock
Voice 2: And the Chinese plate
Voice 1: Appeared
Together: To know as sure as fate.

The climax of the opera coincides with "They ate each other up," sung together over quartal chords in the piano and followed by an "Eeyuk!" in voice 2. They close by telling their audience that the Chinese clock told them so, "It told me." The piano postlude moves from pianissimo to fortissimo, with sustained chords in the left hand and rocking quartal figures in the right, to close with a fortissimo chord, B flat, C, D, and B flat.

Around the same time, Belmont School of Music dean Jerry Warren convinced Pursell to make a set of choral psalm arrangements for him too, and these became "Show Me, O Lord," "There Is a River, and "Arise, O Lord." "Show Me, O Lord" was published in 1985 by Laurel Press Choral Series. This was quite different from the work Pursell had been doing for Word throughout the 1970s, arranging hymns for chorus and orchestra with conventional melodies and traditional harmonies. "Show Me, O Lord" is a meditation on Psalm 39 for unaccompanied solo/alto/tenor/bass choir (SATB) with occasional mixed meter and harmonies that reach beyond the established key of C Minor. The eerie, modernist choral work is characterized by a short-long motive and sustained chords. The other two works were not published.[11]

The year 1985 was a fruitful one for Pursell, compositionally speaking. That year also saw commissions to write a Horn Trio and the *Homecoming Overture* for the Nashville Symphony. The Horn Trio was commissioned by Dr. William Ewers in honor of his ninety-year-old mother, who heard the work in its entirety in July. The work was also performed at Belmont in October.[12]

Pursell was initially hired by Belmont at the associate professor rank, without tenure.[13] After eight years of teaching he decided to apply for tenure, which was granted despite his lack of a completed doctoral degree.

PLATINUM

In late 1985, the Nashville Symphony embarked on an unprecedented project, to record an album of twenty country and popular songs that had hit platinum status on the charts (each selling over a million copies).

The symphony had made only one recording before, *Themes from the Great Symphonies* (Dot Records), in 1960.[14] A meeting to plan the concert and recording was held on December 24, and a small group of arrangers and symphony staffers discussed a list of potential guest performers to be invited, details about who would do the musical arrangements, who would plan the social aspects of the event, and so on.[15] Pursell attended this meeting and was involved in the event through its planning stages.[16]

The concert, which was billed as a benefit concert for the Nashville Symphony, was held on March 11, 1986. Buddy Killen, president of Tree International recording company, produced the event, and several music stars participated in the concert as soloists with the symphony: Chet Atkins, Charlie Daniels, Danny Davis, Mickey Gilley, Charlie McCoy, Ricky Skaggs, and of course, Bill Pursell. Pursell arranged two tunes for the event, "King of the Road" and "Shenandoah." His hit "Our Winter Love" was also featured on the concert, in his own arrangement and with Pursell himself playing piano. The songs were presented as a pops concert at the Tennessee Performing Arts Center downtown, and the concert was recorded digitally and later produced as an album.

Pursell heard from his friend Tony Migliori that Buddy Killen had been present at the final mixing session for the album. Migliori told Pursell that they had finished mixing and that he had said he thought they were done. But then Buddy said, "Wait a minute, no let's go back to the fifth take; I want to hear that. I want to hear the drums, because you know the melody is in the drums on that particular take." Migliori told Pursell that the assistant conductor began to say something (perhaps that drums are not melodic instruments), but that Tony kicked him under the table to silence him. Pursell's take on the matter is philosophical: "We have people in this town who were in the power positions that knew about as much as Bill Justis used to say, 'you know as much about music as my pet dog.'" Buddy Killen now has a famous namesake traffic circle in Nashville at the end of Music Row, complete with a (somewhat controversial) bronze sculpture by Alan LeQuire of nine naked dancing people called *Musica*.

The *Nashville Platinum* album, touted as a celebration of the Symphony's fortieth anniversary, was released in 1986 by Columbia. In the liner notes, Pursell is characterized as a Music Row pianist and symphony booster. His associate professor position at Belmont College is not mentioned. The album includes ten songs from the original concert of nineteen; "Our Winter Love" and "Shenandoah" made the cut. *Nashville Platinum* today is out of print, but copies can still be found. It is another example of the blending of the commercial and classical music worlds between which Pursell traveled so freely. And what better city than Nashville, Tennessee, Music City U.S.A., for a classical symphony to cut an album of orchestral arrangements of country hit tunes? And who better to take part in this project than Bill Pursell? Unfortunately, the high cost of the album would come back to haunt the Nashville Symphony.

HOMECOMING

Pursell's next project with the Nashville Symphony was a less adventurous commission. The symphony took part in the statewide "Homecoming '86" celebrations, and Pursell received a commission from the prominent Nashville patron of the arts, Martha Ingram, to write an overture for the symphony's concert "Prelude to Homecoming." Homecoming '86 was an effort by Tennessee governor Lamar Alexander to celebrate local history and culture, and hundreds of towns in Tennessee participated, with events such as folk song festivals, storytelling, and even a Sweet Tater Day.[17] Homecoming committees were approved on the state level, but all events were locally organized and supported. It was an opportunity for communities to clean up their parks and public spaces, and to celebrate their own local histories.

The "Prelude to Homecoming" concert was held in Nashville on December 3, 1985, and featured works by Tennessee composers. In addition to Pursell's *Tennessee Homecoming Overture*, there were pieces by John Work, a composer and musicologist at Fisk University ("Night in La Vallee"); Kenton Coe, composer ("Yellow Leaf," an aria from his opera *Rachel*); Kenneth Schermerhorn, artistic director of the Nashville Symphony (Jubilee); and arrangements of folk tunes by Associate Director Amerigo Marino. The symphony also performed the Largo and Finale from Antonin Dvorak's Symphony No. 9, "From the New World," a work well known for its use of southern American folk tunes.[18]

Pursell sought out native Tennessee music for his overture, and made use of four different spirituals in a three-part structure.[19] From the program notes:

> The first, heard just after the opening fanfare, is "Lay This Body Down." Found in a collection at Peabody [Nashville music academy], it contains songs used in the Fisk Jubilee Singers' fundraising tour of

the United States in the 1870s. It is joined in counterpoint with the spiritual "When the World Ketch Afire" from Barton, Tennessee. The second and third sections of the piece use two white spirituals from a 1937 collection notated by Lucien L. McDowell called "Songs of the Old Campground." Used for revival meetings in the 1800s, the old campground was a cemetery hill overlooking Hickory Nut and Gum Spring Mountains near Spring Hill. "Come Sing to Me of Heaven," the chief funeral hymn used at the old campground, is used in the central section of the overture. Pursell tries to capture the ghostly "lining-out" and "surging singing" styles used in the spiritual. The final section employs a more upbeat spiritual, "Promised Land."

Henry Arnold reviewed the concert for the *Banner*, and had this to say: "Pursell has created a thoroughly American sound that will likely assure an enduring popularity for the work not only here in Tennessee but throughout the country. It has all the right ingredients: profound brass fanfares, singable tunes, a rich orchestral texture, and the appealing clichés of percussive 'clip clops' and military snare drums."[20] He knew how to please his audience.

Pursell dedicated the overture to Lamar Alexander and the 95th General Assembly. This piece was in a different vein from some of his previous work for the Nashville Symphony, his orchestration of "Our Winter Love," his *Two Orchestral Impressions on Country Tunes*, and the arrangement of the *Star Trek* music. The *Tennessee Homecoming Overture* was a newly composed piece in the classical idiom, and was the first of Pursell's original compositions to appear outside the pops series. The "Prelude to Homecoming" concert was a special event outside the symphony's normal season, but it was clearly not a pops concert. His good relationships with the musical power brokers (and others) of Nashville were paying off; Pursell seemed to have become one of the people the symphony turned to when it needed a new classical work with local flavor. His next commission would be a complete symphony, to be performed during the regular concert season.

HERITAGE

In 1988 Victor S. Johnson, chairman emeritus of Aladdin Industries, decided to celebrate the 40th anniversary of his company's success in

Nashville with a gift to the city of a piece of music. Johnson approached Pursell with the idea of writing a piece that would include "all the various elements of music in Nashville." Thus, the commission came from Aladdin, but the piece was to be performed by the Nashville Symphony, as a gift to the city itself. Today Pursell laughs at this—how can a symphony be a gift? "How do you do that? Do they publish it down in the mayor's office?" Instead, District Attorney Tory Johnson later presented a score of the completed symphony to Mayor Bill Boner.[21] Pursell received a formal proclamation of thanks from the city.

There was only one problem with the commission: on February 3, 1988, the symphony voted to close its doors, due to a budget shortfall of $400,000, and cancelled its remaining seven concerts.[22] Pursell had a commission (for the following season), but no symphony to play it. The *Tennessean* noted that the commission "bears no relation to the future of the Nashville Symphony Orchestra," and quoted Pursell saying, "My job right now is to write it. We'll look at the question of getting it performed a little further down the line."[23] The commission came from Johnson, not the symphony, and Pursell got to work.

Extensive negotiations on how to save the symphony began, and the future of the ensemble was uncertain. The symphony filed for Chapter 11 bankruptcy protection in early June. An article in the *Belmont Vision* noted that almost one-third of its deficit of $400,000 had resulted from the *Nashville Platinum* album project, and that Bill Pursell, along with his then Belmont colleague, Jerry Warren, were recording radio public service announcements in support of the Nashville Symphony, for the organization Save the Symphony.[24] In May, Pursell received a thank-you note from Kathleen McCann: "I am writing on behalf of the entire Nashville Symphony Players Assembly. We wanted to express our sincere gratitude for your support during this very discouraging time. Your PSA [public service announcement] was an encouragement to all of us."[25]

The city of Nashville agreed to donate funds to the symphony, and after extensive union negotiations, they were able to return in November 1988 with a greatly reduced budget, season, and number of musicians (down to 70 full-time players from 86). The players also took a substantial salary cut (from $17,500 to $14,002).[26] Music director Kenneth Schermerhorn called the symphony's return "a vindication of a belief in Nashville," and they opened the season with a pops concert featuring the music of Sousa, Strauss, and Nashville's perennial favorite, Gershwin. After a short season on a tight budget, the symphony announced a small surplus.

The 1989–90 season that followed opened with a classical concert billed as "The Curtain Rises." An editorial in the *Tennessean* noted that the best news about this new season was that the symphony was back.[27] Pursell's Symphony No. 2, subtitled "The Heritage," opened the regular classical series on September 15 and 16, 1989, in War Memorial Auditorium. The work received substantial promotional attention in the press, with lengthy articles in both the *Banner* and the *Tennessean*.[28] Pursell is characterized in these features as a two-time Grammy nominee, an associate professor of music at Belmont University, and a local history buff. This is the first press attention that noted Pursell's university position (though he had held it since 1980), perhaps because this music was more "classical." Even if he himself barely acknowledged the classical/commercial music divide, the differences between the musical worlds emerge in the various portrayals of Pursell for his different projects with the symphony. There was no need to mention his academic credentials during his work on the *Platinum* album, but here was a commissioned work in the Beethovenian symphonic tradition. Studio producer Bill Justis might have called him "Vladibilly" (after the classical pianist Vladimir Horowitz) in the recording studio, but in symphony circles Pursell's educational credentials were desirable, even necessary, and his twenty years' experience in area recording studios made him a legitimate Nashville local.

Pursell was able to indulge his interest in Nashville history with the commission of "Heritage," which he planned as a traditional four-movement symphony. The first movement, "The United Electric Railway—1890," was inspired by Pursell's discovery of a late nineteenth-century photograph of an electric train car on West End Avenue. "I saw a picture of a trolley car coming up West End Avenue in 1892, and that blew my mind, because I love streetcars. I didn't know they had streetcars here. I got to studying about this and looking at it, and it's a description of the United Electric Railway System, here in Nashville. The music is very minimalistic sounding; you hear the car bouncing along."

Pursell did some research, and wrote in his program notes: "In the late 1800s, Nashville had a series of railway and trolley systems which were consolidated in 1890 to become the United Electric Railway. It became the most convenient way to get around Nashville and a model for other cities." He writes that riding the trolley car was often a social activity, that people struck up acquaintances, and sometimes even began love affairs there, thus the romantic lyricism of the middle of the movement. Pursell's love for trains did not begin in Nashville; frequent childhood visits to San

Decorated wagon at the Tennessee Centennial

Francisco and his memories of the steam train coming through Tulare engendered in him a love of trolley cars and trains from his earliest years. So it is fitting that he began his Second Symphony with a movement about trains. Pursell says that it is the closest thing to a minimalist piece that he ever wrote. The minimalist influence can be heard in the steady eighth-note motive in thirds that begins in the violas and is echoed in the cellos and bass. Pursell gives the movement a sense of urban busyness with wind flourishes above the motor rhythm, alternating between reedy punches and brass calls. The motor rhythm drops out for a brief B section, but returns at the end after a plaintive oboe solo and closes the movement.

The second movement, a waltz, is entitled "Centennial 1897" to commemorate Nashville's celebration of the Tennessee Centennial in that year. Pursell found a picture of what he thought was two young girls from Ward-Belmont College, which was at that time a finishing school, riding in a flower-covered wagon to the Centennial celebrations. Even the horse, Pursell noticed, had ribbons woven in his mane. "(The girls) both have parasols, and they look very young, just exactly as we have over at school, and they're on their way to the park. It was the same year that Brahms died, 1897, so there's a little Brahms in there." Pursell writes that he tried to make the music sound just a little like what those two girls might have heard on their way to the fair.

The movement opens with horn and glockenspiel solos, echoed by a clarinet and then a warm string melody. Pursell's skills in orchestration shine through in this second movement as they did in the first, but here the lyricism reflects a late nineteenth-century romantic feel, where the first movement was more modern. The lyrical melody connects to the first movement in its rising and falling thirds, echoing the motor motive. The harmonies and orchestration are lush and filmic. The strings dominate, with occasional violin and woodwind solos.

If you live in Nashville long enough, you will hear a ghost story. The third movement, "Aftermath—December 18, 1864," moves backwards in time a little further, to 1864, and the Civil War. Nashville was the site of a famous Civil War battle, and thousands of men died in a brutal Confederacy defeat. Pursell learned that most of the soldiers were very young, most of them in their teens, and so this movement is an elegy for them. Pursell's longtime Nashville residence on Curtiswood Lane rests on part of that battlefield, and he calls it hallowed ground. He and his children used to find spent shells and other detritus of war in their yard. There is some family history behind this movement.

One December, Pursell's stepdaughter, Ellen, came home from college for a visit, and was staying in an upstairs room. The next morning she told him that she had seen the house next door burning in the night, around 1:00 a.m. But the house was still there. Father and stepdaughter walked next door, and the neighbors were out of town, and the house was unharmed. This was on December 18.

Two years later, Pursell's son Bill was staying in the same room and also saw the house burning, around 1:00 a.m. also on December 18. Pursell remembers:

> This is interesting, because the Civil War battle was on Dec 15 and 16 in 1864, and Dec 18 is when they came in here and cleaned out, carried all the bodies back up into Nashville. So Bill, two years later, on the same day, at the same time in the morning, saw this fire out here, and this time it was a big bonfire. He had the feeling there was some activity around it. Go fast forward 3 or 4 or 5 years, when I would be working on the charts in the back room, and the alarms would go off. I would go upstairs to these electric clocks, and I would go up and turn them off. Though it was four o'clock in the morning, the clocks said 1:15. We started to put this together, and it turns out that possibly there was some kind of a message here, having to do

with the time that they came in here to take all of these people out, who had been killed right here in the front yard.

So I came across this idea for the third movement, of getting this two-note figure, which would be like a lost soul, a young man who had just been killed, who did not want to realize it, and all he wanted to do was go home. He's wandering around and he's thinking to himself, 'I want my Mom,' that kind of thing. So I fashioned this movement of this symphony, the third movement, to describe this wandering figure. Then it goes on into the movement of the people very sadly and stately carrying the people out of this area up to Nashville, to a place to put the bodies. I found myself, as I was composing the thing, getting more and more into the actual battle itself. The screaming shells and all that sort of thing. That's the reason for the third movement of that Second Symphony. It's all historic, and the fact that my family seems to have run into these things. Bill and Ellen both have seen, what would you call them, apparitions in uniforms? I don't know.

The two-note motive, a dotted quarter note E to an eighth note F, followed by a half note (or longer) F, is supported by sustained chords in the strings. A slight military tinge is given by dotted rhythms in the brass, and by occasional punctuation by the field drums. This movement, like the second movement, is string-dominated (strings are a specialty of Pursell's) and ends the same way it began, with a solo oboe, the instrument that traditionally signals death, repeating the two-note motive over sustained chords in the strings. A note on the manuscript says that Pursell completed this on September 2, 1989, at 2:45 a.m.

"The Ryman" is the fourth and final movement of the symphony, and a tribute to the famous Nashville landmark, built in 1892. Pursell recalls: "Now it's not the description of the Ryman as we know it; it's the one that was built for Sam Jones from Cartersville, who was the Methodist minister, that saved Colonel Tom Ryman. Colonel Tom built it; it was called the Union Gospel Tabernacle. Then later, they called it the Ryman Auditorium, because Colonel Ryman in 1914 was killed in a buggy accident, right outside where the train station was. I'm describing Sam Jones talking about perdition. That's what the last movement's about."

The auditorium was not just a place of worship; its central downtown location and acoustics soon made it one of the most popular concert halls in Nashville, hosting not only religious revivals, but Grand Ole Opry

The Ryman. Courtesy of Grand Ole Opry, LLC.

performances and countless types of music concerts. Pursell's music for this movement, with its rhythmic persistence, wide-open harmonies, and brass flourishes, is a reminder of the hall's origins and a tribute to American folk music. Upon hearing this movement, one might think of Aaron Copland's wide-open spaces. But it also has the spirit of a fanfare, with its quick tempo and frequent cadences. Pursell's orchestration again shines in this movement, as just about every wind instrument enjoys a featured passage. Here, though, the brass dominates. "The Ryman" almost sounds more like an overture, an opening rather than a finale. It is sufficiently grand and tonal to please Nashville concertgoers.

Pursell insisted on conducting his symphony himself at its premiere, and had made this a condition of his acceptance of the commission. When he had written the *Homecoming Overture* for the symphony, and was attending a rehearsal of the work, Schermerhorn had asked Pursell for advice on balance and tempo. However, Pursell remembers that when he got up to the stage and started to discuss his ideas, Schermerhorn rushed him along, saying that he didn't have much time (this might not surprise anyone who has enjoyed conversations with the garrulous Pursell). Pursell did not want that to happen with his Second Symphony, and so he made sure that he would conduct this work himself. Later, when the Symphony performed the piece at one of their park concerts, with Schermerhorn conducting, Pursell admitted that he liked Schermerhorn's tempos better than his own, and told him so. He thought it was a better performance than the premiere had been.[29]

The other pieces on the September 1989 program were both by Mozart, the Overture to *The Marriage of Figaro* and the Flute Concerto No. 1, played by James Galway. That the symphony could afford a prominent guest artist was a sure sign of its return to fiscal health. Pursell had known Galway, the world-renowned flutist, for some time before they shared a concert with the symphony at War Memorial Auditorium. Galway had come to Nashville in years past to make recordings, and he and Pursell got to be good friends. Galway visited Pursell's house on Curtiswood Lane several times, one time even forgetting his gold flute there (and calling in a panic to retrieve it). He asked Pursell to write something for him, and Pursell began to compose a Suite for Flute and Piano, but it was never finished. He later made an arrangement of the song "Don't It Make My Brown Eyes Blue" for flute and piano for Galway.

The concert review by Jerome Reed in the *Tennessean* gave more attention to Galway's performance of Mozart than to Pursell's piece, but Reed did remark that the symphony was "very listenable," and that the most beautiful movement was the third movement. This slight, shallow mention seems almost an insult for a work that was a special commission for a local composer in honor of the city of Nashville, especially when one considers the amount of attention Pursell had received for his performances with the symphony in the 1960s, and all of the promotion that this premiere had received before the concert. Whether this was the result of a starstruck reviewer, dissatisfaction with Pursell's symphony on his part and a reluctance to criticize a well-publicized piece, or an editorial decision that "The Heritage" had already gotten enough attention is unclear. In spite of this, the concert was a success, and for Pursell an opportunity to exercise his compositional and orchestration skills in a full-length classical work in the Beethovenian symphonic tradition.

Pursell's decades-long relationship with the Nashville Symphony Orchestra reflected his comfort in diverse musical settings, classical and popular. He performed George Gershwin's *Rhapsody in Blue* with them several times, under different conductors. *Rhapsody in Blue* itself crosses easily between the classical and popular musical worlds, its status as a piano concerto, a classical genre, blending with its use of jazzy rhythms and harmonies. The work often appeared on Nashville Symphony pops concerts alongside Broadway songs and other works in the popular style.

Left to right: Kenneth Schermerhorn, music director and conductor of the Nashville Symphony; William Pursell; Mayor Bill Boner; Victor S. Johnson III, vice chairman of Aladdin Industries; David Wilson, chairman, Tennessee Performing Arts Foundation; Ben Rechter, president-elect, Nashville Symphony Board of Directors

Pursell, now in his early nineties, can still play the piece at any given moment, and he can also play the Rachmaninoff Third Piano Concerto with ease. For the Nashville Symphony, Pursell also wrote commissions on everything from arrangements of country tunes to an original classical symphony, and even, as a representative of the Nashville recording scene, served as their public advocate. Newspaper articles that announced his collaborations with the symphony mentioned both his classical training at the prestigious schools, the Peabody Conservatory and the Eastman School of Music, and his active life in the Nashville recording industry, as he worked with big stars like Johnny Cash and Patsy Cline. Even this small section of his musical life betrays the weakness of the division between the musical labels "classical" and "commercial" or "popular." For Pursell, it was all music, and a way to earn a living.

Like the Cumberland River, the crooked river of Pursell's musical life made a full arc around downtown Nashville and touched just about every corner of the musical life of Music City U.S.A. During his years in Nashville, Pursell had a hand in just about every aspect of American musical life, from jingles to religious albums to classical concerts. His music traveled from Nashville to London and around the world, one success after another, but always down a different bend.

9. DR. PURSELL

From the late 1980s, Pursell settled into a routine as a university professor, worked to finish his doctorate degree, and continued to make an extraordinary variety of music. At a time when many might have been looking forward to a not-too-distant retirement, he was just gaining momentum.

Pursell's work as a freelance musician brought him into contact with all kinds of interesting people. When he used the same studio over a long period of time, such as the Anvil Studio in London, he not only met new people; he got to know others quite well. John Williams is just one example. Ken Medema and Kurt Kaiser are others. These relationships brought him more work and often turned into lifelong friendships. Pursell's connections in the music industry led eventually to invitations for membership in some of the most exclusive clubs in the world: the Savage Club in London and the Bohemian Club in San Francisco. Most people don't even know these clubs exist, but their membership includes some of the most powerful men in the world. His membership in these clubs was a direct result of his music making. Pursell was invited to visit the Bohemian Club in 1986 to help with the musical productions here, and after rendering a great deal of service to the club in the form of gratis orchestrations and performances, was invited to become a member.

The Bohemian Club was founded in 1872 by a group of California journalists who wanted to promote appreciation of the arts. Based in San Francisco, the Bohemian Club is known as a refuge for some of the most powerful members of American society, including George Bush and George W. Bush, Newt Gingrich, William F. Buckley, Henry Kissinger, George Schulz, David Rockefeller, and Arthur Schlesinger. Author Allan Drury (*Advise and Consent*) was also a member. Pursell remembers seeing George Bush (Senior), Ronald Reagan, and Gerald Ford all together one summer at the Bohemian Grove. Pursell, a staunch Democrat, laughingly calls it a Republican stronghold, though there is some degree of political diversity in its membership. Like the Savage Club, the Bohemian Club supports artistic life, so there were also many who were members by virtue of their artistic abilities. The filmmaker Ken Burns was a guest at the

Grove in the summer of 2012. Sergei Rachmaninoff also visited and played there, though he was not a member. Both the Bohemian and Savage Clubs have a vested interest in welcoming artists—they pay their dues, meet the bar minimum, pay for their dinners, and provide professional-level entertainment for no fee. And though the membership of both is strictly limited to men, they host regular ladies' nights so that the wives can satisfy at least a little of their curiosity about the goings-on.

The Bohemian Club has a building in San Francisco on Post and Taylor Street, called the City Club. The dining room and library there host dinners, luncheons, theme nights, concerts, and holiday parties throughout the year. There are also hotel-like rooms for members to stay in when they are in town. But the Bohemian Grove, set in ancient California redwoods, is the heart of the Bohemian Club, and is what distinguishes it from any other exclusive gentlemen's club. Pursell's summer visits to the Bohemian Grove were both the source of his eventual membership and the basis of many close friendships and a real sense of connection to Bohemian life.

Every July, Bohemians from far and wide travel north from San Francisco to the Grove, a large campground set within a redwood forest. The camp used to have its own rail line that would bring members up from San Francisco. Now members drive or are flown up in a private jet owned by a Bohemian for a nominal fee. Each Bohemian has a home "camp," which is essentially a place to relax, sleep, and drink. The camps have witty names, such as Tunerville, where the orchestra musicians stay, and Hill Billies, the home camp of the Bush men and other Republican dignitaries.

Pursell was adopted into the Totem In camp, which is also known as a camp for accomplished musicians and artists. The Totem In camp features a stage with two Steinway grand pianos. The Aviary camp is for the singers. Some of the other camp names are: Valhalla, Whoo Cares, Wild Oats, Wohwohno, Woff, and Derelicts.[1] The camps are each autonomous, and the facilities vary widely from one camp to another, depending upon the wealth of its members. In general, the barracks are very comfortable, and the bars are well stocked. Open-top buses travel the Grove all day, transporting men from camp to camp.

The symbol of the Bohemian Club is the owl, and the Grove season opens with the "Cremation of Care," at which a giant owl appears and a giant dummy, representing the cares of the outside world, is burnt. This particular ceremony has been the subject of prurient attention by the press, which tends to portray it as some sort of Satanic ritual.[2] Pursell wrote the music for the ceremony one summer in the early 1990s. He points out that the purpose of this ceremony is to say farewell to the outside world, so that the men can enjoy their time in the forest. Pursell also says that this is not a dangerous ritual, just a harmless gathering of "a bunch of old men with hearing aids." These men, mostly highly placed in society, come to the Grove to drink, laugh, socialize, and to forget about the high seriousness of their lives for a time. It is a treasured refuge and a safe retreat.

The Bohemian motto, "Weaving spiders come not here," makes explicit the informal nature of the camp—no business is supposed to be conducted, although Pursell says that important deals are certainly made there from time to time. The most famous of these deals was the birth of the Manhattan Project in 1939, from a meeting convened with Luis Alvarez, J. Robert Oppenheimer, and other scientists in the French Chalet at the end of River Road in the Bohemian Grove. Yes, the atomic bomb got its start at the Grove, a story much beloved in Bohemian lore.

The main events of the summer encampment, after the Cremation of Care, are an orchestra concert, a band concert, the Low Jinks (comic theater), a concert by the Jinks band, and the Grove Play. Considerable resources are used for these entertainments; Pursell thinks that the costumes for each Grove Play alone cost upwards of $100,000 each year.[3] The Grove Play always is newly composed (both script and music), performed by area professional musicians (all of them Bohemians), and lavishly staged. Typical topics remind one of seventeenth-century Roman operas—stories from antiquity and the Bible, characters mythological and historical. And as was common in early theatricals, including the plays of Shakespeare, males play all of the female characters, due to the men-only nature of the camp. Pursell's first musical contributions to the Grove's extensive musical offerings were performances on the evening concerts and impromptu jam sessions with fellow pianists, but he did write the music for an entire Grove Play in 1990, *The Prophecy*.

Pursell's first visit to the Grove was in the summer of 1986, when he participated in a Saturday night musical show. Beverly Landstreet, a close family friend in Nashville, invited him to attend as a guest. When he told Pursell, a working musician, that he would not be paid for his performance, and that the club would not pay for his plane ticket to California, Pursell thought this was so crazy that he just had to go. At concerts there, he performed his Second Piano Sonata and his record hit "Our Winter Love."[4] His performances must have been well received, for a letter from

Pursell (right) performing at The Grove

Bohemian (and Postmaster General) Robert Setrakian said, "I hope the ovation received at the Last Saturday Night gave you some indication of the pleasure you bestowed on all of us. My little Spinet at Bald Eagle Camp never sounded so good."[5]

Pursell was invited back to the Grove as a guest for the 1987 encampment, and he served as the orchestrator (also on a volunteer basis) for the Grove Play of that year, *Talleyrand*.[6] In 1988 Pursell was asked to do more arrangements for the Low Jinks show, and returned for a third time as a guest. After this visit, Stuart Morshead (then captain of Totem In) and John O'Connor (husband of Supreme Court Justice Sandra Day O'Connor) sponsored Pursell in an application for membership in the club. Their letters, and those of two other members (James D. Walters and D. Griffith Harries III), mention Pursell's virtuosity and versatility as a pianist and composer, and his all-around personable nature.

From these letters, it is clear that Pursell's musical skills helped him gain notice at the club, and his convivial personality sealed the deal. Harries, who is referred to as "waffle fingers Harries" in a letter from another Bohemian, wrote that Pursell "wowed the audience" on his first visit to the Grove, has done a large amount of work for Grove music since, and is "a tremendously great guy."[7] Another letter from James D. Walters called Pursell "without peer . . . an enormous talent . . . willing to give far more than he takes... already a major contributor to the Grove and City Club productions... and, a wonderful, congenial human being to boot!"[8] The letters mention fun times spent hopping from camp to camp, weekend visits during the year, and friendships gained. Pursell seems to have managed to have a good time but also to make himself available for spontaneous musical evenings and much work as an orchestrator and composer.

Pursell was given associate (nonresident) membership, which gave him a significant fee discount but also obligated him to contribute to the musical life of the encampment each summer through providing orchestrations, new music, or performances. He maintained this status for twenty years, and in 2009 was granted honorary membership, which freed him from any professional (musical) obligations at the Grove, and he could simply visit and enjoy the retreat. In the summer of 2013, Pursell was honored by a "Munch-In Brunch-In Memorial Lunch-In: A Special Program in Recognition of Bill Pursell." Many of his compositions were performed, and Pursell himself played some selections on the piano. The poster for the event featured images of album covers and described Pursell as "Bohemian, Californian, Student, Professor, Composer, Writer, Performer, Husband, Dad, and Campmate." Pursell was eighty-seven years old at the time, and thoroughly enjoyed himself.

The most significant musical contribution Pursell made to the Bohemian Grove was the 1990 play *The Prophecy*. J. Thomas Rosch and Peter Arnott wrote the book, and Pursell composed all-original music for the production.[9] The play tells the story (taken from the Hebrew Bible) of Saul, Jonathan, David, and Goliath. Rosch describes the production at the Grove as "thoroughly professional," utilizing seventy professional musicians in the orchestra and principals from the San Francisco Opera and Symphony Chorus.[10] The cast list separates the chorus into a Tabernacle Choir and "Villagers and Soldiers," and members of the various Bohemian camps are listed as members of the twelve tribes of Israel.

An examination of the playbill, which includes extensive personnel lists that include dancers and Bohemians themselves, brings to mind the court ballets of Louis XIV, with extravagant costumes and sets, when the courtiers themselves would dress up and perform as part of the spectacle. The production of *The Prophecy* indeed seems every bit as extravagant as a French court drama would have been. The playbill also lists twelve set painters, thirteen members of the makeup crew, and a stage crew of fourteen. Considering that the spirit of levity prevailed at the Grove, the listing of so many crew members may have included encampment

Playbill for *The Prophecy*

guests or members who simply lent a hand at some point. Two of the stage crew bear the last name of Morshead, and it is hard to believe they are not related to the Stuart Morshead who sponsored Pursell's membership. Regardless, it is clear that the eighty-fifth Grove Play, *The Prophecy*, was the major event of the summer encampment, as the play usually is. Pursell's favorite piece of music from *The Prophecy* is his setting of Psalm 23, which ended the show. It is set for a baritone and tenor, and has been used for several Bohemian funerals since.

Pursell continued to provide music for various events, but his second significant contribution was the 1997 quasquicentennial Grove Play *Time and Again*, for which Pursell provided both arrangements and new music. This was "a compendium of highlights from Grove Plays over the years celebrating the 125th anniversary of The Bohemian Club."[11] *Time and Again* drew on choruses, solos, and small ensemble pieces from Grove Plays from 1970 (*The Bonny Cravat*) to 1996 (*Runnymeade*). Pursell

Official portrait of Pursell as a Grove Play composer. Courtesy of Phyllis Shuptine Best

conducted the orchestra in the production, and he remembers having to wear white gloves so that the orchestra could see his hands. The Play was always held outside, among the redwoods, and the musicians played up on a hill, with cordless microphones.

All of the music that Pursell composed for the Grove resides in the City Club library in San Francisco, available only to Bohemian Club members. The libretto of the play is sent out to all of the members, but the music remains unpublished and archived. A detailed history of the music of the Grove Plays has not yet been written for public eyes, and due to the private nature of the Club, may never be.

Pursell's musical contributions to Bohemian life were significant, both in terms of new compositions and service in orchestration and performance, and were as important a part of his musical life as his days in the Columbia studio. A Bohemian slogan is that "Midsummer sets us free from Dull Care." Although many of Pursell's hours in the Grove were spent doing the same work that he did at home as a professional musician, arranging, orchestrating, rehearsing, and performing, he does remember the Grove as a place where he could leave Dull Care (the worries of the working world) behind for a time.

FINISHING THE D.M.A.

After teaching at Belmont for several years, Pursell decided, with much encouragement from Jerry Warren and other colleagues, to finish his doctoral degree at the Eastman School of Music. He first got the idea from the then Eastman director Robert Freeman, whom he met at the Bohemian Grove in 1989. Freeman suggested that he finish the doctorate, and upon learning that Eastman would accept his coursework and only require comprehensive exams and a thesis, Pursell decided to push through and finish his D.M.A. in composition.

Belmont gave him a year of study leave (1992–93), and Pursell devoted himself to an intense study of music history. He remembers enjoying this year of study even more than he did as a student at Eastman. He had time to study, and was getting paid to do so. Normally, for a doctoral comprehensive exam, faculty members will give the student some sense of how to prepare, and the coursework would be fairly fresh in her mind. For Pursell, though, who had left Eastman over thirty years before, the task of preparing for comprehensive exams was very different and entirely self-directed. "I just went back and got all my outlines out, the Gleason outlines, and I must have used about twenty-two, twenty-three books. I was just diving in, studying." Eastman did send him a sample of an old exam, so he would be prepared for the format. Samuel Adler, a composer, was selected to be his major advisor.

Pursell was asked whether he wanted to take the new exam or the old exam, and he chose the new exam. He was asked to analyze some Wolf and Mahler songs. Unfortunately, his theoretical analysis techniques were not up to date (he was not very familiar with Schenkarian analysis, a method of analyzing music very much in vogue in the 1990s), and the theory professor failed him on that exam. He was then advised to switch to the old exam, and take it after a three-month period. He continued to study, and passed with distinction. Pursell remembers having to identify several music scores and recognized all but an Eliot Carter string quartet, which he identified through his signature technique of metric modulation. He completed his exams in 1993.[12]

Pursell was required to perform a solo piano recital as part of the completion of his degree. Pursell performed his recital on November 20, 1992, with works by Scarlatti, Mozart, Bach, Rachmaninoff, and Poulenc. He closed the recital with his own compositions, *Felis Domesticus* (from

Pursell in Tulare at the premiere of *Kaleidoscope*

his Peabody days) and Piano Sonata No. 2 (the work he had composed as Composer of the Year for TMTA).[13]

Pursell composed a piano concerto, *Kaleidoscope*, for his doctoral thesis. *Kaleidoscope* was not premiered until 2005 in Pursell's hometown of Tulare, California, on a concert by the Tulare County Symphony. The promotional article that appeared in the *Visalia Lifestyle Magazine* says (inaccurately) that it was a piece he composed in his spare time while teaching at Belmont and does not mention its role in Pursell receiving his doctorate. Pursell performed *Kaleidoscope* as piano soloist in Tulare; he also performed one of his perennial favorites, Gershwin's *Rhapsody in Blue*, at the concert.[14] In October 2012, the piano concerto received its Nashville premiere with the Belmont Symphony Orchestra, as part of a yearlong series of celebratory concerts for the opening of the new concert hall, the McAfee Concert Hall. Pursell's daughter Shari passed away unexpectedly just a week before the concert, but ever the professional musician, Pursell insisted on playing regardless, and he did. He later said that he was disappointed in his own performance as pianist, but in the circumstances, to play at all was a feat.

Manuscript page of *Kaleidoscope*

The "Performance Directions" at the beginning of the score to *Kaleidoscope* note that a tone row shapes the melodic and harmonic materials. A tone row is a linear statement of all twelve pitches in a particular order. Composers from the 1920s on have used tone rows as a way of structuring harmony without using major/minor scales or functional chords. The choice of a tone row by Pursell for his D.M.A. thesis makes perfect sense: even as late as the 1990s, the use of a tone row had serious academic connotations. Like Sam Adler, his thesis supervisor, Pursell chose to use a tone row in a more friendly way: rather than strict adherence to the order of the tone row, he used it as a guide to melodic shapes and chord structures. Thus, although *Kaleidoscope* uses a tone row, it is not, strictly speaking, a serial work. The tone row does mark it as a modernist, somewhat academic work.

The tone row is first stated in the French horn (his 2012 revision shifts this line to the English horn): D/B flat/D flat/E/E flat/C/G/A flat/C flat/A/G flat/F. The intervals in this row avoid the tritone, an interval commonly used in atonal composers. There are several minor thirds and half steps, and no perfect fifths. As the work progresses, one hears many quartal chords (chords based on the interval of a perfect fourth) that can be derived from the intervallic structure of the tone row.

Kaleidoscope is in three sections, following a typical ABA form. Pursell's instructions to the performer are that the A sections are played very strictly and the B section can have more rhythmic freedom and expressivity. Indeed, the A section is dominated by rapid sixteenth-note figures in the piano, echoed by sixteenth-note bursts (three or four notes) in the winds and strings. The B section is more lyrical, with sustained chords and reed (clarinet and oboe) solos. The pianist has a cadenza fairly early in the piece, at rehearsal C (measure 57), and another cadenza near the end of the B section, beginning at measure 195. A typical piano concerto would have a single cadenza, just about where Pursell's second cadenza appears; since *Kaleidoscope* is a single movement, the extra cadenza makes up for the lack of the two subsequent movements that a more traditional concerto would include.

Significantly, Pursell does not include any jazz or popular music references in *Kaleidoscope*. This choice highlights the purpose of this work—to complete a doctoral degree in music. Pursell must have felt himself to be under some level of constraint; this piece was for a grade, and a committee would evaluate its appropriateness as a culminating work. Pursell was not a typical D.M.A. student; he was well beyond his student years and had vastly more compositional tools at his disposal than a less experienced student might. These circumstances make *Kaleidoscope* stand out in his oeuvre—a purely academic work, but with plenty of the complexity in orchestration and musical thought that signify his ever-questing musical mind. But not a bit of influence from his years in the Nashville recording studios is allowed to peek through.

Pursell received his doctorate from the Eastman School of Music in 1995 and in doing so, completed a musical and educational journey he had begun in 1942 when he moved to Berkeley to study music with Elizabeth Simpson and then abandoned when he left the Eastman School of Music to go on the road with the Jerry Jaye Trio in 1956.[15] Along the way, he participated in just about every type of musical experience that life as a pianist and composer in America could offer. And although he would continue to compose, arrange charts, record, and perform from time to time, the great majority of his energies were now devoted to teaching, another bend in the crooked river of his musical life.

TEACHING

Pursell says that he likes to keep an open mind when a student brings him a new composition.

> First, I try to see what they've got; it's kind of like putting a stethoscope on somebody. A doctor will do that, put his stethoscope on you and he will listen really hard to see what your heart is doing, lub-dub-lub-dub. I believe that's the way to teach composition. I've studied with enough composition teachers in school to have seen the differences in the way they all approach it. Hanson's attitude was more or less, "What have you got?" He was open to it. But then on the other hand, with Wayne Barlow, who was very open to ideas and seemed to throw out little feelers and ideas that would help a student, say, "I've never thought of it that way before," this kind of thing. With me, I just simply don't make up my mind, when a student comes in.

Pursell disagrees with the schools of composition that are looking for a particular style or sound; he only wants to find what works for each composer. In this sense, his teaching philosophy mirrors his life as a

Pursell with Dean Freeman at his D.M.A. graduation from the Eastman School of Music

professional musician, embracing whatever comes and avoiding prejudice toward or against any particular musical style.

Pursell is a people person; he can talk to someone for hours, not only telling stories, but listening to those of his students. People fascinate him, and this is one thing that makes him an effective teacher. His strong sense of fair play also means that he does not insist on being right all of the time; rather, education is a process of discovery, and he and his students are partners on the journey. He asserts: "The trouble is, lots of times people will say, 'That's not right, this is right but that's not right.' Well my attitude is 'What isn't right? Why is it not right?' I don't believe in right and wrong in music. I believe in degrees of development in music, but there is no right or wrong in composition."

It is difficult to pin Pursell down on how to determine exactly what works and what doesn't in composition. His acute awareness of music history and changes in musical style and technique over the centuries gives him an appreciation of traditional styles but also of the important role innovation plays in musical change over time. Above all, there is craft.

Well, you build on things that have worked over a period of time. But on the other hand, somebody will jump up and say, "Why is that valid today? That craft? Why is it valid today?" So does that point to something inexorable that is a constant running truth that goes through centuries and centuries? Is that what we're talking about? I don't know. I think it's a very interesting idea. When you look at the *Pieta* of Michelangelo, I'm just astonished by the folds in the cloth, which looks nothing like marble. He makes it look like cloth. That was a technique that people knew in those days. If you look at *David*, you can marvel over that fact that that Carrara marble ended up looking like that. So that's a craft. And the Italians knew what it was and how to use it and what to do with it. So is there a kind of internal truth that exists whether you apply it to sculpture or to art or to music that we have to look at and say, "This is what we must go through before we even become great?" Is that a possibility? I don't know.

ADVICE

When asked if he has any advice for his students who are trying to make a life for themselves in the music business, Pursell says persistence is key. Most people in the music business will advise young musicians to make good contacts, and Pursell admits that most successful people will say they have succeeded because of the contacts that they have made. Connections and networking made a real difference in the crooked river of his own career. But Pursell cautions students that they must be prepared and competent: "If you know these people and you don't have your act together, it can be very embarrassing, especially because these people are expecting the best out of you. And they expect you to be able to total it up, and be able to deliver, and if you can't do that, you might as well just forget about the contacts, because these people are seeing people every day that really are good."

Pursell also firmly believes that talented young people should go to a big city, where there are not only the best teachers, but also the best places to perform, and people to listen. "I have no doubt in my mind that there are hundreds of prodigies in this country that simply are born in small towns and everybody regards them as extremely odd, because they could do this and that. But even the music teachers in those small towns aren't geared to giving them what they need as much as a person in New

York." Pursell is speaking here from his own experience, having grown up in a small town and then, upon arriving in Berkeley for advanced study, being told he was three years behind where he needed to be, and having to work twice as hard to catch up.

Another piece of advice Pursell offers to his students is to listen to the best music and the best performers of all styles, and learn from them. Careful listening is especially important when learning how to write for the orchestra, a skill that Pursell developed during his time in the Air Force. As an orchestration teacher, Pursell will bring music into his class and after listening together, he will ask his students what they notice.

> We were talking about the French horn, and I was saying that it was a straight horn without valves in the early days, you know, operating on a column of sound that was generated on the harmonic series. But at the same time, they had these little crooks that they would put in and change the column of air. So I played them this third movement of the Mozart Horn Concerto. I said, in those days, you were lucky if you could play a chromatic scale. Well, that concerto defied everything I said, because here's Mozart writing chromatic scales. So evidently he had a friend that must have been one hellacious horn player. It's all a common sense thing. Everything in orchestration, basically, you have to look at the century and the time that it occurred to realize that it mirrored pretty well what they had to work with at that time.

Close listening combined with historical awareness are just a matter of basic common sense to Pursell. If one writes for orchestra, there is so much to know.

Pursell had a great deal more at his disposal in his own century. He had not only the traditional classical orchestra, with its strings, winds, and percussion, but he also had instruments more commonly used in the commercial music world, electric guitar, bass, drum set, and an incredible variety of stylistic development through the years. Having been born in 1926, his lifetime coincided with the rise of popular music in America, and he somehow managed to take advantage of every kind of music that he encountered during his long and fruitful life. Pursell's diverse musical experiences from an early age gave him that rare ability to arrange and orchestrate in a variety of musical styles. And these skills, when he came to Nashville, made him an important figure in the rise of the Nashville Sound.

A Popular and Jazz Theory class at Belmont College, 1985

As a teacher, Pursell brought many experiences and skills to the table: a versatile and imposing piano technique, great facility in orchestration, a keen ear for music regardless of its style, and most importantly, a sense of comfort in whatever musical style students would bring to him. This was especially important when teaching at Belmont, whose mission is to value and nurture a diversity of musical styles. One student might have a strong classical background, and another might have grown up playing bluegrass with her family and not really knowing yet how to read music. The musical culture at Belmont allowed Pursell to fully explore and take advantage of a lifetime lived in classical, country, jazz, and other kinds of popular music, and share with students what he had learned along the way. This particular bend in the crooked river of Pursell's musical life took him in all of the various musical directions he had experienced during a lifetime of professional music making as a composer, arranger, orchestrator, and performer. The teaching position at Belmont brought everything together into one place, and allowed Pursell to pass on his skills to new generations.

THE VERY LAST DANCE HALL

In December 2014, at the Tracking Room recording studio in Nashville, Tennessee, I stood just behind Pursell in the piano booth, turning pages for him as he played his part for "The Very Last Dance Hall Left in L.A.," an original song that Bill, his daughter Laura, and his songwriter friend Fred Burch had written for his new album. The eighty-eight-year-old pianist banged out a funky rhythm at top volume, and I turned the pages quickly as he made his way through the chart. I didn't have earphones, so I could not hear the rest of the rhythm section, which had already been laid down, or the comments of the session leader. The Yamaha piano sounded too loud and rather harsh to me, as I looked through the soundproof windows toward the engineer's booth. But the music was lively, bright, and fun. Presumably the timbre would be edited in the mixing process. Maybe it sounded better through the microphone; I was a newcomer to the recording studio. I was surprised by how casually Pursell played through his part, throwing his hands and fingers every which way on the keys, not worried about subtleties of voicing or timbre. A few takes, and then they were on to the strings.

The album, also called *The Very Last Dance Hall Left in L.A.*, was released shortly after, and became available on Amazon and ITunes. It includes Bill, Laura, and Fred's original song, but also Pursell's arrangements of many country and jazz standards. His brother, Ray Clawson, financed the venture, and they had hopes that the album would make them some money.

The release party took place in the Tracking Room in May 2015, and Bill and Laura (with help from drummer Paul Leim and bassists Steve Mauldin and Jim Ferguson) performed several standards, country and jazz, and some of the songs that were on their album. But in spite of calls from the crowd to perform "The Very Last Dance Hall," they refused to do it, because they said, it needed all of the bells and whistles, winds and strings and other things. Their pick-up trio just wouldn't do it justice.

The song tells the story of a dance hall in Los Angeles that was closing that year, and Laura Pursell, who lives and works in L.A. in the music industry, says that it was indeed the very last dance hall left in L.A. She used to perform there. It's a tune that celebrates the music and the couples who came there regularly. One of the regulars, Roger, lost his wife, but still sat in the hall and listened to the music. The story is both sad and happy, full of loss and nostalgia but also joy and music.

Working at the Tracking Room, December 2014. Photographs by the author

Cover of *The Very Last Dance Hall Left in L.A.*

Laura Pursell told her audience at the release party in Nashville that the entire album seems to be about loss and grief, from "Strange," to "I Can't Help It (If I'm Still in Love with You)," to "If I Could Reach You." Her childhood home on Curtiswood Lane was sold in the summer of 2014, and that summer she moved back and forth from the recording studio, where she recorded the first three tunes of the album, to her home to help her parents pack up forty years of belongings. This album could very easily be seen as the end, the last father-daughter collaboration, the last time in the studio for William Pursell.

But it isn't. As of the summer of 2017, he is freshly retired from teaching but remains as active and energetic as ever. His opera, *Crooked River Town*, having been performed at Belmont in spring 2016, needs attention, and he has several other projects brewing. Age seems to be completely irrelevant for this man who has spent his life composing, performing, and arranging music. Musicians rarely retire; they may leave one job for another, but most never quit making music. Perhaps music is a fountain of youth, of sorts. Or maybe a river.

The crooked river of Pursell's musical life, meandering from classical piano music to rhythm and blues to disco and more, left behind a rich and varied legacy. It led Pursell far away from the conservatory environment that he had first encountered through his studies with Elizabeth Simpson in Berkeley, California, and then with Alexander Sklarewski at the Peabody Conservatory. It led him to military service in Washington, D.C., to clubs in Hagerstown, Maryland, and Boca Raton, Florida, and the recording studios of Nashville, Tennessee. Eventually, however, it led him back to the familiar institution of a university school of music, where he could share what he had learned with students eager to follow their own rivers.

POSTLUDE

Crooked River Town

On a hot July day, I am sitting in the front study of Bill's hundred-year-old house, and Bill is sitting at the piano. "How does your opera end?" I ask him. "Tell me about the final scene." Bill grabs the score, finds the right place, and begins to play and sing:

> And the General left with his guns that night,
> to turn the tide of insult to make a wrong so right.
> And Rachel howled a tune of sun and creek and moon,
> a lady so defiled, she saw her end begin too soon.

This "bluegrass opera" is Rachel's story much more than that of Andrew Jackson. The events take place before his inauguration as president and end with Rachel's death. *Crooked River* is a love story, and an odd one—Rachel's ex-husband haunts the lovers, but Jackson's rival seems to be the Poltroon rather than the Cuckold (the ex-husband).

In some ways, though, the opera is a classic tale of doomed love, because Rachel will not survive. From the opening scene, set in a Nashville tavern, Rachel's weakness from a heart condition is front and center. At the ball at the Hermitage (Andrew Jackson's home, which you can still visit today), she insists on dancing ("That Crooked River Bump") but faints from weakness. And Act I closes with a walk along the Cumberland by Rachel and her false friend, Missy Prissy (yes, that is her name), where Rachel sees "something" coming to carry her home, but Missy sees nothing. To a gentle Siciliano rhythm, Rachel sings and her words refer to the classic verses about Babylon and waters:

> Weeping we sit beside this river
> Thinking of Thee O Jerusalem.
> We have put away our lyres by hanging them

Pursell with the cast of *Crooked River Town*, Courtesy of Belmont University

Pursell and Fred Burch, watching the workshop premiere of *Crooked River Town*, Belmont University, April 11, 2016. Photograph by the author

on willow limbs O Jerusalem.
Has my savior come to take me
if it's so I pray I go

... and still Missy sees "nothing." This haunting music returns at the very end of the opera after her death.

At the end of Act II, General Andrew Jackson goes off to fight a duel with the Poltroon and Rachel waits with trepidation in her bedroom. Her doctor is with her, and her servant Hannah, and Missy Prissy, who is cruelly hoping the Poltroon will shoot Jackson. There are two knocks on the door, and both times Rachel thinks it is Death coming to get her. But the first time it is Red Eagle, who reports on the results of the duel—Jackson wounded, but the Poltroon killed. Behind a scrim, the audience sees the duel as Red Eagle narrates it to her, and the theme "guns, guns, guns" from Act I returns, in a slow 2/4 meter. Like the words, the harmony is simple, a straightforward F minor, nothing much outside the key. As Red Eagle announces the General has been shot but the Poltroon killed, the harmony becomes more agitated and dissonant and Missy's plan is foiled. After the Poltroon's death, the music returns to the plodding F minor chords, back and forth, back and forth, a poignant three-note motive, and the second knock on the door is heard.

It is Jackson himself, and Rachel falls into his arms, weak from her heart condition and worry. After a beautiful love duet (a reprise of "This Kiss" from Act I), she dies rather suddenly, and Jackson falls silent. The Cuckold, her ex-husband, enters and is quickly expelled from the room.

I get a little choked up every time I hear the music of the final scene. It introduces a plaintive three-note motive that winds around and around, through the sung music and the accompaniment, pulling everything together. There are melodies recalled from earlier moments in the opera, the "Guns, Guns, Guns" of the horse race, the love duet from the first act ("This Kiss"), the Cuckold's brazen, insane music, and Hannah's earthy lines. The melody from Rachel's Act I ghost vision scene rises in the harmonica, underpinned by the strings and the mandolin playing the love melody and the three-note death motive. Everything comes together here, including the bluegrass ensemble and the strings.

A skillful composer, Pursell draws together the various threads of the opera's story in the final scene. The main characters each get a say (except for the Poltroon, who is killed in the duel with Jackson), and at the very end, when Rachel dies, it is Missy Prissy, her jealous rival, who gets the

Hannah with a white apron; Missy Prissy with a parasol; Narrator with his guitar.
Courtesy of Belmont University

last word, reprising the end of Act I, when Rachel had a premonition of her death: "Weeping we sit beside the river," while the chorus of bluegrass girls sings over the sweet siciliano "I am His; I am ready." The key shifts from the F minor of the death scene to the original G major, the central key of *Crooked River*. This time, Missy Prissy sings that she *does* see something, and the audience sees Rachel standing behind a scrim, wearing the white dress she had planned for Jackson's inauguration. The bluegrass girls sing over the gentle siciliano rhythm "Yonder, yonder, yonder it gleams." The shift to G major evokes a spark of redemptive hope.

And the stage fades, and we are no longer listening to an opera, or even to a composer playing through his opera on the piano while roughly singing all of the parts. We are in Rachel's bedroom, mourning her passing with the rest of them.

At the very end, Pursell's music, like this opera, is not bluegrass, or opera, or rhythm and blues, or classical, or country. It is music. This is the story that he knows, the story that shaped his crooked river of a musical life, and the story of how a life in music can be shaped in twentieth-century America. Pursell's natural gifts, rigorous training, and a lifetime of hard work made him a versatile and prolific composer, arranger, and performer. The last act of *Crooked River Town* has been written, but it is not the last turn in the long and winding path Pursell has followed. I can't wait to see what lies around the next bend.

COMPOSITIONS

		(all unpublished unless noted)			
Year	Work	Genre/ instrumentation	Commission/ Dedication	Where composed or first performed	Notes
JUV	Encore Petite	Piano		Tulare	Juvenilia; brown spiral notebook
JUV	Lullaby	Piano		Tulare	Juvenilia; brown spiral notebook
JUV	Melody Fantasia, fragment	Piano		Tulare	Juvenilia; brown spiral notebook
JUV	Monk Dirge	Piano		Tulare	Juvenilia; brown spiral notebook
JUV	Rem (fragment, sketch)	Piano		Tulare	Juvenilia; brown spiral notebook
JUV	The Dead	Piano and voice		Tulare	Juvenilia; brown spiral notebook
1941	A Day in the City (opus III)	Piano		Berkeley	manuscript in archives; multiple copies
1941	The Dead	Lied		Tulare	Text by Stockman; prize-winning song
1941	Wanderer's Night Song	Lied		Tulare	Text by Goethe; prize-winning song
1943	A Dream	Piano		Tulare	Juvenilia; manuscript in archive
1943	Fragments from First Movement of a Piano Concerto	Piano Concerto		Berkeley	manuscript in archive; written during high school for fellow student Janice Whipple
1944?	Mad Player Piano	Piano		Tulare	Wrote at home in the summer
1944?	Waltz Conflict	Piano		Berkeley	
1945	Piano Sonata No. 1	Piano Sonata		Peabody	Composed at Peabody; first movement played at Town Hall, NYC by Shura Dvorine; only first movement finished

COMPOSITIONS

Year	Title	Type		Location	Notes
1950	Felis Domesticus	Piano		Peabody	1. Lost Kitten, 2. Siamese; Alfred Mouledous played at Town Hall, NYC; dedicated to Cecile Genhart
1951	Prelude and Toccata for Piano and Orchestra	Piano and Orchestra	Eastman	Rochester	Inscribed: "To Brother 'Daylight' From Brother 'Mohawk' Feb 27th 1951 in the year of our Landlord"
1952	Introduction and Toccata	Piano		Eastman	On a 9-tone scale, while studying with Howard Hanson
1953	Symphony No. 1	Symphony		Eastman (written)	Unfinished, I. (partial); II. Rondo (sketch); written under Hanson
1953	Three Biblical Scenes for Orchestra	Tone poems		Eastman	I. Christ Looking over Jerusalem; II. Suffer the Little Children; III. Trial, Crucifixion, Resurrection; manuscript of II in archive
1955	Bluebeard	Tone poem		Eastman	Unfinished manuscript of tone poem for orchestra
1960	Beatnik Beat	Piano		manuscript in archive	
1960?	Poem for Guitar on the Lullaby Theme "Hush My Babe"	Guitar		Nashville	manuscript in archive
1960/61	Poem for Guitar on the tune "Sweet William and Lovely Nancy"	Guitar	Chet Atkins	Nashville	Arrangement for guitar for Chet Atkins; manuscript in archive
1968	Two Symphonic Tone Poems	Tone poems; arrangements	Nashville Symphony, Thor Johnson	Nashville	1. Wabash Cannonball; 2. I Can't Help It If I'm Still in Love with You
1975	A Decent Thing, Honestly Made	Industrial Film	McDonald & Little; for Coca-Cola	Atlanta	Film, history of Coke commercials/original music and Coke themes; composed to play for Coke employees
1975	High Country	Television	McDonald & Little; for Coca-Cola	Birmingham	Original music, television use

COMPOSITIONS

Year	Title	Type	Commissioned by / For	Location	Notes
1975	Six Flags over Georgia	Theme park music	Six Flags	Nashville	Theme park music for the carousel
1976	Circus World	Theme park music	Ringling Bros.	Nashville	Pre-recorded music for Florida show
1977	Cypress Gardens Music	Theme park music	Cypress Gardens	London	Theme park music
1979	Montage on Three Gospel Tunes	Piano duet	Neilson and Young	Nashville	Composed for Neilson and Young, gospel piano duo team
1980	Sabina Airlines	Jingle	McDonald & Little	London	Original music, television and radio use
1982	Don't It Make My Brown Eyes Blue	Arrangement; piano and flute	James Galway	Nashville	Arrangement for James Galway, flute and piano, manuscript in archive
1982	The Towers of the Brazos	Incidental music	Baylor University	Waco, TX (Waco Hall, Baylor University)	Overture, Entr'acte, 19 cues for play; commissioned to celebrate Baylor's history, with Kurt Kaiser and Ted Nichols
1985	Concert Trio for Violin, French Horn, and Piano	Trio	Dr. William Ewers, for his mother	Nashville	1. Theme and Variations, 2. Largetto y Dolce, 3. Andantino y Rinforzando
1985	Homecoming Overture	Overture, symphonic	Nashville Symphony; Mr. and Mrs. E Bronson Ingram	Nashville	Dedicated to Lamar Alexander and members of 91st Tennessee General Assembly, 1985
1985	Piano Sonata No. 2	Piano Sonata	TMTA, Composer of the Year commission	Johnson City	1. Allegretto con Spirito; 2. Toccata
1985	The Duel	Chamber Opera	Linda Ford and Sherry Kelly	Nashville	Based on a poem of same name by Eugene Field; written for Belmont faculty colleagues
1985	Three Psalms for A Cappella Chorus	Choral	Belmont Chamber Singers	Nashville	Dedicated to Jerry Warren; 1. Show Me O Lord, 2. There Is a City; "Show Me" was published
1985?	Aprés Sergei R	Piano	Nashville	Planned companion piece (not done) Apres Sergei P	

COMPOSITIONS

1989	Symphony No. 2, "Heritage"	Symphony	Aladdin Industries, Victor Johnson	Nashville	I. The United Electric Railway—1890, II. Centennial 1897, III. Aftermath—December 18, 1864, IV. The Ryman; premiered by Nashville Symphony, Bill Pursell conducting
199?	The Four Seasons of Marrcrest	Orchestra	Daniel Landes, composer	Nashville	Orchestration for his colleague Daniel Landes; Robert Marler played piano
1990	The Prophecy	Grove Play music	Bohemian Club	Bohemian Grove	Pursell conducted its only performance at the Grove, outside San Francisco, California
1995	Kaleidoscope for Piano and Orchestra	Piano Concerto	DMA thesis work	Eastman/ Nashville	Single movement; doctoral thesis composition for Eastman D.M.A.
1997	Celebration Overture	Overture; orchestra	Dedicated to Dr. Robert Gregg and the Belmont Symphony Orchestra	Nashville	Dated 9/3/1997
2006	Paraphrase on a Mozart Minuet String Quartet in D K. 575	String Quartet	Elisabeth Small, Belmont	Nashville	Inscribed: "for Betty Small" (violinist)
2016	Crooked River Town	Opera	Nashville	Opera on the life of Andrew Jackson and Rachel Robards; first performance as a workshop by Belmont Opera, spring 2016	
<2016>	Busch Gardens	Theme park music	McDonald & Little	Nashville	Original music, television use
<2016>	Creomulsion	Radio music	Tucker-Wayne	Nashville	Original music, radio use
<2016>	Firestone	Television	Herston Ent	Nashville	Original music, television; Henry and Harvey series

<2016>	Laura's World	Song	Laura Pursell	Nashville	Planned suite for daughter; one piece in manuscript
<2016>	Our Lives, our Fortunes, our Sacred Honor	Incidental music	Word, Inc.	Los Angeles	Paul Harvey, speaker

*Pursell also composed several jingles for radio and television use through the early 1970s for the advertising firm McDonald & Little.

DISCOGRAPHY

Bill Pursell was a session musician, arranger, and producer on countless albums recorded in Nashville in the 1960s through the 2000s. Finding them all would be impossible, even if Nashville union records were available (for unknown reasons, in 1974 all of the union timesheets in Nashville were thrown out). The discography herein includes a selection of albums, using data from the Pursell archives, the Library of Congress Sonic database, and various websites. It includes all of his solo work and albums where he was the sole arranger or producer. Undated albums and selected 45s appear at the end of the list.

Year	Album	Artist	Studio	Catalog Number	Notes
1959	Music for Quiet Listening	Eastman-Rochester Orchestra	Mercury	MG 50053	Christ Looking over Jerusalem by Pursell; other composers including Ron Nelson, Kent Kennan, Wayne Barlow
1960	Subtle Swing	Hank Garland	Sundazed Studios	N-3901/3902	Bill Pursell, piano; jazz
1962	Our Winter Love/A Wound Time Can't Erase	Bill Pursell	Columbia	CW 281 163	45/Pursell single
1962	She's Got You/Strange/The Wayward Wind/So Strange It Hurts	Patsy Cline	Decca	ED 2719	Pursell, organ
1962	So Wrong/You're Stronger Than Me/Heartaches/Your Cheatin' Heart	Patsy Cline	Decca	ED 2729	Pursell, organ
1962	The Unforgettable Guitar of Hank Garland	Hank Garland	Columbia	CL 1913	small-group jazz; Pursell, piano

Year	Title	Artist	Label	Catalog	Notes
1963	Blood, Sweat, and Tears	Johnny Cash	Columbia	CS 8730	Pursell, piano
1963	Our Winter Love	Bill Pursell	Columbia	CS 8792	Pursell first solo album; reissued in 1992; this was the 1963 hit single and album
1963	Chasing the Dream	Bill Pursell	Columbia	CL 2077	Pursell second solo album
1963	Farewell to Adra/Pride	Bill Pursell	Columbia	4-42832	45/Produced by Don Law and Frank Jones
1963	Inverno/Dolce Stagione (Our Winter Love)	Bill Pursell	CBS	BA 121017	Italian 45/ Pursell single
1963	Loved/Stranger	Bill Pursell	Columbia	4-42780	45/Pursell single
1963	The Christmas Spirit	Johnny Cash	Columbia	CS 8917	Pursell, arranger, piano, organ
1963	Top Pops	Armed Forces	Armed Forces Radio and Television	RL 7-4	Pride by Pursell
1964	Crying	Bill Pursell	CBS	CBS 5939	Portugal release; Crying; I'll Never Be Free; Quiet Nights of Quiet Stars; You've Lost That Lovin' Feelin'
1964	Hip Boots!	Boots Randolph	Monument	MC 6601	Pursell, piano on most tracks; Produced by Fred Foster
1964	I'll Never Be Free/Crying	Bill Pursell	Columbia	4-43090	45/promo
1964	Orange Blossom Special	Johnny Cash	Columbia	9109	Pursell, piano; re-released in 2002
1965	A Remembered Love	Bill Pursell	Columbia	CL 2421	Pursell third solo album
1965	A Remembered Love: The Romantic Bill Pursell	Bill Pursell	Columbia	CS 9221	Canadian release of A Remembered Love
1965	Heartbeat/I'm in a Very Romantic Mood	Bill Pursell	Spar	9008	45/Pursell single
1965	I Walk the Line/Our Winter Love	Bill Pursell	Columbia	4-33077	45/Pursell single

1965	Quiet Nights of Quiet Stars/ You've Lost That Lovin' Feelin'	Bill Pursell	Columbia	4-43380		45/Pursell single
1965	Sings the Ballads of the True West	Johnny Cash	Columbia	CK 86789		Pursell on harpsichord for The Blizzard; Reissue 2002
1966	It's Superman/ Love Theme from Superman	Ned Odum Boys/Bill Pursell	Columbia	4-43570/4-43593		45/promo/Pursell, arranger
1966	Soul Shall It Be/ Love Theme From Superman	Bill Pursell	Columbia	zsp 113569/4-43593		45/Produced by Don Law and Frank Jones
1968	Funny How Time Slips Away/The Shadow of a Girl	Kathy Dee	Decca	32372		45/Bill Pursell, arranger
1968	The Nashville Guitars at Home	Various Nashville musicians	Monument	SLP 18093		Pursell, piano
1969	A Country Dream	Eric Andersen	Vanguard	VSD 6540		Pursell, piano on "Deborah," "I Love You," and "Devon, You Look Like Heaven"
1969	A Man Away from Home/I've Got Today to Live For	Van Trevor	Royal American	RA 283		45/ Pursell, arranger
1970	Heartbeat	Bill Pursell and the Nashville Sweat Band	Spar	9008		45/Northern Stomp
1970	Spend Some Time with Me	Pozo Seco	Certron	CS-7007		Pursell, piano
1970	You Can't Put the Leaves Back on the Trees/ Freedom Is America	Arthur Godfrey	MTA	MTA 175		45/ Pursell, arranger and conductor
1971	He Even Woke Me Up to Say Goodbye/	Lynn Anderson	Chart	5136		45/ Pursell, arranger
1971	Today	The Four Galileans	Canaan	CAS 9693		Pursell, organ; hymns
1972	Blues for Baby Jesus	Gary Mann	Educator and Executive Insurance	EE-101		Pursell, arranger, electric piano, organ, sleigh bells; Christmas album

Year	Title	Artist	Label	Catalog #	Notes
1972	Christmas with Gary Mann	Gary Mann	Educator and Executive Insurance	EE-102	Pursell, piano, electric piano, organ, sleigh bells; arranger, first four songs
1972	He's an Indian Cowboy in the Rodeo/Not the Lovin' Kind	Buffy Saint-Marie	Vanguard	VRS 35156	45/ Pursell, arranger
1972	Home Free	Dan Fogelberg	Columbia	PC 31751	Pursell, arranger "Hickory Grove"
1972	Show Me How to Love/ The Highway Narrows	Linda Willingham	Gallery	G-107	45/Pursell, producer and arranger
1972	Soft and Gentle/ Richer in Love	Harry Robbins	Royal American	RA 60	45/Pursell, producer and arranger
1973	The Century Men in Nashville	The Century Men	Broadman	CHM 82	Pursell, piano
1974	Hymns That Live	various	Tempo	R-7092	Pursell, orchestra arrangements
1974	Listen—The Music of Ken Medema	Ken Medema	Word	WST 8613	Pursell, arranger and conductor; first Grammy nomination
1974	Nostalgia	Young Church Singers	Word	WST 8610	Pursell, arranger and conductor; Rodeheaver publisher songs
1974	Raw Sugar/ Sweet Sauce/ Banana Pudd'n'	Al Hirt	Monument	KZ 32913	Pursell, piano
1975	Down Home Singing	Sego Brothers	Heart Warming Records	R3336	Pursell, piano
1975	Harpin' the Blues	Charlie McCoy	Monument	KZ 33802	Pursell, piano; arranger, "St. Louis Blues"
1975	Music for Quiet Listening	Eastman Orchestra	Eastman Rochester Archives	ERA 1003	Re-release of same title
1975	The Big Steel Guitar	Lloyd Green	Steel Guitar Record Club	4	Pursell, percussion
1975	The Longer I Serve Him	Kurt Kaiser	Word	WST 8671	Pursell arranger, piano

1976	Bill Pursell and the Nashville Sweat Band and Aides	Nashville Sweat Band	Alston Records	4405	TK Productions; pictures on album of all musicians working in the studio wearing "The Nashville Sweat Band" sweatshirts; CD now available, remastered
1976	Bump Me Baby (El Cumbanchero)/ Now	Bill Pursell and the Nashville Sweat Band and Aides	T.K. Disco	17	45/May be Mexican release? Produced by Gene Nash
1976	It Will Be Different the Next Time	Sego Brothers and Naomi	Heart Warming Records	R3433	Pursell, piano
1976	Lillie Knauls reaching	Lillie Knauls	Paragon	PR-33006	Pursell, conductor
1976	Nashville City Limits	Bill Pursell	Fonit Cetra	IS 20189	45/Italy release of Now and Déjà vu
1976	Now	Bill Pursell and the Nashville Sweat Band	RCA Victor	26.11.410	Disco album; also released as Quality2199X
1976	Now	Bill Pursell and the Nashville Sweat Band and Aides	Alston	3721	Released in the UK by Spark (SRL 1142); Netherlands by EMI (5C 006-97773)
1976	Troubadour	J.J. Cale	Shelter Records	6317 904	Pursell piano on "You Got Me On So Bad"
1977	Barbershop Days	Various artists	National Geographic	07798	Pursell, arranger and conductor; with SPEBSQUA (Society for the Preservation and Encouragement of Barbershop Quartet Singing in America, now Barbershop Harmony Society)
1977	An American Christmas	Various artists	National Geographic	07799	Pursell, arranger and conductor; second Grammy nomination
1977	Through the Eyes of Love	Ken Medema	Word	WSB-8748	Pursell, arranger and conductor; Recorded at Anvil Studio, Denham, England, Eric Tomlinson engineer (worked with John Williams on Star Wars films)

Year	Title	Artist	Label	Catalog #	Notes
1978	On Parade	Starburst Concert Band; New World Chamber Orchestra	National Geographic	07808	Pursell, arranger and conductor; National Geographic album on the music of John Philip Sousa; recorded at Anvil Studio, Denham, England
1978	Simply Beautiful	Bud Tutmarc	Word	WST-8802	Pursell, hymn arrangements
1980	Each Step of the Way	Westminster Symphonic Orchestra, Bill Pearson conductor	CMP Recordings	CMP-87906	Pursell, hymn arrangements
1980	Romans 8:28	Westminster Symphonic Orchestra	CMP Recordings	CMP-87916	Pursell, hymn arrangements
1980	Theme from a Summer Place/ Our Winter Love	Percy Faith and His Orchestra/Bill Pursell	Old Gold	9059	45/UK re-release
1982	A Part of Me	Kurt Kaiser	Word	WSB 8792	Pursell, orchestration
1982	Spirit Wings	Joni Eareckson	Word	WSB 8878	Pursell arranger (some tracks)
1982	The Wayward Wind	James Galway	RCA	AFL1-422	Pursell compositions "Winter Sunset," "Shaman"
1984	A Heritage in Hymns	Westminster Phil Orchestra; UM Festival Chorus	Light	LS-5832	Pursell, conductor and arranger
1986	George Beverly Shea and friends	Kurt Kaiser, conductor	Word	7-01-896010-X	Pursell's hymn arrangements
1986	Nashville Platinum	Nashville Symphony Orchestra, various artists	Columbia	CK 40440	Pursell, arranger "Shenandoah" and "Our Winter Love"
1991	The Patsy Cline Collection	Patsy Cline	MCA Records	MCAD4-10421	Compilation of recordings 1955–63; Pursell, organ
1993	Music to Remember	Various	Plymouth	3285-2	Compilation including "Our Winter Love"
1993	Those Wonderful Instrumentals	Various	K-Tel	3091-2	Compilation including "Our Winter Love"
1996	Symphonic Elvis	Memphis Symphony Orchestra	Teldec	4509-94573-2	Pursell, piano on "Are You Lonesome Tonight?"

DISCOGRAPHY

1998	The Essential Johnny Cash	Johnny Cash	Columbia	C3K 65557	Re-release; Pursell on tracks recorded in 1962
2000	The Guitar Legend: The RCA Years	Chet Atkins	Buddha	74465 99673 2	Compilation; Pursell, piano on "Early Times," "Satan's Doll," "So Rare"
2002	Four Seasons of Marrcrest	Chattanooga Symphony and Opera	Elephantr		Pursell orchestration of Dan Landes composition. Audio and enhanced CD-ROM. Bob Marler on piano.
2004	Romance in Paris	Various	Green Hill Productions	GHD 5390	Pursell, piano
2015	The Very Last Dance Hall Left in L.A.	Bill and Laura Pursell	Netcommusic		Pursell, piano and arranger; Steve Mauldin, producer; financed by brother Ray Clawson
2016	Millennium	Bill and Laura Pursell	Netcommusic		Pursell, piano and arranger; Standards, country and light rock; with Laura Pursell and various studio musicians
2016	A Remembered Love/Madrilena	Bill Pursell	Columbia	4-43255	45
2016	Almost There/ Almost There	Andy Williams	Columbia	4-43128	45/Pursell, arranger; Produced by Rob Mersey
2016	An Old Fashioned Nashville Christmas	The Music City Choir, Boots Randolph, and Bill Purcell [sic]	Halo	1002	Pursell, piano, arranger
2016	Becky Sings Until Then	Becky Lozano	Christian Faith Recordings	6703	Pursell, piano
2016	Bill Pursell at the Piano: The "In" Sound of Country and Western Music	Bill Pursell, solo piano	Spar	3010	Produced by William Beasley, recorded at Spar Studio
2016	Chapters/ Chapters	Bobby Hudson	Rhythmic Sound Productions	PRP-40372/ RSP-1000-B	45/Pursell produced, arranged, wrote liner notes; picture on back of album taken on Pursell's property, the old farm office porch

2016	Dark Alley/ Autumn Magic	Bill Pursell	Columbia	4-42876	45/Produced by Don Law and Frank Jones; Radio station copy
2016	Earl Gregory plays Somewhere My Love	Earl Gregory	Columbia		Pursell, piano, vibes, producer
2016	Emmons Guitar Inc.	Buddy Emmons	Emmons Guitar Inc.	ELP 1001	Pursell, piano
2016	Faded Love/I Really Don't Want to Know	Bill Pursell	Spar	9010	45/Pursell single
2016	Gonna Get On/ It's a Rainy World	Rob Chartier	Cinda	3102370	45/Pursell, arranger; produced by Chuck Cellman
2016	Heartbreaker/ Scandalous	Interludes	Valley Records	V 1005	late 1950s; Pursell, arranger
2016	I Was Born to Love You/ Heartbeat	Herbert Hunter/Bill Pursell	Spar	9009	45
2016	I'm a Freak for You/Gray Matter	Bobby Rock	Rhythmic Sound	RSP 2064	45/Pursell, arranger; produced by Bobby Rock
2016	I'm Coming Home/Storybook Castles	Larry Othello/ Diane Minor	LPS Records	R 1002/1003	45/Pursell, arranger, co-producer (with Jim Barkley)
2016	I'm from Missouri Too/ Nine Hundred Ties	The Don Cross Strings	Dearborn	ZTSC 141803	45/Pursell, arranger; produced by Howard White
2016	Let's Build a New World Now/ Wrapping Paper Dreams	Rob Chartier	Cinda	4102370	45/Pursell, arranger
2016	Never Let Freedom Die/ Guess Who's Happy at Home	Maureen Reagan	Lincoln Records	L-1004	45/Pursell, producer, arranger
2016	Never on Sunday/Brown Sugar	Bill Pursell	Epic	5-10148	45/promo record
2016	Our Winter Love/I Walk the Line	Bill Pursell	Columbia	4-32077	45
2016	Sandee's Prayer/ Storybook Castles	Diane Minor	LPS Records	R 1001/1003	45/Pursell, arranger, co-producer (with Jim Barkley)

2016	Sånger Vi Gårna Minns	Samuelsons	Pilot (5)	PLP 1014	Pursell, piano
2016	Sincerely/Snap Your Fingers	The Sinceres	Columbia	4-43110	45/Pursell played on this; radio station copy
2016	Sleep, Baby Sleep	Various artists	Columbia Special Products		Children's Album; Pursell, arranger, producer
2016	Storybook Castles/Pink Ice	Diane Minor/ Larry Othello	LPS Records	R 1004/1003	45/Pursell, arranger, co-producer (with Jim Barkley)
2016	Sunday in Madrid/Satin and Velvet	Bill Justis/Bill Pursell	Smash	S 1851	45/Instrumental; arranged by Bill Justis; "For Broadcast Only; Not for Sale"
2016	The Goodyears of Music	Bill Pursell	Radio Records	32194-4	Piano jazz album; Pursell, piano and Kurzweil; Buddy Harmon, drums; Craig Nelson, bass
2016	Train of Love/ Walk Easy, You're Stepping on my Heart	Janet Johnson and Anita Kerr Singers	Phil-Jam Records	1002	45/ Pursell, producer, arranger
2016	We've Got to Get It on Again	Addrisi Brothers	Columbia/ Blackwood Music Inc.	4-45521	45/ Pursell played on this; radio station copy
2016	What Went Wrong/A Woman's Hand	Jean Shepard	Capitol	2779	45/ Pursell, arranger
2016	When a Prayer Wings Its Way to Heaven/Symbol of Our Times	Jay Ferrell	J&J Records	804B-2914	45/ Pursell, arranger, producer
2016	Winter Waves/ Geary Street	Bill Pursell	Dot Records	45-17217	45/Produced by Buddy Killen

NOTES

INTRODUCTION

1. This lies in stark contrast to Charlie McCoy's career. Charlie McCoy is a virtuoso harmonica player and also plays guitar and sings. He is considered one of the "Nashville Cats." McCoy and Pursell both studied aural skills and theory with Madame René Longy, but Pursell says that McCoy carefully (and intentionally) concealed his formal musical training. "He had a game plan," Pursell says, and he certainly was able to quickly blend in to the Nashville scene, unlike Pursell. See McCoy's biography on the Country Music Hall of Fame and Museum, where McCoy was inducted in 2009.

2. You can find their live performance of this song for the 2000 Academy of Country Music award show on YouTube.

CHAPTER 1: CALIFORNIA CHILDHOOD

1. Locals pronounce "Tulare" to rhyme with the word "carry." Steinbeck even mentions Tulare in his novel.

2. William Pursell, autobiographical fragment, Biographies folder.

3. Letters from these institutions in the family archive attest to this.

4. Arthur Pursell described his wife this way in his autobiography.

5. Tulare Historical Museum, "Tulare History: Rankin Field." http://www.tularehistoricalmuseum.org/rankin.html. Accessed March 6, 2017.

6. Several recital programs with Miss Lee's studio survive in Pursell's childhood scrapbook, including a recital in 1937 where he played a Clementi Sonatina and in 1942 where he played the Rachmaninov Prelude in G Minor (among other selections).

7. "Elizabeth Simpson Presents an Afternoon of Piano Music," June 20, 1943/44?, Recital programs folder. This document lists three recitals, two of solo music and the third of piano concertos.

8. Name of composition teacher from "Scholastic Background and Professional Activities" (From Pursell's Belmont tenure application) in Biographies folder; name of harmony teacher from unidentified newspaper clipping on the May 28, 1944, recital, also Biographies folder.

9. Undated news clipping, Biographical Clippings folder; I assume that this is from the *Tulare Advance Register*, and it must be dated May 1944 because it mentions his parents leaving "this Friday" to attend his May 28 recital in Berkeley.

10. The chord pattern in the first several measures is I-VI-V$\flat$9.

11. "William Pursell to be Guest Soloist at Gavlan Symphony's Concert Here Saturday." Undated news clipping in Biographical Clippings file.

12. The recital program can be found in his childhood scrapbook.

13. *Tulare Advance-Register*, November 14, 1944, "Mattie's Midway: Orchestra Billed $6,000 for Piano." This symphony was founded by teenage co-conductors Aristotle Gravras and Kenneth Lange, and was only in existence from 1943–45 (Biographical Clippings folder). A clipping in Pursell's childhood scrapbook, also presumably from the *Advance Register*, describes the beginning of this youth orchestra. Pursell's performance took place during their second concert.

CHAPTER 2: TWO FATHERS

1. The boy was Henry Bramer's brother; Bill cannot remember his first name.

2. Clawson was convicted in 1952 and fled to Mexico, where he lived on a yacht for six years before returning to America and being met by FBI agents at the airport. For example, "FBI Arrests Fugitive L.A. Playboy Clawson," *Star News* (Southern California), August 21, 1959. The text of Clawson's self-written brief in appeal of this conviction is No. 13105, U.S. Ninth Circuit Court of Appeals, January 31, 1952.

3. From an unfinished attempt by Pursell to write about this experience. Three chapters exist (Raymond Clawson folder).

4. For example, he gives his mother's real and false names (Elinor Humphrey, Elinor Henry) and his birth father's real name (Raymond Clausen or Clawson), even though his mother's husband at the time of birth (Robert Humphrey) was listed as father on the birth certificate as Donald Humphrey. Several attempts at this letter are extant and remain in the Before Chuck folder in the William Pursell archives.

5. These documents are all found in the After Chuck folder, Pursell archives.

6. Pursell would later meet his half-brother, Russell, and become good friends with him.

7. Nancy O'Neill, note to Bill, Before Chuck folder.

8. Raymond entered San Quentin on June 22, 1927, and was given a twenty-year sentence on June 15, 1929, according to court documents. Meeting of the State Board of Prison Directors, June 15, 1929. Document in court documents folder, Raymond Clawson folder.

9. The brief and court record are today available on Amazon.com as part of their Making of Modern Law historical series. *Raymond W. Clawson, Petitioner, v. United States of America. U.S. Supreme Court Transcription of Record with Supporting Proceedings*. Gale, 2011. A copy of the original brief exists in the Pursell archive, *S.F. No. ____ In the Supreme Court of the State of California in the Matter of the Application of Raymond W. Clawson for a Writ of Habeas Corpus*, November 15, 1930.

10. "Parole Ruling Brings Joy to 3,000 Convicts," *Oakland Tribune*, February 2, 1930.

11. When cleaning out Pursell's basement in the summer of 2014, we came across a book-length tract on the dangers of alcohol in Arthur's papers. Pursell smiled and said, "That's my dad."

12. Eulogy, Tom Hennion, Arthur Pursell folder.

13. The history of the observatory can be found on their web page at http://tulareastro.org/about-us/history/. Accessed March 7, 2017.

14. Arthur's journal and letters from his soldier days, as well as pictures he took in France, survive and are a treasured part of the family archive.

15. *A Modern History of Tulare County* offers a biography of Arthur Pursell on pages 105–6. California State Archives, Sacramento, California.

16. Arthur's photo albums survive, replete with original photos of some of these extensive hikes. Pursell family archive.

CHAPTER 3: HIGH FLIGHT

1. Nabokov's autobiography, *Bagazh* (1975), paints a fascinating portrait of Russian émigré life in the United States in the mid-twentieth century.

2. Franz Bornschein, letter "To Whom It May Concern," January 8, 1946, Peabody folder.

3. It is likely that this recital took place in mid-November, because a letter from Arthur Pursell dated November 26, 1945, says "Congratulations on your successful recital!" Although Bill remembers playing on recitals constantly during his time at Peabody, it is likely that this recital is one he would have mentioned in a letter home.

4. Mme. Longy is a famed American pedagogue in music. Her father was the founder of the Longy School of Theory in Boston.

5. Arthur Pursell, letter to Bill Pursell, December 22, 1945.

6. I have reconstructed this timeline from letters to and from his parents, and the exact dates are unclear. Bill has told me that he enlisted well before Christmas 1945, but that he did not tell his parents until January.

7. Arthur Pursell, letter, November 7, 1945.

8. Arthur Pursell, letter, January 27, 1946.

9. Bill insists that he began military service on January 1, 1946, but his discharge papers list an enrollment date of February 18, 1946. He also remembers being discharged on January 1, 1949, but the date listed is February 17, 1949. The date "January 1, 1949" is typed on the document below his rank, Technical Sargent. What is clear is that he began military service in early 1946 and left in early 1949.

10. A letter from Bernie Lipshitz dated May 7, 1946, urges Bill to get the sample scores to Washington as soon as possible. (The letter also includes a mouth-watering description of the mess hall at Bolling Field, to encourage Bill even further.)

11. In 1973 a fire destroyed 75 percent of all Air Force personnel records for those discharged between September 25, 1947 and January 1, 1964, whose names follow alphabetically after Hubbard, James, E. Bill's records were in this group. The National Archives maintains information on this event at http://www.archives.gov/st-louis/military-personnel/fire-1973.html.

12. The U.S. Air Force Band maintains an archive in Washington, D.C., and lists several of Pursell's arrangements in their card catalog. There are also several uncatalogged boxes in a room; these likely contain many of Pursell's arrangements,

and perhaps those of Fred Kepner and Glenn Miller as well. Personal communication from Technical Sergeant Devon Landis, March 12, 2014.

13. The only recording of this piece that exists, as far as I have found, is an Air Force 33 rpm disc owned by Bill. It is a copy of a copy, and there is a loud hissing throughout. It is very difficult to hear the orchestra; the narrator's voice is strongly in the foreground. If the score survives, it is in the Air Force archives, uncatalogged.

14. Arthur Pursell, letter, May 25, 1946.

15. Arthur Pursell, letter, July 14, 1946; This was the first letter addressed to Bolling Field.

16. Delia Pursell, Christmas card, December 23, 1946.

17. Arthur Pursell, letter, June 9, 1948.

18. Arthur Pursell, letter, June 13, 1948.

19. Various letters from Arthur Pursell from December 1945 mention Bill's illness.

20. Pursell's manuscript of "Powder Your Face with Sunshine," complete with cross-outs, is in the Pursell archive.

21. His commanding officer, Colonel George Howard, wrote him a glowing letter of recommendation, stating that his arranging talents grew immensely during his military service and that further training at Eastman would help him "go far indeed." George Howard, letter, March 1, 1949.

22. Arthur Pursell, letter, January 30, 1949.

CHAPTER 4: A STUDENT AGAIN, AND THEN, NOT

1. This study is mentioned in Allen Cohen, *Howard Hanson in Theory and Practice* (Westport: Praeger, 2004), 14.

2. A resource for Howard Hanson's Eastman years is Vincent A. Lenti, *Serving a Great and Noble Art* (Rochester: Meloria Press, 2009). It includes lists of professors who served at Eastman and their dates of service, lists of major artists and conductors who performed there, many stories about Hanson, and three discographies of Hanson's recordings.

3. The Doctor of Musical Arts degree was approved by the National Association of School of Music (of which Howard Hanson was the president) in 1951, and was instituted by the Eastman School, Northwestern University, and the University of Michigan the following year (Latimer 2010). Pursell left Eastman in 1956 to join the Jerry Jaye Trio on tour as a keyboardist, and would not complete his D.M.A. until 1995.

4. "Eastman School Gives New Award," *New York Times*, May 11, 1953. This prize is also discussed in Perone, pp. 5 and 147.

5. Interview, September 21, 2012.

6. A pylonidal cyst is a boil or growth at the end of the tailbone, most common in young men under forty years of age. It's possible that Pursell developed this as an irritation from all of the hours he spent sitting, whether on the piano bench or behind the wheel of a car.

7. Pursell says that this name change was Mickey's idea.

CHAPTER 5: NASHVILLE SESSIONS

1. The rise of the Nashville Sound is a phenomenon much examined by scholars of country music, as I note in the introduction. Further sources include Bill Malone, *Country Music U.S.A.* (Austin: University of Texas Press, 2010); Paul Kingsbury, *Will the Circle Be Unbroken: Country Music in America* (New York: Dorling Kindersley, 2006); and Paul Hemphill, *The Nashville Sound: Bright Lights and Country Music* (Athens: University of Georgia Press, 2015).

2. The Carousel is mentioned in Hemphill 2015 (62) and Malone 2010 (257).

3. Henry Haynes, a guitarist, and Kenneth Burns, a mandolin player, formed a highly successful country music duo known for making up new words to popular country music songs.

4. Pursell points out that this was a different case than in New York or Los Angeles.

5. See chapter 6.

6. WSM, a radio station that was founded in 1925 by the National Life and Accident Insurance Company (their motto, "We Shield Millions," thus the call letters WSM), is the birthplace of the weekly Grand Ole Opry show and helped many country music greats get their start in the music business. It remains a national advocate for country music and broadcasts today from the Gaylord Opryland Hotel and Convention Center in Nashville. An excellent history of the station and its contributions to the music life of Nashville was written by Craig Havighurst, *Air Castle of the South: WSM and the Making of Music City* (Urbana: University of Illinois Press, 2007).

7. Travis Stimeling is writing a book about the Nashville string session players. His lecture also discusses this phenomenon: "When Maurice Ravel Met George Jones: Orchestral Strings in Commercial Country Music, 1960–1980," Music and Discourse Lecture, Belmont University, February 10, 2016.

8. Program, Fifth Nashville Arts Festival, 1961, Nashville Symphony folder.

9. Sydney Dalton, "Opening Concerts Win Praise," *Nashville Banner*, May 15, 1961; Louis Nicholas, "'Twas a Beautiful Day for a Delightful Concert," *Tennessean*, May 15, 1961.

10. Louis Nicholas, "Symphony Cats Swing it," *Tennessean*, May 2, 1962.

11. "Page Says Farewell in Gershwin 'Pop' Redo," *Tennessean*, June 6, 1962.

12. "Symphony's Concert Thrills Large Crowd," *Nashville Banner*, June 13, 1962.

13. Hemphill (2015) tells a funny story about a Chamber of Commerce member who loved country music, and his wife who did not, as an illustration of this classical/country divide (32–33). He later asserts, "Galloping capitalism overcame country music during the Sixties" (238).

14. Malone (2010, 257) and Streissguth (1997, 171–72) both refer to the cliquish nature of the Nashville session musicians.

15. Pursell actually did work in a brewery, unloading trucks, one summer during his college years in Rochester. He also faced this kind of discrimination during his years of service in the Army (See chapter 3).

16. A very brief history of the Quonset Hut can be found in Kingsbury (2006, 234).

17. Pursell had to join the union in 1949 in Rochester, New York, in order to play with Jack End's dance band, a job he took to earn money during his student years.

18. Read more on Pursell's relationship with W. O. Smith in chapter 7.

19. The program for the dinner is in the Biographies folder. Pursell is not listed by name but is listed as a "guest" of Chet Atkins at Table 1. Other entertainment included Betty Cannon's Beauty Dots (a Rockettes-like dance troupe), Jane Morgan (singer), Augie and Margo (dancers), Alan King (comedian), and the NBC Orchestra. The United States Navy Band provided the dinner music.

20. Bill Pursell, letter to Mom and Dad, May 23, 1961, Biographies folder. The two other musicians were Bob Moore and Buddy Harmon.

21. Fan Fair is a Nashville tradition, a music festival created for fans of country music that includes concerts, merchandise booths, and opportunities for the fans to meet major artists at autograph booths.

CHAPTER 6: OUR WINTER LOVE

1. Michael Kosser tells this story in *How Nashville Became Music City, U.S.A.* (Milwaukee: Hal Leonard, 2006), 159–60. Kosser's version claims that the engineer had just connected Martin's guitar and had asked him not to play until he adjusted the levels, but Martin gave a single "tic" of his signature "tic-tac" bass, and blew the circuit. Kosser also relates that Glen Snoddy was the engineer who developed the fuzz box, and that he sold it to Gibson.

2. Eddy Arnold's description of this easygoing process can be found in Streissguth (1997, 172–73).

3. Justis nicknamed Pursell "Vladimir" after Vladimir Horowitz because of his skills at the piano, sometimes even calling him "Vladibilly."

4. The first album to use the distorted bass sound, according to Pursell, was Marty Robbins's *Don't Worry*.

5. *Billboard*, January 5, 1963, 43. The statistics are taken from a survey of *Billboard*'s online archive of issues from the stated dates.

6. March 30, 1963.

7. Here is a complete list of songs that appeared on the album: "Our Winter Love" (J. Cowell); "There'll Be No Teardrops Tonight" (Hank Williams); "Four Walls" (M. Moore and G. Campbell); "A Wound Time Can't Erase" (B. Johnson); "Born to Lose" (T. Daffan); "Loved" (Grady Martin); "Stranger" (I. Stanton and W. Walker); "I Walk the Line" (Johnny Cash); "Love Can't Wait" (Marty Robbins); "Bye Bye Love" (F. Bryant and B. Bryant); "I Can't Help It (If I'm Still in Love with You)" (Hank Williams); "Dark Alley" (Bill Pursell).

8. "Col's Gold Guitar Award to Pursell for Cramart Tune," *Music Reporter* VII, No. 37 (April 6, 1963): 8. Pursell archives, Our Winter Love folder.

9. Arthur Pursell, letter, April 16, 1963.

NOTES   211

10. Linda Peterson, letter, April 14, 1963.

11. Amber Nicole Shavers discusses the results of recoupment clauses when artists do not fully understand the subtleties of the contracts they are signing in *The Little Book of Music Law* (Chicago: American Bar Association, 2013). One of the issues is exactly what the studio claims as expenses. Another issue is that the bulk of the royalties go to the writer and publisher. In the case of "Our Winter Love," the writer was Johnny Cowell, not Pursell.

12. Letters, January 22, 1966, from Pursell to Columbia (marked "copy for myself"), and October 21, 1966, from Columbia to Pursell. Pursell archives, Columbia folder.

13. Shari, Bill and Marion's daughter, was one of the first infants to be diagnosed with fetal alcohol syndrome, due to her mother's alcoholism. Under the impression that she would never develop normally, Pursell would later place her in a children's home. Shari eventually came home to Nashville to live with Pursell and his third wife Julie, went to public school, and was able to live independently as an adult until 2012, when she died of undiagnosed cancer at the age of fifty-two.

14. Pursell archive, Royalties folder.

15. "Pops Show to Feature Bill Purcell [sic]," *Tennessean*, August 2, 1963.

16. Pursell's appointment books from this time survive, with the times of sessions and names of artists clearly marked. Pursell archive, Appointments box.

CHAPTER 7: NASHVILLE AND BEYOND

1. The program for the 1963 concert does not survive, as is common for concerts given in Centennial Park. It is likely no programs were printed for these outdoor concerts, as I found none in the Nashville Symphony archives. The program for the 1966 concert is in the Nashville Symphony folder.

2. Program, Nashville Symphony Orchestra, Spring Pops Concert, May 17 and 18, 1968, Nashville Symphony folder.

3. Draft of Pursell letter to Joseph Habig, April 26, 1929, Nashville Symphony folder.

4. "Symphony Seeks Brass Bell," *Tennessean*, May 16, 1968.

5. Louis Nicholas, "Enthused Crowd Gets Johnson; Symphony," *Tennessean*, May 19, 1968. Courtesy of Nashville Symphony Archives. See also Werner Zepernick, "Symphony's Pops Concert Enchanting," *Nashville Banner*, May 20, 1968.

6. Concert program, September 24 and 25, 1971, courtesy of the Nashville Symphony archives.

7. Bill Pursell, letter to Mike Casey, November 23, 1968, Maureen Reagan folder.

8. Mike Casey, letters to Bill Pursell, December 10, 1968, and February 4, 1969, Maureen Reagan folder.

9. Bill Pursell, letter to Stanley Ballard, September 1, 1969, Maureen Reagan folder. Ballard sent a reply (also in the Maureen Reagan folder), September 16, 1969, acknowledging that the demand would be sent to Reagan.

10. The 45 was released as Spar 9008. One can find it listed in a catalog of Spar 45s at http://www.blueslandproductions.com/giant_catalog.html#spar45s (accessed May 15, 2014).

11. A recent history of the Northern Soul movement is Elaine Constantine and Gareth Sweeney, *Northern Soul: An Illustrated History* (London: Virgin, 2013).

12. While in Nashville, Tupper Saussy taught English at the Montgomery Bell Academy, the school that was the basis for the movie *Dead Poets' Society*. He then founded an advertising agency and became a prominent businessman. At the time of the concerto, he had left the business world to become a full-time composer. Saussy would later become notorious for refusing to pay his taxes and becoming a federal fugitive, and would go on to later write books about government control. He composed orchestral music, art songs, and popular songs.

13. "Don't Quote Me: Party Weekend for Jane, Randy," December 29, 1968; "Don't Quote Me: Kay and Ray Name Big Day," January 12, 1969; and "Our Girl Friday Says: She'll Board Jet for Washington," January 17, 1969.

14. Pursell had divorced Marion Lumpkin in 1964 and had custody of their child, Shari. His 1965 marriage to Julie, who had two daughters herself, created a blended family that is still together today.

15. Louis Nicholas, "Nashville Talents Spark a Busy Week," *Tennessean*, January 12, 1969; Werner Zepernick, "Symphony to Perform Tupper Saussy Original," *Nashville Banner*(?).

16. Kathy Sawyer, "Now it's 'T. Saussy, Composer,'" *Tennessean*, Sunday Showcase, January 12, 1969.

17. "After the Concert," *Nashville Banner*, January 14, 1969.

18. Louis Nicholas, "Saussy Premiere Fills the House," *Tennessean*, January 14, 1969; Werner Zepernick, "'Hausgeists' Premiere Well Liked," *Nashville Banner*(?), January 14?, 1969.

19. "Critics' Choice—Tupper Saussy," *Nashville Banner*, January 17, 1969. Courtesy of the Nashville Symphony Archives.

20. As mentioned before, Travis Stimeling writes about this. "When Maurice Ravel Met George Jones: Orchestral Strings in Commercial Country Music, 1960–1980," Music and Discourse lecture, Belmont University, March 23, 2016. Also see interview, February 13, 2012.

21. "Trevecca Slates Bill Pursell," *Tennessean*, November 12, 1969; "Youth Symphony to Feature Pursell," *Tennessean*, January 27, 1970; both articles Nashville Banner Archives, Nashville Public Library.

22. The Cocktail Piano series continues to this day; as many as six different volumes are available on Amazon.com as of May 2014.

23. From his obituary: "From 1959, when he joined the Cine-Tele Sound (CTS) studios in Bayswater, Tomlinson helped to revolutionise film music recording techniques and was held in awe for his ability to deliver a finished soundtrack as a live mix (the process of blending together multiple sound sources as they are produced using a

mixing console) during recording sessions." *Telegraph*, December 16, 2015. Apparently this was his signature technique.

24. Letter to Kurt Kaiser, February 27, 1974, Word folder. Bill became close friends with Kaiser and worked with him on several projects, not just for Word.

25. "Age-Spanning Album," *Christian Life*, August 1974; "Nostalgia," *Christian Review*, August 1974, Word folder.

26. Douglas Childress, letter to Bill Pursell, September 5, 1975. Pat Dunn, letter to Douglas Childress, December 11, 1975. Word folder.

27. As of the spring of 2016, Ken Medema will write you a "personal song" for $159.99. You can fill out a form on his website.

28. This incident is referred to in a letter from Raymond Mosley, October 5, 1980, Raymond Mosley folder.

29. Aaron Watson's *The Savage Club* (1907) begins with an entire chapter celebrating "Bohemia" and its vagaries.

30. A letter from Raymond Mosley details Pursell's pending membership and names Praosnitz. February 20, 1978, Raymond Mosley folder.

31. Letters requesting honorary "lady" membership for wife Julie and daughter Laura and bills and receipts for their stays are in the Pursell archive, Savage Club folder.

32. Two contact lists of members exist in Pursell's archive, 1988–89 and 1990–91. Wednesday Night Club folder.

33. The personnel list for the Nashville Sweat Band remains in Bill's personal archive, along with union session records.

34. Handwritten list of instrumentalists, Nashville Sweat Band folder. Phonograph Recording Contract, American Federation of Musicians, February 18, 1976, and March 24, 1976, photocopy in Nashville Sweat Band Folder.

35. Review, *Music Week*, April 10, 1976, Nashville Sweat Band folder.

36. Mike Stuart, memo to Veronica, April 1976. Richard Spinks, letter to Veronica, April 12, 1976. Grammatical errors and capitalization his. Richard Searling, telegram to Jon Smith, Spark Records, April 15, 1976. Pete Owen, memo to Veronica, date replied April 20, 1976. Dave Caff, handwritten note to "all at Sparks," no date. All in Nashville Sweat Band folder.

37. Paul Crabtree, "The Day the Circus Came to Town," script, Circus World folder.

38. Dick Kuegeman (Ringling Brothers and Barnum and Bailey, Circus World), letter to Bill Pursell, March 2, 1976, Circus World folder.

39. Paul Crabtree, memorandum to Bill Purcell [sic], February 22, 1976, Circus World folder.

40. Notes, first line "1322 bars," Circus World folder.

41. "Nashville Sound Backs Circus World Show," *Tennessean*, March 24, 1976, Circus World folder.

42. Bud Davis, letter to Bill Pursell, April 15, 1976, Circus World folder.

43. Dick Kuegeman, letter to Bill Pursell, May 12, 1976, Circus World folder. Multiple copies of Circus World's check to Bill are also in this folder.

44. The exact total is $1,161.84, including Bill's own session leader fee of $366.72.

45. All Cypress Gardens documents can be found in the Cypress Gardens folder.

46. Promotional articles appeared in the *Tennessean* in April ("Galactic Concert," April 16, 1978; "Laser Patterns Light up Opry at 'Star Wars,'" April 25, 1978; "Ready for a 'Star Wars' Symphony?," April 30, 1978). The concert was announced to be sold out on May 2 in the *Tennessean*. Nashville Symphony folder and Courtesy of Nashville Symphony Archives.

CHAPTER 8: HERITAGE

1. The tunes in order are (Side 1): "The Thunderer," "My Wild Irish Rose," "Summertime Medley" ("The Sidewalks of New York," "I Don't Want to Play in Your Yard," "In My Merry Oldsmobile"), "Wait Till the Sun Shines, Nellie," "On the Banks of the Wabash, Far Away," "Meet Me in St. Louis, Louis"; (Side 2) "Grandfather's Clock," "Hello, Ma Baby," "Evening in the Park" ("The Band Played On," "Love's Old Sweet Song," "Daisy Bell"), "I Love You Truly," "In the Good Old Summertime," and "Sweet Adeline." Bill arranged and conducted all tunes except "My Wild Irish Rose," "Wait Till the Sun Shines, Nellie," "On the Banks of the Wabash," "I Love You Truly," and "Sweet Adeline."

2. Kurland was a string session player in Nashville in the 1960s and, like Pursell, was an important part of the changes in country music that led to the rise of the Nashville Sound.

3. The master tape of this recording can be found in the William Pursell Archive, Lila Bunch Library, Belmont University.

4. Judy Fernbach Simon, letter, May 31, 1997, Pursell archive, National Geographic Sousa folder.

5. These projects are listed on Bill's résumé, Biographies Folder. Business correspondence for Sabena Airlines and Coca-Cola is extant in their own folders in the Pursell Archive.

6. Barbara Burch, "Sunset Throng Gets Warmed up as Governor Displays Virtuosity," (Memphis) *Commercial Appeal*, May 30, 1982.

7. Letter to Bill Pursell from Lamar Alexander, June 14, 1982, Nashville Symphony folder.

8. Letters in Composer of the Year folder.

9. Teresa Boyce, "Tuning up for 'The Towers,'" *Baylor University Report*, January 1982, 8–10.

10. Bob Darden, "Microcosm of BU Past Blooms in Towering Play, *Waco Tribune-Herald*, February 3, 1982.

11. There is a letter from Pursell to Lynn Phillips of Cumberland Hill Music Corporation, noting that "Show Me" was part of an intended set of three, with a verbal agreement with the publisher to publish the works as a set. "Show Me" was the first completed and was published before the other two were ready; upon receiving a rejection to publish the other two psalm works, Pursell asked for the rights of "Show Me" back so that he could take the set elsewhere.

12. Tenure application, Belmont folder.

13. College faculty ranks are: Assistant Professor (tenure track), Associate Professor (tenured), and Professor ("full"). Pursell was hired at the middle rank to give credit for his many years of experience as a professional musician.

14. "Stars Sign up for Symphony's 'Platinum' Album Taping," *Tennessean*, February 16, 1986.

15. Matthew Maddin, "Memo," December 24, 1985, Platinum folder.

16. The upcoming concert was promoted in two *Tennessean* articles: "Stars to Join Symphony in Disc Debut," January 8, 1986; "Stars Sign up for Symphony's 'Platinum' Album Taping," February 16, 1986.

17. Sweet Tater Day was a revival of the old seed potato day in rural Gladeville, Tennessee. Descriptions of Homecoming '86 can be found in the Tennessee Encyclopedia of History and Culture, http://tennesseeencyclopedia.net/entry.php?rec=645 (accessed June 9, 2014); and an article in the *Chicago Tribune*, Jack Hurst, "Tennessee Homecoming '86," June 22, 1986, http://articles.chicagotribune.com/1986–06–22/travel/8602140671_1_volunteer-state-tennessee-homecoming-native (accessed June 9, 2014).

18. "Symphony's gift reflects Tennessee talent, support," *Tennessean*, December 1, 1985. Also, the concert program of the December 3 concert can be found in the Nashville Symphony archives.

19. Pursell's working notes for the *Homecoming Overture* can be found in the Pursell archives, Homecoming folder.

20. Henry Arnold, "Homecoming '86 Musically Welcomed," *Nashville Banner*, December 4, 1985.

21. Mark Valenzuela, "Symphony's Opening Night Makes Grand Impression," *Vanderbilt Hustler*, September 8, 1989.

22. The archives of the Nashville Symphony includes a binder of news clippings on this period of bankruptcy. At the front is a list of the cancelled concerts.

23. "Aladdin Commissions Symphony," *Tennessean*, July 13, 1988.

24. Marilyn Phillips, "Pursell and Warren aid Symphony," *Belmont Vision*, March 25, 1988.

25. Kathleen McCann, letter to Bill Pursell, May 27, 1988, Nashville Symphony folder.

26. Beth Morton, "Fall and rise of symphony leads '88 arts news," *Nashville Banner*, December 29, 1988. Courtesy of Nashville Symphony archives.

27. Editorial, *Tennessean*, September 15, 1989. Courtesy of Nashville Symphony archives.

28. Bobby Hearn, "Nashville Gets Own Symphony," *Nashville Banner*, September 11, 1989; Sandy Smith, "Nashville History Inspires Composer," *Tennessean*, September 14, 1989; Henry Arnold, "State's History Relived Through Pursell's Music," *Nashville Banner*, September 14, 1989; Wheat Williams, "Symphony Performs Pursell's Piece," *Belmont Vision*, September 15, 1989.

29. "Heritage" was performed in the "Centennial Park Concert" series on September 24.

CHAPTER 9: DR. PURSELL

1. Map of Bohemian camp, Bohemian Club folder. The 1989 map notes that the camp encompasses 2,700 acres. It also lists all of the members of the various camps.

2. One can find excerpts from radio host and filmmaker Alex Jones's 2000 documentary *Dark Secrets: Inside Bohemian Grove* on YouTube. An essay on negative media attention can be found in Richard K. Arnold, "Public Relations Sweet and Sour," in Jerry C. Cole, editor, *Annals of Bohemia, Volume VII: 1988–1996* (San Francisco: Bohemian Club, 1997), 107–15. Arnold describes a conversation with a television reporter who accused Bohemians of running naked around the Grove. He admits that they peed on the trees, but that wasn't equivalent to running around naked.

3. This number cannot be verified, due to the closed nature of the Bohemian archives. Other information on the Club in this chapter comes from its Annals, of which Pursell owns several, and various letters and documents in the Pursell archive.

4. He was invited by William P. Jaeger Jr., of Rutherford Hill Winery. His May 7, 1986, letter to Pursell is in the Bohemian Grove folder.

5. Robert Setrakian, letter to Bill Pursell, August 18, 1986, Bohemian Grove folder. Setrakian refers to a Friday night performance on the spinet, and a Saturday night performance on two grand pianos, according to Pursell.

6. The composer was Andrew Imbrie.

7. D. Griffith Harries, letter to William C. Green, April 28, 1989. The "waffle fingers" comment appears in George Alexander, letter to Bill Pursell, March 23, 1989. Both letters Bohemian Club folder.

8. James D. Walters, letter to Membership Committee, May 4, 1989. Ellipses his.

9. *The Prophecy* playbill, Bohemian Grove folder. Also, J. Thomas Rosch, letter to Robert C. Weinbaum, February 4, 1991, Bohemian Grove folder.

10. Rosch, letter to Weinbaum. This letter was an attempt to gain financial backing for a Broadway production of the play, which was never accomplished.

11. *Time and Again* playbill, Bohemian Club folder.

12. A copy of these exams can be found in the Eastman folder.

13. The recital program is in the Eastman folder.

14. The concert was called "Roman Holiday" and closed with two Italy-themed pieces: Respighi's *Roman Festival* and Tchaikovsky's *Capriccio Italien*. "Tulare County Symphony Presents Roman Holiday," *Visalia Lifestyle Magazine*, September 2005.

15. He was awarded the degree in the fall semester of 1995 but walked through graduation in May 1996. James Undercofler, letter to William Pursell, December 7, 1995, and Commencement program, Eastman folder.

BIBLIOGRAPHY

ARCHIVES

William Pursell Archive, Lila D. Bunch Library, Belmont University, Nashville Tennessee

The Pursell archive includes countless documents, including most surviving manuscripts of his music; recordings; newspaper and magazine clippings; personal and business correspondence; unfinished biographies written by Bill, his father, and his mother; recital programs; photographs; and official documents such as his military discharge papers, proclamations, session pay lists, etc.

The Nashville Room, including the Banner Clippings Archive, Nashville Public Library, Nashville, Tennessee
California History Room, California State Library (Sacramento)
The Library of Congress Sonic Catalogue
The Eastman School of Music
The National Archives (United States)
Nashville Symphony Archives
National Geographic Archives
The Peabody Conservatory of Music
United States Air Force Band Archives
Word Records

PERSONAL COMMUNICATION

Interviews with William Pursell, October 2011–December 2013
Interviews with Jerry Warren, Julie Pursell, Laura Pursell, and Harold Bradley
Email communications with William Pursell and others

NEWSPAPERS AND MAGAZINES

Baylor University Report
Belmont Vision

Billboard
Chicago Tribune
Christian Life
Christian Review
Music Reporter
Music Week
Nashville Banner
New York Times
Oakland Tribune (California)
Star News (Southern California)
Telegraph (London)
Tennessean
Tulare Advance Register (California)
Vanderbilt Hustler
Visalia Lifestyle Magazine (California)
Waco Tribune-Herald (Texas)

SECONDARY SOURCES

Bomar, Scott, Randy Poe, Ribert Price, Dwight Yoakam, et al. *The Bakersfield Sound: Buck Owens, Merle Haggard, and California Country*. Nashville: Country Music Foundation Press, 2012.

Clawson, Raymond. *Raymond W. Clawson, Petitioner, v. United States of America. U.S. Supreme Court Transcription of Record with Supporting Proceedings*. Making of Modern Law historical series. Gale, 2011.

Cole, Jerry C., ed. *Annals of Bohemia, Volume VII: 1988–1996*. San Francisco: Bohemian Club, 1997.

Cohen, Allen. *Howard Hanson in Theory and Practice*. Westport: Praeger, 2004.

Constantine, Elaine, and Gareth Sweeney. *Northern Soul: An Illustrated History*. London: Virgin, 2013.

Country Music Foundation. *Country: The Music and the Musicians from the Beginnings to the '90s*. New York: Abbeville Press, 1994.

Havighurst, Craig. *Air Castle of the South: WSM and the Making of Music City*. Urbana: University of Illinois Press, 2007.

Hemphill, Paul. *The Nashville Sound: Bright Lights and Country Music*. Athens: University of Georgia Press, 2015.

Holt, Fabian. *Genre in Popular Music*. Chicago: University of Chicago Press, 2007.

Ivey, Bill. "The Bottom Line: Business Practices that Shaped Country Music." In *Country: The Music and the Musicians*. New York: Abbeville Press, 1994. 280–311.

Jensen, Joli. *The Nashville Sound: Authenticity, Commercialization, and Country Music*. Nashville: Vanderbilt University Press, 1998.

Kienzle, Rich. "The Forgotten Hank Garland." *Journal of Country Music* 9, no. 3 (1983).

Kingsbury, Paul. *The Grand Ole Opry History of Country Music.* New York: Villard, 1995.

———. *Will the Circle Be Unbroken: Country Music in America.* New York: Dorling Kindersley, 2006.

Kosser, Michael. *How Nashville Became Music City U.S.A.: 50 Years of Music Row.* Milwaukee: Hal Leonard, 2006.

Latimer, Marvin. "The Nation's First D.M.A. in Choral Music." *Journal of Historical Research in Music Education* 32, no. 1 (October 2010): 19–36.

Lenti, Vincent A. *Serving a Great and Noble Art.* Rochester: Meloria Press, 2009.

Levine, Lawrence. *Highbrow/Lowbrow: The Emergence of Cultural Hierarchy in America.* Cambridge: Harvard University Press, 1988.

Malone, Bill. *Country Music U.S.A.* Austin: University of Texas Press, 2010.

Nabokov, Nicolas. *Bagazh: Memoirs of a Russian Cosmopolitan.* New York: Atheneum, 1975.

Norgate, Matthew, and Alan Wykes. *Not So Savage.* London: Jupiter Books, 1976.

Pecknold, Diane. "Heart of the Country? The Construction of Nashville as the Capital of Country Music." In *Sounds in the City: Popular Music, Place, and Globalization.* London: Palgrave Macmillan, 2014.

Perone, James. *Howard Hanson: A Bio-Bibliography.* Westport: Greenwood, 1993.

Schafer, Stephanie. *Cashville: Dilution of Original Country Music Identity through Increasing Commercialization.* Hamburg: Diplomica Verlag, 2012.

Schulenberg, Richard. *Legal Aspects of the Music Industry.* New York: Billboard Books, 1999.

Shadinger, Richard. *Music on the Beautiful Mountain: A History of Music at Belmont.* Nashville: Fields Publishing, 2016.

Shavers, Amber Nicole. *The Little Book of Music Law.* Washington, DC: American Bar Association, 2013.

Smith, W. O. *Sideman: The Long Gig of W. O. Smith.* Nashville: Rutledge, 1991.

Stevens, Ray. *Ray Stevens' Nashville.* Tallahassee: Father & Son, 2014.

Stimeling, Travis. "When Maurice Ravel Met George Jones: Orchestral Strings in Commercial Country Music, 1960–1980." Music and Discourse Lecture, Belmont University, February 10, 2016.

Streissguth, Michael. *Eddy Arnold: Pioneer of the Nashville Sound.* Jackson: University Press of Mississippi, 1997.

Washburne, Christopher, and Maiken Derno, eds. *Bad Music: The Music We Love to Hate.* New York: Routledge, 2004.

Watson, Aaron, and Mark Twain. *The Savage Club.* London: T. F. Unwin, 1907.

Zak, Albin. *I Don't Sound Like Nobody: Remaking Music in 1950s America.* Ann Arbor: University of Michigan Press, 2011.

INDEX

Abbey Road, 122, 127
Acuff, Roy, xi, 83
Adler, Samuel, 170, 173
adoption, 3, 6, 24, 33, 52, 84–85, 164
Air Force, xii, 44–50, 53, 54–58, 67, 93, 115, 141, 177, 207–8n
Air Force Orchestra, xii, 44–48, 50, 54, 110
Alexander, Lamar, 149, 153, 154, 191, 214n
American Federation of Musicians, 86, 116, 133, 213n
Anita Kerr Singers, ix, xii, xiv–xv, 96, 203
Anvil Studio, 122, 125–26, 143, 163, 199, 200
Apollo Theater, 71, 106
Army Band, 36
Arnn, John, 148
Arnold, Eddy, ix, xi–xii, xiv, 9, 74–77, 82, 84, 86–87, 92, 210n
ASCAP, 55, 90
astronomy, 9, 34, 35
Atkins, Chet, ix, xii, xiii, xiv, 75–79, 82–83, 85, 87–89, 94, 152, 190, 201, 210n

Balanchine, George, 40
Baltimore, Maryland, 22–23, 39, 41–43, 53, 79
banjo, xi, 91
Barber, Samuel, 66, 150, 170
Barbershop Days, 140–43, 199
Barlow, Wayne, 62, 174, 195
Baylor University, 123, 150, 191, 214n
BBC Symphony Orchestra, 128

Beasley, Bill, 117, 201
Beatles, 106, 107, 122
Belle Meade (Nashville, Tennessee), 118–19
Belmont College, 146–48, 178
Belmont Mansion, 119
Belmont University, vii, ix, xii, xvii, xix, 148–52, 155–57, 170–71, 178, 181, 184, 186, 191–92, 205n, 209n, 212n, 214–15n
Benjamin Award for Quiet Music, 65, 89
Berkeley, California, 6, 13–14, 17–20, 22–23, 28, 31, 42, 57, 174, 177, 182, 189, 205n
Bernstein, Sid, 105–8
Berry Hill (Nashville, Tennessee), 146
Bierley, Paul, 142, 144
Billboard, xiv, xv, xix, 92, 97–99, 105, 117, 210n
Blood, Sweat, and Tears (album), 91, 196
BMI, 89, 90, 109
Boca Raton, Florida, 46, 182
Bohemian Club, 163–70, 192, 216n
Bolling Field (Washington, D.C.), 46, 47, 49, 207–8n
Bornschein, Franz, 39, 40, 207n
Borodin, Alexander, xvii, xviii, 5
Bradley, Harold, ix, xi–xv, 77, 78, 80, 83, 86, 87, 95, 96, 97, 112, 122
Bradley, Owen, ix, xii, 76, 83, 86, 95
Brahms, Johannes, 20, 124, 142–43, 157
Broadway, xvii, xviii, 114, 161, 216n
Burch, Fred, xvii, 179, 184
Burton, Flora, 51, 59
Busch Gardens, 146, 192

California, vii, ix, xi, xx, 3, 6, 9, 20, 23, 31, 33, 35, 37, 42–43, 78, 82, 84, 92, 99, 100, 114–16, 124, 163, 164–65, 167, 171, 182, 192, 206–7n
Camp Tulequoia, 10
Campbell, Charles, 34
camping, 4, 8, 10, 11
Carlson, Mrs., 31
Carlson, Raymond (Clawson), 31
Carousel, xii, 77, 83, 87, 129, 209n
Carter family, xi
Cash, Johnny, ix, xv, xx, 26, 79, 84, 87, 90–92, 99, 101, 105, 112, 162, 196, 187, 201, 210n
Centennial Park, 79, 80, 82, 211n, 215n
Challenger (space shuttle), 50
Chasing a Dream (album), xv, 109
"Christ Looking over Jerusalem" (orchestra), 62–65, 89, 190, 195
Christmas, 6, 43, 47, 51–52, 97, 104, 145, 196–99, 201, 207–8n
Circus World, 132, 134–36, 191, 213n
Civil, Alan, 128
civil rights movement, 87, 110, 129
clarinet, 10, 36–37, 50, 81, 158, 173
Clawson, Raymond, 24, 26, 27–33, 37–38, 206n
Cline, Patsy, ix, xx, 87, 101, 112, 162, 195, 200
Coca-Cola, 146, 190, 214n
Cocktail Piano Time (album), 120
Coffeen, Selby, 96
Collins, Jay, 146, 148
Columbia Records, x, xii, xix, 76, 90–95, 97, 99, 105–12, 152, 169, 195–98, 200–203, 211n
Columbia Studio B, ix, xii, 86, 94–95, 101
Composer of the Year, 149, 171, 191, 214n
concertos, xv, xviii, 13–14, 58–59, 76, 79–82, 114, 118–19, 161–62, 171, 173, 177, 189, 192, 205n, 212n
contracts, xii, 11, 55, 90, 105–6, 112, 116, 137–38, 211n, 213n
Country Music Association (CMA), xiv

Country Music Hall of Fame, ix, 83, 205n
Cowell, Johnny, 94, 99, 210n, 211n
Crabtree, Paul, 132–35, 213n
Cramart Music, 93–94, 99, 210n
Cramer, Floyd, ix, x, xii–xv, 78, 83, 85, 88–89, 94, 112
Crooked River Town (opera), xvii, xviii, xx, 181, 183, 184, 187, 192
Cumberland River, xx, 80, 113, 139, 162, 183
Curtiswood Lane, vii, 147, 158, 161, 181
Cypress Gardens, 137–38, 191, 214n

"Dark Alley" (song), 99, 101, 202, 210n
"Day in the City" (piano), 14, 189
Debussy, Claude, 50, 61, 65, 125
Decca Records, xii, 112, 121, 195, 197
divorces, 74, 108, 212n
Doctor of Musical Arts (DMA), 63, 67, 192, 208n
"Don't Worry" (song), 95, 210n
"Dream, The" (piano), 14, 189
Duel, The (opera), 150, 191
"Duel, The" ("The Gingham Dog and the Calico Cat") (poem), 150

Eastman School of Music, 9, 26, 51, 56–63, 65–67, 70, 118, 162, 170, 174–75, 190, 192, 195, 198, 208n, 216n
Ed Sullivan Show, 107, 109
Evans, Sally, 7–8

"Fall Tenderly Roses" (song), 142–45
"Felis Domesticus" (piano), 63, 65, 170, 190
Field, Eugene, 150, 191
Florida, xi, xiv, 46, 74–76, 130, 132–33, 182, 191
flying, airplane, 11, 50, 93, 111, 130
Frugoni, Orazio, 59
fuzz box, xiv, 95–97, 210n

Gabhart, Herbert, 149
Garland, Hank, xiii, 77, 79, 83, 86–87, 93–94, 195

INDEX

Genhart, Cecile, 59, 190
Gershwin, George, x, xviii–xx, 79, 81, 110, 113–14, 119, 155, 161, 171, 209n
G.I. Bill, 57–58
Gilkyson, Charles, 29
"Girl with the Flaxen Hair, The" (piano), 125
Grammy Awards, 122, 125, 145, 156, 198, 199
Grand Ole Opry, xi, xiii, 9, 82, 84, 92, 138, 159, 160, 209n
Grieg, Edward, x, 79, 80
Grove Play, 165–66, 168–69, 192

Habig, Joe, 114, 120, 211n
Hagerstown, Maryland, 68–69, 72, 182
Hanson, Howard, 56–59, 61–63, 65, 89, 174, 190, 208n
Harlem (New York City), 71
Harman, Buddy, 95
"Hausgeists" (piano concerto), 118, 212n
"Heartbeat" (song), 117, 197, 202
Hennion, Tom, 34–36, 207n
"High Flight" (poem), 49–50
hiking, 4, 10, 19
Hoiby, Lee, 65–66
Homecoming Overture, 148, 153–54, 160, 191, 215n
Homer and Jethro, 78
Horn Trio, 151
Horowitz, Vladimir, 41, 65–66, 156, 210n
Humphrey, Donald, 27–28
Humphrey, Eleanor (Elinor) (birth mother), 27–30, 206n

"I Can't Help It (If I'm Still in Love with You)" (song), xv, 99, 114, 181, 190, 210n
Interludes, xi, xiv, 66, 73–75, 202
Introduction and Toccata for Piano, 65–67, 190–91
Ives, Charles, xix

Jackson, Andrew, xvii–xviii, 183, 185, 192
James, Standard (Stanley Rochinski), 55–56

jazz, x, xii, xv, 17, 38, 48, 76, 77, 79, 83, 86–87, 99, 101, 129, 148, 161, 173, 178–79, 195, 203
Jerry Jaye Trio, 66–68, 71–73, 106, 174, 208n
Johnson, Thor, xx, 114, 119, 190
Justis, Bill, 93–94, 96, 97, 152, 156, 203, 210n

Kaiser, Kurt, 122–23, 126, 127, 150, 163, 191, 198, 200, 213n
"Kaleidoscope" (piano concerto), 171–74, 192
Keesler Field (Biloxi, Mississippi), 44, 46, 85
Kennedy, John F., 63, 88–90
Kenton, Stan, 46, 67
Kepner, Fred, 45–46, 54, 208n
Kerr, Anita, 96
Killen, Buddy, 130, 152, 203
"King of the Road" (song), 152

Lavery, John, 140, 142, 144, 145
Law, Don, x, xii, 90, 95, 97, 99, 105, 107–9, 196, 197, 202
Lee, Lucy, 12–13, 205n
LeQuire, Alan, 152
Lila D. Bunch Library (Belmont University), vii, viii, 214n
Lipshitz, Bernie, 44–46, 207n
Liszt, Franz, 17, 41
London, England, 110, 113, 120–22, 127–29, 138, 140, 143, 145, 147–48, 162–63, 191, 212n
"Long Island Sound" (song), 94, 97
Longo, Alfred, 111
Longy, René, 42, 205n, 208n
Lumpkin, Marion (second wife), 74, 75, 211–12n

"Mad Player Piano" (piano), 14–15, 17, 189
"Madrilena" (song), 111–12, 201
Manhattan Project, 34, 165
Marcellus, Bob, 50, 54, 56

Martin, Grady, ix, xiii, xiv, 93–95, 99, 113, 210n
McDonald and Little, 113, 118, 146, 190, 192–93
McGee, Lizzie, 7–9
Medema, Ken, 125–27, 163, 198–99, 213n
Mennini, Louis, 60, 62, 65
military, xx, 6, 26, 40, 46, 49, 51, 56–57, 85, 93, 142, 154, 159, 182, 207–8n; draft, 14, 30, 36, 39, 42–44
Moore, Bob, ix, 95, 210n
Moseley, Raymond, 128, 138, 143
Mozart, Wolfgang Amadeus, xvii, 12, 161, 170, 177, 192
Muenzer, Edgar, 54, 57
Music City U.S.A., xi, 129, 153, 162, 210n
Music Row, xi, xiii, 152
Musica (sculpture), 152

Nabokov, Nicolas, 39, 40, 207n
Nash, Gene, 77, 130, 199
Nashville Platinum (album), 130, 151–52, 155–56, 200, 215n
Nashville Sound, ix, x–xv, xix, xx, 76–77, 82–83, 87, 94, 96, 99, 120, 130, 177, 209n, 213–14n
Nashville Sweat Band, 130–32, 197, 199, 213n
Nashville Symphony, vii, ix–x, xv, xx, 76, 79, 80–81, 110, 113–14, 118–19, 120, 130, 138–40, 148–49, 151–55, 161–62, 190–92, 200, 209n, 211–12n, 214–15n
National Geographic, 113, 140, 144–45, 199–200, 214n
New York City, 55–56, 63, 65–67, 69, 73, 76, 97, 99, 106–7, 120, 208–9n, 210n, 214n
Northern Soul, 117, 212n
Nostalgia (album), 122–25, 198, 213n

Oakland, California, 3, 5, 14, 32, 206n
Omni Music, 93–94
On Parade (album), 142–43, 145, 200

Our Winter Love (album), xv, 92, 93–94, 99–100, 109, 196, 210n
"Our Winter Love" (song), xii, xiv, 83, 92, 93–112, 117, 120–21, 131–32, 152, 154, 165, 195–96, 200, 202, 210–11n

Page, Willis, xx, 79, 82, 110, 113–14
Peabody Conservatory of Music, 9, 14, 23, 26, 39–44, 46, 51–53, 56, 58–59, 118, 162, 171, 182, 189–90, 207n
Pell, John, 148
Peterson, Naomi (aunt), 20, 124–125
Phillips, Susan (first wife), 66, 73–74
Porter, Bill (Jerry Jaye Trio), 67, 70–72
"Powder Your Face with Sunshine" (song), 55–56, 208n
Presley, Elvis, xiii, 72, 200
Prophecy, The (play), 165, 167–68, 192, 216n
Pursell, Arthur (father), xix, 3, 5–7, 24–27, 33–34, 36, 37, 42–43, 51, 56, 67, 101, 205n, 207–8n, 210n
Pursell, Bill (son), 146
Pursell, Delia Peterson (mother), 3, 5, 6, 9, 23–24, 26, 27, 30, 33, 37, 43, 51–52, 67, 85, 124–25, 208n
Pursell, Ellen (daughter), 146, 158, 159
Pursell, Julie Hollobaugh (third wife), 54, 118, 146, 211–13n
Pursell, Laura (daughter), 30–31, 146, 179, 181, 193, 201, 213n
Pursell, Margaret (daughter), 146
Pursell, Shari (daughter), 108, 146, 171, 211–12n
pylonidal cyst, 72, 208n

Quonset hut, xi, xii, 86, 210n

Rachmaninoff, Sergei, x, xviii, 17, 79, 101, 128, 131, 162, 164, 170
Radio Hour, 45–46, 50, 55
Rankin Aeronautical Academy, 11, 205n
RCA Victor, xii, 17, 78, 114, 199–200, 201
Reader's Digest, 120

INDEX

Reagan, Maureen, 115–16, 202, 211n
Red Cross, 3, 5–7, 14
regional breakout, 97–98
Rhapsody in Blue, xviii, 79, 81, 113–14, 120, 161, 171
Robbins, Hargus "Pig," xiii
Robbins, Marty, ix, 95–96, 112, 198, 210n
Rochester, New York, 56–59, 65, 66, 72, 190, 195, 198, 208n, 209n, 210n
Rodeheaver, 122, 198

Sabena Airlines, 146, 214n
Sacramento, California, vii, 27, 28, 207n
San Francisco, California, 5–7, 13, 20, 31, 38, 115, 121, 157, 163–64, 167, 169, 192, 216n
San Quentin State Prison, 28, 31–32, 206n
Saussy, Tupper, 118–19, 212n
Savage Club, 128–29, 163–64, 213n
Schermerhorn, Kenneth, xx, 153, 155, 160, 162
Serkin, Rudolph, 20, 22–23, 89
Shepard, Jean, ix, 92, 203
"Show Me, O Lord" (mixed choir), 151, 191, 214n
Sierra Nevada Mountains, xi, 4, 7, 9–10, 12
Simpson, Elizabeth, 13–14, 18–19, 20, 22–23, 174, 182, 205n
Six Flags Over Georgia, 137–38, 191
Sklarevski, Alexander, 23, 39, 40–41, 53–54, 59, 79, 128
slapback, xiv, 94, 96–97
Slatkin, Felix, 99, 117
Smith, W. O. "Smitty," 87–88, 110, 129, 130, 210n
Society for the Preservation and Encouragement of Barbershop Quartet Singing in America (SPEBSQSA) (Barbershop Harmony Society), 140, 199
Sousa, John Philip, 142–45, 155, 200, 214n

Spar Records, 117, 121, 196, 197, 201–2, 212n
St. Louis, Missouri, 97–98, 140, 198, 214n
Stan Williams (stage name), 67–68, 72
Star Trek (1979), 138–39, 154
Station Inn, xviii
Steinway piano, 13, 19, 164
Stewart, Reginald, 39, 41, 53

Talleyrand (play), 166
Tchaikovsky, Pyotr Ilych, 4, 14, 80, 216n
telescopes, 9, 34–35, 37
Tennessee Agricultural and Industrial Normal School (Tennessee State University), 88, 110
Three Biblical Scenes for Orchestra (orchestra), 63, 190
Through the Eyes of Love (album), 125, 199
Time and Again (play), 168, 216n
Time to Heal, A (television movie), 146
Tomlinson, Eric, 122, 199, 212n
Toscanini, Arturo, 48, 89
Towers of the Brazos, The (incidental music), 149, 150, 191
Tracking Room (Nashville, Tennessee), 179, 180
trains, 3, 4, 7, 20, 22, 23, 31, 44, 57, 114, 115, 125, 132, 156, 157, 159, 213n
Trevecca, 120, 212n
Trutner, Herman, 14
Tubb, Ernest, xi
Tulare, California, 3, 6–7, 9, 11–12, 13, 19, 25, 31, 33–37, 39, 50–52, 57, 67, 100, 114, 124, 157, 171, 189, 205–7n, 216n
Tulare Astronomical Society, 34
Two Orchestral Impressions on Country Tunes (orchestra), 114–15, 154

unions, musicians, vii, ix, xix, 86, 113, 116, 120, 122, 127, 130, 133–38, 155, 195, 210n, 213n
United States Army, 5, 11, 36, 20, 43, 45, 130, 209n

Vanderbilt University, 110, 129, 215n
Very Last Dance Hall Left in L.A., The (album), 179–80, 181, 201
Vogt, Roy, 148

"Wabash Cannon Ball" (orchestra), 114–15, 190, 214n
Waco, Texas, 123, 150, 191, 214n
Walker, Jeannine, 148
"Waltz Conflict" (piano), 14, 16–17, 189
Warren, Jerry, 151, 155, 170, 191
Washington, D.C., 33, 44, 46, 51–53, 55–56, 88, 182, 212n

Wednesday Night Club, 88, 129, 213n
Whitney, Bill (Pursell), 73
Williams, Hank, 83, 99, 210n
Williams, John, 122, 163, 199
Wimbledon, 109
Woodland Studios, 134, 137
Word Records, 113, 122–23, 125, 127, 150–51, 193, 198–200, 213n
WSM radio, xi, xiii, 79, 209n

YouTube, 101, 205n, 216n

www.ingramcontent.com/pod-product-compliance
Lightning Source LLC
Chambersburg PA
CBHW030619230426
43661CB00053B/2066